Springer Series on Social Work

Albert R. Roberts, D.S.W., Series Editor

School of Social Work, Indiana University, Indianapolis

Vol. 1 **Battered Women and their Families:** Intervention Strategies and Treatment Programs, *Albert R. Roberts, D.S.W.*

Vol. 2 **Disability, Work, and Social Policy:** Models for Social Welfare, *Aliki Coudroglou, D.S.W., and Dennis L. Poole, Ph.D.*

Vol. 3 **Social Policy and the Rural Setting**
Julia M. Watkins, Ph.D., and Dennis A. Watkins, Ph.D.

Vol. 4 **Clinical Social Work in Health Settings:** A Guide to Professional Practice with Exemplars
Thomas Owen Carlton, D.S.W.

Vol. 5 **Social Work in the Emergency Room**
Carole W. Soskis, M.S.W., J.D.

Vol. 6 **Task-Centered Practice with Families and Groups**
Anne E. Fortune, Ph.D.

Vol. 7 **Widow-to-Widow** *Phyllis R. Silverman, Ph.D.*

Vol. 8 **Edler Abuse and Neglect:** Causes, Diagnosis, and Intervention Strategies, *Mary Joy Quinn, R.N., M.A., and Susan K. Tomita, M.S.W.*

Vol. 9 **Law and Social Work Practice**
Raymond Albert, M.S.W., J.D.

Vol. 10 **Information and Referral Networks:** Doorways to Human Services *Risha W. Levinson, D.S.W.*

Vol. 11 **Social Work in the Workplace:** Practice and Principles
Gary M. Gould, Ph.D., and Michael Lane Smith, Ph.D.

Vol. 12 **Foundations of Social Work Practice**
Joseph Anderson, D.S.W.

Vol. 13 **The Human Bond:** Support Groups and Mutual Aid
Harry Wasserman, D.S.W., and Holly E. Danforth, M.S.W.

Vol. 14 **Social Work: The Membership Perspective**
Hans S. Falck, Ph.D.

Harry Wasserman is an associate professor at the School of Social Welfare at the University of California, Los Angeles. He teaches social work microtheory and practice and the history and philosophy of social welfare. Prior to his academic appointment, Wasserman was the Director of Social Services at Denver General Hospital, and Chief Social Worker of the Children's Asthma Research Institute and Hospital in Denver, Colorado. He also was social work consultant to the Evergreen Residential Treatment Center for Children, in Evergreen, Colorado.

Holly E. Danforth received her Master of Social Welfare in 1985 from the University of California, Los Angeles (UCLA). She was employed as a clinical social worker at the UCLA Neuropsychiatric Institute and Hospital's Adolescent Service. Presently, she is pursuing her Doctorate of Social Welfare at the University of California, Berkeley.

THE HUMAN BOND
Support Groups and Mutual Aid

Harry Wasserman, D.S.W.
Holly E. Danforth, M.S.W.

Springer Publishing Company
New York

Springer Publishing Company, Inc.
536 Broadway
New York, NY 10012

88 89 90 91 92 / 5 4 3 2 1

Library of Congress Cataloging-in-Publication Data

Wasserman, Harry.
The human bond.

(Springer series on social work ; v. 13)
Includes bibliographies and index.
1. Self-help groups—United States. 2. Social group work—United States. 3. Stress (Psychology) I. Danforth, Holly E. II. Title. III. Series.
HV547.W386 1988 361.4 88-3226
ISBN 0-8621-5980-X

Printed in the United States of America

Contents

IV Looking Forward

Preface

This is a book about social support and how people who share a common situation can help each other as members of groups. The helping professions are just beginning to take this idea seriously. The content of this book provides testimony to the increasing use of support groups led by professional human services workers.

We conclude from what we have read about American beliefs and attitudes that at the very heart of our way of life is a profound ambivalence that revolves around the individual as an autonomous person and the individual as a member of a community to which she or he belongs. It would seem, judging by recent sociological writings, that this ambivalence is weighted toward the side of the autonomous individual, unimpeded by social obligations inherent in human ties.

The sociologists who wrote *Habits of the Heart* (Bellah et al., 1985) describe the split in the American psyche as "the deep desire for autonomy and self-reliance combined with an equally deep conviction that life has no meaning unless shared with others in the context of community" (p. 150). One of the main themes (and laments) of *Habits of the Heart* is that we Americans hardly possess a vocabulary with which to express our longing for a life "shared with others in the context of community" (p. 150).

The helping professions, including our own profession of social work, reflect quite forcefully this ambivalence, this duality. The individual seeking and receiving psychological help from a counselor or therapist has been and currently is in the treatment of choice. This choice reflects

Bellah, R.N., Madsen, R., Sullivan, W.M., Snidler, A., & Tipton, S.M. (1985). *Habits of the heart*. Berkeley, CA: University of California Press.

the values and wishes of both parties. The various forms of group treatment under professional auspices—group psychotherapy, social work with groups, family treatment—have only now begun to challenge the supremacy of the dyadic arrangement.

Professionally led support groups of people burdened by a common life situation are a relatively recent development. We do not make any claims that group work in any of its forms is superior to individual psychotherapy or that a support group is the equivalent of a small community in action. We do think that a meaningful support group experience signifies an experience in human solidarity, even though its duration may be brief. In some small way a genuine support group strengthen the bonds between and among people. When people join a support group in quest of help, the group process naturally transforms many of them into helpers. When this happens, we then can speak reasonably about human solidarity and the reinforcement of the human bond. One's own and other people's pain become moral reference points of human connection.

In choosing to write about social support and support groups, we wish to celebrate the human bond as the main source of human decency, our capacity to feel and share with others. This book is testimony to our belief in the possibility of a more humane world, though we live in the shadow of a great darkness.

Harry Wasserman, D.S.W.
Holly E. Danforth, M.S.W.

Acknowledgments

Preliminary work on this book began in the academic year 1980–1981. By virtue of being a member of an academic faculty, Harry Wasserman, the senior author, spent a three-month sabbatical during the academic year 1984 working on this project. The University of California, Los Angeles (UCLA) provided further support by awarding Wasserman two monetary grants in 1984 and 1985 to hire a research assistant and pay for incidental expenses. Holly E. Danforth was that research assistant. She became one of the authors in recognition of her contribution to this book. The authors extend their gratitude to UCLA for its indispensable support.

There are a few people who deserve special mention. They either read parts or all of the manuscript and offered important commentaries and criticism of the working drafts. Included among these people are Harry's brother, Sidney Wasserman, D.S.W.; Edith Sherman, Ph.D.; Rosalyn Bernstein, M.S.W.; Professor Robert S. Nevin; and Professor Albert R. Roberts, Social Work Series Editor of the Springer Publishing Company. The later two are both faculty members at the Indiana University School of Social Work, and they suggested new ideas and fresh departures in the content of the book and indicated needed changes in its organization.

Denise Wasserman typed some of the early drafts and read these carefully as a good editor would. She paid attention to clarity of thought, errors in grammar and syntax, and typographical and spelling mistakes. Denise also did an excellent job of organizing the bibliographic material into categories for analytic purposes. Her emotional investment in the success of this book was as great as the authors; and her support was the unique kind of a loving wife.

Harry Wasserman expresses his gratitude to the members of his extended family and friends who believed in the validity and relevance of this work and in its eventual execution. Together we comprise a mutual aid network, one tiny but significant strand in the larger fabric of the human bond.

The authors have chosen to use the masculine and feminine pronouns in reference to social workers, group leaders, clients, and group members. The decision to use both forms was made for two reasons. First, recognizing that the majority of social workers are women, the traditional exclusive usage of the male pronoun did not make much sense. Secondly, in keeping with the spirit of the human bond and dignity, we felt a commitment to utilize nonsexist language.

Special thanks are extended also to two excellent typists, Valentina Stewart and Junghee Kim, for their efficiency and, above all, their cheerful demeanor.

Introduction

In the present literature on "helping groups," no text specifically addresses the support group modality, particularly as conceptualized for use in the social work profession. As a result of the topic's relative newness, this book serves, in part, as a "how-to" manual, but it also presents an important aspect of any practice method—that is, the rationale and justification of a theoretical base. In fact, a primary step in the development of a professional social worker involves the evolution of an individual with a natural helping stance to one who articulates the process of helping.

Part I proposes a theoretical foundation for support group work. Chapter 1, "Social Support: An Overview," discusses the general concept of support from various disciplines. Chapter 2, "Stress and Support Systems," reviews the research relating the concepts of stress and support. Chapter 3, "Why Do We Need Support Groups?" presents a case as to the appropriateness and effectiveness of support groups in today's world. Chapter 4, "Understanding Stress: Implications for Support Group Need," suggests a conceptual formulation unique to the use of support groups in the context of stress.

With this foundation, Part II moves on to the practical application of support group theory. For a fuller grasp of support group work, these chapters integrate theoretical material with rich examples of existing support groups. Chapter 5, "Planning a Support Group," tackles the process of group formation and design. Chapter 6, "Leading a Support Group," focuses on the components of mutual aid and how it becomes an integral part of the support group process. Support group phases are identified. Similarities and differences between support group and therapy group phases are noted as are the structure and dynamics of long-

and short-term groups. The group leader role in terms of purpose and activity is delineated.

Part III (Chapters 7, 8, 9, 10) discusses professionally led support groups in four fields of social work practice: health, the frail elderly, child and family, and mental health. Target populations, the planning process as applied to each field, and the problematic issues specific to each field of practice are the foci of analysis.

In Part IV, Chapter 11, "Possibilities for the Future," takes up the theme of professionally led support groups as an important component of a reconstructured social work. Finally, some suggestions are proffered in regard to the kinds of research the profession of social work might undertake in the future.

The deepest need of man is the need to overcome his separateness, to leave the person of his aloneness.

ERICH FROMM

Individuals need the nurture of groups that carry a moral tradition reinforcing their own aspirations.

ROBERT BELLAH

Social morality depends upon man's capacity to give and to receive love, to be kind and to be empathic.

KENNETH CLARK

The idea of community excludes paranoia. A group willing to accept criticism and go on thinking and talking can be a community.

ROBERT M. HUTCHINS

Thus the sum of things is ever being renewed, and mortals live dependent one upon another.

LUCRETIUS

Two basic needs of the human being—besides the physical one of survival—are the needs for self-respect and for belonging, which is the acceptance of the "I" and the "You" and the finding of the bridge between the two.

GISELA KONOPKA

I Basic Foundations for Social Support Groups

1 Social Support: An Overview

In this beginning chapter, the reader will be introduced to the concept of social support and the sources of its current popularity, particularly in the field of social work.

This chapter explores the "good fit" between traditional social work values and the application of social support in theory and practice. Recently, within and outside the mental health professions, there has been a convergence of ideas, research findings, and "new" helping modes which indicate the importance of the "social support" concept. The fascinating aspect of this development is the new scientific and professional interest in a homely and commonplace human interaction that frequently comes naturally to people. Not often do the social sciences and associated professions become enraptured with such a nonesoteric concept. It may be defined similarly to Louis Armstrong's definition of jazz: Everyone understands social support who has experienced it both as giver and receiver. Without question, social support has been a natural, spontaneous portion of humanity's inherent helping process.

However, the scientific and professional interest in social support and in another concept connected with it, the social network, is of recent vintage, perhaps in the past 10 to 15 years. A host of thinkers from a variety of fields whose principal intellectual concern is in human ecology, as well as a rapidly proliferating number of self-help groups share a common interest in these concepts. This convergence on the themes of social support and social network offers an exception to the social sciences and mental health professions' proclivity to generate their own concepts with little regard to their transmittable value to allied disciplines. The sharing of these concepts across disciplines such as social anthropology, sociology, community psychology, and social work is unusual. Despite this unique sharing of ideas, a difficulty has been the lack of clarity surrounding the concepts of social support and social network.

In practice, terms such as *social network, personal network, social support system,* and *support network* are being used interchangeably, a habit that promotes confusion. In this book, the term *social network* is used to connote all of a focal person's relationships with people, in effect, every person she knows. This includes members of the nuclear and extended families, friends, neighbors, acquaintances, colleagues at work, or fellow congregants of a church. However, obviously all individuals known to a focal person do not constitute a *support system,* since not all contacts serve in a supportive role. Yet within the social network there are some members of the focal person's actual support system, while others are only potential members. Whether or not a focal person's actual or potential support system is activated may depend, for instance, on the particular nature of a crisis; the physical propinquity of any given member; the ability of a social worker to help a client mobilize her support system; and a host of other personal, interactional, and structural factors.

Thus, the distinction between *social network* and *social support system* is a critical one. Social network is a more global concept than social support, and its practical utility is to provide the social worker with the focal person's total social world, from which a support system can be mobilized. A brief discussion of social network and support system theory will further clarify this distinction.

SOCIAL NETWORKS

Anthropology's Contribution

Anthropologists have traditionally been interested in the ties and connections among human beings that constitute the social relations of communities. The intricacies of kinship structures and the centrifugal and centripetal forces that separate or connect people are among their primary foci. Thus, the term *social network* in its broadest sense signifies a set of relationships among people without inputing any positive or negative values. Gottlieb (1981) provides the following definition:

> The social network is a unit of social structure that includes all of an individual's contacts. The network can be studied from the point of view of a single member or it can be studied as a whole. Its composition can be broken down in a number of ways, based on formal sociological classifications (such as nuclear family, extended family and peers), or based on psychological dichot-

omies (such as intimate versus casual ties), or based on the settings from which ties originate (such as neighbors, workmates, domestic relations, volunteer associations and the community's health, welfare, and educational institutions). [p. 203]

Barnes (1972) was among the first anthropologists to use the concept of social network. He used it to distinguish the ties of friendship, neighborliness, and kinship in a Norwegian town. His analysis also included an examination of the ties within the formal framework of the town's social institutions such as the parish and the workshop. Barnes's definition of social network was "the set of concrete interpersonal relations linking individuals with other individuals" (p.2).

Bott's (1971) analysis of sex-segregated roles among English working-class married couples elaborated Barnes's definition of establishing a correlation between rigidly defined sex roles and closely knit social networks. In a closely knit network, the individuals within it know each other and have high rates of interaction. In a loose network the opposite is true: Many of the individuals do not frequent each other, and their ties exist only by virtue of their connection with a focal person. A closely knit network is more predictive of its members' behaviors than their membership in the same social class. Bott's analysis was refined by Mitchell in his definition of a social network as "a specific set of linkages among a set of persons with the . . . property that the characteristics of these linkages as a whole may be used to interpret the social behavior of the persons involved" [quoted in Mitchell, 1969, p. 2].

The concept of social network has been subjected to rigorous analysis, making a differentiation between a personal network and a whole network. The former is one in which a focal person is the starting unit of analysis. A person can be chosen from any population and a map or any pictorial device can be constructed which designates all of the persons to whom the focal person is connected.

The whole-network strategy, as used by Craven and Wellman (1973), portrays all of the linkages among all persons in any given interacting population. This strategy is most efficiently used to depict the totality of ties in a clearly bounded, small population such as a village.

For social work purposes, both strategies can be used, depending on the unit of analysis. However, given the preponderance of clinical social workers and group workers within the ranks of social work, it would seem that the concept of personal network would have the greatest research and practical utility.

Personal networks have many characteristics and dimensions. In interactional terms, a distinction is made between uniplex and multiplex relationships. In the former, links between the focal person and others are characterized by a single type of content or by a single role relation, such as borrowing money, giving advice, or casual conversation. Multiplex relationships signify more than one type of content or role relationship.

Another interactional dimension is that of the direction or directionality of relationships. This dimension refers to the flow of relationships in a dyad. A relationship can be unidirectional, with one person being a giver and another the receiver; or the relationships can be reciprocal in nature, where that which is exchanged between two people approaches a higher measure of equality.

Personal networks can also be analyzed in terms of structural characteristics such as ''density,'' which refers to the closeness or looseness of the network. Another characteristic is ''degree,'' which refers to the average number of interactions members have with each other.

Sociology's Perspective

Sociology's current interest in social networks emerges out of a discontent with Weberian and structural-functional theories. Such concepts as bureaucracy, socialization, social structure, or reference group do not sufficiently convey human interactions in detail. Individual actors, their ties to others, and the ruptures of these, for instance, are not well understood through traditional sociological analysis, nor are the conditions under which people can be expected to be of help or of little or no help to each other. While there is no social network theory per se, the concept itself seems to be sufficiently powerful to have launched a rather large number of researchers into investigating the relationships of people in their everyday settings.

Social network theorizing and research have begun to indicate, contrary to the Parsonian emphasis, that significant groupings of people and social worlds bridge the gap between the nuclear family and society's formal social structures such as government, schools, and corporations, which are all bureaucracies. Clearly, the extended family has not disappeared in American life: People still form family like friendships as part of their social network; people still come together around common troublesome circumstances as in a self-help group; and people in the workplace still give each other emotional support. Thus the worlds of bureaucracy and the nuclear family are not inevitably separated from each other. But it is not clear at this time how a family's social network and the agents of a given bureaucracy can perceive each other as interdependent entities.

SOCIAL SUPPORT SYSTEMS

Defining "Social Support"

In examining social support, many scientific workers begin with the research of the epidemiologist John Cassel and his seminal work, which links together stress and susceptibility to organic disease and/or psychological distress. Cassel (1974) stated his principal hypothesis as follows: "The circumstances in which increased susceptibility to disease would occur would be those in which, for a variety of reasons, individuals are not receiving any evidence (feedback) that their actions are leading to desirable and/or anticipated consequences" (p. 405).

Of importance here is the notion that people can become physically, mentally, or socially debilitated if they do not receive or perceive signs from significant others that make them feel safe and valued. One aspect of health is people's capacity to know what others expect of them and how they are generally evaluated by others. When individuals experience a failing sense of coherence in their world, then their susceptibility to disease increases. People's sense of coherence depends in part on a solid feeling of confidence in the positive outcome of their actions.

Cassel (1974) further contends that "the nature and strengths of available group supports" (p. 407) can be protective of health. This health-protective hypothesis has prompted various definitions of social support, all of which tend to feature the same elements. Caplan (1974) writes as follows:

> Support *system* implies an enduring pattern of continuous or intermittent ties that play a significant part in maintaining the psychological and physical integrity of the individual over time. The various elements of the support system may be spontaneous, that is, not organized in a planned way by someone who is interested in promoting the health of the individual or the population, but emerging from the needs of the individual and the natural biosocial responses of the people in his community or from the values and traditions of his culture and society. [p. 7]

As to the elements of a support system, Caplan says,

> Both enduring and short-term supports are likely to consist of three elements: The significant others help the individual mobilize his psychological resources and master his emotional blinders; they share his tasks; and they provide him

with extra supplies of money, materials, tools, skills, and cognitive guidance to improve his handling of his situation. [p. 6]

Barrera (1981) has constructed the Arizona Social Support Interview Schedule (ASSIS) and has formulated the components of social support as follows:

1. Material aid: providing material aid in the form of money and other physical objects
2. Physical assistance: sharing of tasks
3. Intimate interaction: interacting in a nondirective manner such that feelings and personal concerns are expressed
4. Guidance: offering advice and guidance
5. Feedback: providing individuals with information about themselves
6. Social participation: engaging in social interaction for fun, relaxation, and diversion from demanding conditions. [p. 75]

On inspection, Barrera's view of social support replicates Caplan's, but Barrera's novel feature is that of "social participation for fun, relaxation, and diversion from demanding conditions" (p. 75).

Cobb (1976) formulates the concept as follows: "Social support is defined as information leading the subject to believe that he is cared for and loved, esteemed, and a member of a network of mutual obligations" (p. 300). Support means affirmation that a person is loved and valued, regardless of achievement.

Cobb (1976) and Caplan (1974) also emphasizes the reciprocity inherent in support systems. Those who are helped may someday be helpers, and vice versa. Support of others is characterized by mutuality and mutual aid.

Clearly, the mutuality in a support system is not always evident at any given moment in time. In the worlds of social work, psychiatry, and medicine, the focal person (client, patient) may be temporarily or permanently dependent, regressed, or disabled. Except for those situations of chronic disability—and here, too, no absolute statements can be made—the persons being helped in some later circumstances become helpers, within their support systems. This can also be seen on an everyday basis among our own families and friends, as children who were once dependent upon their parents experience a reversal of roles. The parents, when they become old and sometimes infirm, become dependent upon their children. Thus the factors of mutuality and the balance of forces within a support system are affected by the variables of time and age.

Finally, Bloom's (1982) conceptualization of a support system replicates some ideas of other authorities noted here, but her dimensions of social support are, in a sense, more extensive and elaborate. With the first dimension—the maintenance of social identity—Bloom has in mind both the macro and micro aspects of social identity. The macro "subdimension" carries resonances of Durkheim's (1951) classical formulation, namely, "the degree to which an individual is integrated into the larger society" (Bloom, 1982, p. 136). The micro perspective refers to the "interaction between the target individual and the support system [revealing] the process [by] which an individual's social ties provide social identity feedback" (p. 137). Feedback, according to Bloom, helps the focal person understand that there are often people who face the same circumstances and that some of the focal person's behavior is appropriate due to the experienced strain and tension.

Bloom's (1982) second dimension is emotional support, referring to "behavior which assures the individual that he is loved and valued as a person regardless of achievement." The third and fourth dimensions are tangible or environmental support and information. The fifth dimension Bloom calls "social affiliation," which incorporates the concept of peoples' interdependence in both social and psychological terms. A rather bulky literature on social affiliation exists which examines the preference people have to be with others in stressful and nonstressful situations. Bloom's categories replicate the others, capturing conceptually the human need for affiliation and social identity—the need for attachment, connection, and bonding.

The researchers in the field of human development have promoted the belief that the original mother-child dyad in an "average expectable environment" is the precursor for all consequent human ties and connections. Literally, the person becomes human through the bonding interaction of those early years. Beginning with the infant's dependence upon his mother or mother surrogate and ending frequently in that individual's need to be taken care of, the person's reality is defined essentially through his social relatedness. If the key concept to the understanding of the physical world is the atom, and the keys to the biological world the gene and DNA, the world of psychosocial functioning relies primarily on the human experience of attachment, bonding, and connection, of which social support throughout the life cycle is a principal derivative.

Effects of Social Support

During the past half-century, a small but increasing number of sociologists, anthropologists, social and community psychiatrists, and community psychologists have engaged in a considerable amount of research on the effects of social support. These disciplines are fundamentally interested in the relationship between mental health and social factors. Beginning with Farris and Dunham's (1939) work on the environmental and ecological correlates of mental disturbance in Chicago, and continuing in later works (Langer & Michael, 1963; Leighton, 1959; Srole et al., 1962), a body of knowledge has emerged which points toward a strong association between psychiatric disorder and social disorganization, as well as an association between a lack of social integration or anomie and a sense of bewilderment about normative standards of behavior. A person's mental health and sense of well-being are intimately connected with the nature of his social ties. In brief, these studies have led us to think that the most important determinant of human behavior is the human social environment.

If this hypothesis is correct, and if the fragmentation of social ties or the lack of them is associated with mental disorder, then the current research on social networks and social support systems makes eminent sense. How do the nature of human connections with people and the vicissitudes of those connections affect well-being? More specifically, how does the presence or lack of human support or its inconsistency affect our physical and psychosocial functioning?

What do the researchers in the domain of social support tend to show? The word *tend* is critical here because there are many methodological problems with the research that has been done, and there are still large gaps in knowledge of precisely how social support works. Putting this caveat aside for a moment, what *does* the research tend to show?

As mentioned earlier with respect to Cassell's (1974) work, it appears that social support plays a role in preventing disease and maintaining health. There is a hypothesis that states that social support in some undefined way maintains well-being. This should not be read as a statement of total inoculation against disease and illness. Like good nutrition, it is one of the major determinants in preserving health, but not the only factor. However, once a person has fallen ill, the presence of social support acts as a buffer against the power of the disease or illness. In other words, people who have good, solid support systems regain their health more quickly than those who have weak or fragmented support systems. DiMatteo and Hays (1981) in their review of the research conclude that "social supports may, in fact, be associated with recovery and coping with serious physical illness and injury" (p. 121). Crisis theory and practice also indicate that social support facilitates coping with a crisis. Where a client's support system is not intact or does not seem, for one reason or another, available, he will often be assigned to a "crisis group," which in part acts as a support system.

In a major review, Cobb (1976) cites many research investigations that indicate that social support can protect people who find themselves in critical, stressful situations, including "low birth weight to death, from arthritis through tuberculosis to depression, alcoholism, and other psychiatric illnesses. Furthermore, social support can reduce the amount of medication required and accelerate recovery and facilitate compliance with prescribed medical regimens" (p. 300). Gore (1978) found that a lack of social support exacerbated the sense of stress of unemployed men. "The unsupported evidenced significantly higher elevations and more changes in measures of cholesterol, illness symptoms and affective response than the supported" (p. 157).

Social support can be thought of as interpersonal transactions that include one or more of three key elements: affect, affirmation, and aid (Kahn & Antonucci, 1980). Seen in this way, it is quite clear that the people deprived of these life-giving transactions are those who are the most susceptible to some form of mental, physical, or social breakdown.

TRADITIONAL USES OF SOCIAL SUPPORT IN SOCIAL WORK

As a profession that serves vulnerable populations—frequently those bereft of essential supportive contact—social work to some extent has incorporated supportive aspects into its programs and interventions. At times it would appear that this practice evolved spontaneously, without a clear, articulated appreciation for the support process. Nevertheless, it is important to acknowledge the established forms of support, in order to recognize fully social work's inherent kinship with the support concept.

Formal Support Systems

In the informal support process discussed earlier, people draw upon their personal social networks to form their own support systems. These contain both kin and nonkin relationships, where relatives, friends, and neighbors carry on reciprocal, helpful activities as a normal, expectable, almost routine affair. There is, however, another kind of support system which is formal in nature, a creation of government, and specifically a creation of a government's social policy. This, of course, refers to that vast array of social programs and benefits that have sprung up under the auspices of the welfare state, including Social Security, Medicare, and Workmen's Compensation. These function as formal support systems, created to insure people's safety, security, and health at important transition points and during times of expected and unexpected crisis. It is unthinkable that a contemporary advanced society might meet its citizens' needs without a system of formal programmatic social supports, called social welfare. The basic programs and services of this system encompass income maintenance and security programs, a medical care scheme, and policies supporting decent housing.

These are the fundamentals of a formal support system, but beyond these is a host of programs that reflect—or, better, should reflect— the support people need in order to live decently in economic and social spheres. For instance, if one thinks about families—both two-parent and one-parent families—it is clear from census statistical data and from daily experience that the trend is for most parents to work, in the quest for steady income in order to live decently. This immediately confronts society with many questions concerning child-care needs, some of which must be responded to by governmental social policy and large-scale social programs. Day-care arrangements for children, whether wholly or partially financed or not financed at all by public funds, represent formal support systems for families. Without them, millions of people could not work and would be dependent upon income from sources other than work.

Likewise, school breakfasts and lunches for children are another example of formal social support, the absence of which would deprive some children from poor families of the only decent meal(s) they receive. Obviously, the physical and mental well-being of some children are at stake when these formal supports are cut back. Only governmental funds can assure their continued existence. They are a social support par excellence.

Substitute Support Systems

When a natural support system (nuclear family, extended family, neighbors) has great difficulty in offering one or some of its members love, care, and financial and/or emotional security, social workers insure the fulfillment of those needs by forming a substitute support system. It is recognized that, like natural supports, substitute systems sometimes fail. Nevertheless, "society" has historically assigned professional social work the task of implementing strategies of finding and sustaining adequate, life-giving, substitute placement and care, particularly in child welfare. Social work has not conceptualized foster care placements in individual and group homes as constituting substitute support systems, but in actuality they are precisely that.

Another example of this kind of temporary support system is a social work invention that goes back to at least the latter half of the 19th century, namely, the special group home for pregnant unmarried young women. These young people remain in a group home for varying portions of their pregnancies and usually leave within a month or two after giving birth. Still another type of temporary support system is a foster home for dependent, neglected or abused children. Placement in a foster home sometimes becomes permanent in the sense that the child does not return to his biological parents, but the original intent on the part of the placing agency is usually of a temporary nature.

The adoptive home represents a permanent support system devised for children whose parents have chosen to give them up to adoptive families. This arrangement reflects a general belief that children need a family in which to grow up properly, to assume their rightful place in the world. Parental love and care in this view are the highest sources of physical security and emotional support for children.

Support in Clinical Social Work

In clinical social work itself, the importance of social support has been a persistent theme, although that particular terminology has been used only recently. First, one can think of the clinical relationship as a temporary support system. Clients see a social worker when they are troubled and/or a source of trouble for other people. Among other things, social workers gives clients a great deal of emotional support, by listening to them and trying to understand the way they perceive themselves and others and the situations in which they find themselves. To the extent that clients feel accepted and understood by a social worker, they feel cared for and respected as human beings regardless of the nature of their difficulties.

In a recent article, Nelsen (1980) states that the professional relationship offers a client emotional support by employing protection, acceptance, validation, and education. The social-worker/client relationship is characterized by a dyadic arrangement in which the social worker for a limited period of time provides a client with a relationship that sustains him by using the human virtues of empathy, congruity, acceptance, and positive regard.

Supportive therapy was thought to be an inferior method of treatment 25 or 30 years ago; it was merely a way of placating and soothing the complaints and difficulties of patients suffering from a variety of serious, chronic emotional and thinking disturbances. These ranged from schizophrenic disorders and chronic depressions to lifelong unresolved feelings of dependency, hypochondriasis, and so on. Typically, clinics and hospitals assigned these patients to personnel on the lowest rungs, namely, social work, psychology, and psychiatry students who, as part of their training, had to treat the gamut of psychiatric disorders. Supportive therapy was offered to "uninteresting" and "unchallenging" patients, deemed incapable of achieving insight into their problems or of using that insight in a beneficial way. Thus "supportive therapy"—as contrasted with "insight therapy," with its ultimate goal of "personality restructuring"—was viewed as a rather lowly enterprise designed to keep people afloat and placated.

However, Rogers's (1957) classic work in clinical psychology and the seminal paper by Selby (1956) in social casework had an important and lasting impact on workers in the mental health professions with respect to this previously trivializing attitude toward supportive treatment. Rogers's (1957) hypothesis about the necessary conditions of the therapist's empathy, congruity, acceptance, and positive regard in reference to successful outcomes gave credence to the critical nature of therapeutic support. Selby (1956), influenced primarily by developments within psychoanalytic ego psychology, wrote about the ego-building aspect of supportive treatment. She argued that supportive treatment was not simply a way for clinicians to shore up the "weak egos" of clients, but rather the treatment of choice for those clients with "temporarily impaired" ego functioning. "There . . . seems to be general consensus that support is more than palliative; it can act as a motivation for growth, change, and problem-solving by reducing anxiety, providing the element of hope, and releasing clients' energy to work toward problem resolution" (Selby, 1979, p. 583). In brief, the factor of emotional support in clinical social work and other forms of treatment has gained a certain respectability within the past 25 years.

In a contribution entitled, "An Attempt to Examine the Use of Support in Social Work Practice," Compton (1979) conceptualizes the support phenomenon in social work theory and practice as being based on the ideas of Bernard Bandler (1963). He believed that "life itself" provided the most powerful model for workers in the human services. By "life," Bandler meant "the natural process of growth and development and the rich trajectory of the life span" (p. 31). Bandler thought the therapeutic task consisted of the removal of "blocks and obstacles" in the client's social and psychological development, and in the psychotherapist's alliance with the "progressive forces" within the client, namely the internal processes of "growth and development." Compton (1979) sums up Bandler's formulation thus: "All our efforts within client systems in social work are supportive, as the focus is in development and is aimed on increasing ability to cope with life pressures" (p. 380).

Recent research findings tend increasingly to emphasize the critical importance of the human qualities of the therapist rather than her therapeutic orientation and style. Lambert and DeJulio (1978) write, "The theoretical orientation of a therapist is a highly overrated variable in psychotherapy outcome." They estimate that the theoretical system guiding the therapeutic encounter accounts for only 5% of the variation in treatment outcome (Lambert & DeJulio, 1978). What seems to be of cardinal importance, however, is the client's perception of the therapist, her "credibility and attractiveness." These "therapist-offered conditions," which include the capacity to convey empathy, understanding, warmth, and caring—all components of emotional support—seem to be the *sine qua non* of beneficial results in therapy and presumably in all forms of clinical social work treatment.

Social Work with Groups

The research of sociologists, social and community psychiatrists, and community psychologists into the beneficial effects of support systems can be interpreted as a reaffirmation of the principles and purposes of social work with groups. In reading the contributions of some of the principal theorists on group therapy, one is struck by the similarity and continuity of some major themes: the group as a source of "social responsibility" (Papell & Rothman, 1966, p. 68); the group as a provider of "intellectual and social enhancement" (Hartford, 1976, p. 48); the group as a "helping context in which the individual, aided by the social support of other members, could gain self-understanding" (Hartford, 1976, p. 49); the group as a promoter of "mutual responsibilities and . . . learning and competence in social roles" (McBroom, 1976, p. 271); the group as a potential "mutual aid system" (Papell & Rothman, 1980, p. 7); and the group as a vehicle toward "the strengthening and development of social networks" (Abels & Abels, 1980, p. 25). Unfortunately, given the historical preponderance of clinical social workers within the profession, the philosophy of social work with groups has been considerably neglected. While it is true that many casework agencies, psychiatric clinics, and hospitals have engaged clients and patients in group treatment, in general that method has been identified as group psychotherapy and not social work with groups. This deemphasis on group work theory has clouded the profession's awareness of the essential role of support in a group process.

Theorists of social work with groups have been engaged in an intellectual debate that mirrors a historical debate in democratic political theory; How does a democratic society simultaneously respect, fortify, and promote the rights of individuals while also promoting and implementing a public policy designed to insure order and the fulfillment of responsibilities in collective life? Similarly, theorists who conceptualize group work as a mutual-aid system maintain that the individual's rights and well-being are not to be sacrificed to the authority and power of the collective (group) through the processes of isolation and scapegoating and the strictures of rigid conformism.

It is no historical accident that social work with groups evolved out of the social settlement movement. Coyle (1948) and Wilson and Ryland (1949) were among the early theorists who were closely connected with the settlement experience, and they made the initial attempts to formulate an intellectual base for group practice in social work. Like so many theorists who followed in their path, they did not view people as clients and certainly not as patients, but as *members* of a group who gathered together for a variety of reasons, usually under the aegis and sponsorship of a community agency. Members came together to accomplish specific tasks; to socialize; to confront some common circumstance that created pain; or to pursue a collective purpose, such as the revitalization of a depressed neighborhood. Members in these small groups are the microcosmic equivalents of citizens in the larger society.

When a social agency organizes a single-parents group to work together on a common problem, it does so with the understanding that questions of income, transportation, child care, loneliness, isolation, and the need for love and affection are not simply individual issues but common concerns. When people begin to grasp this, they will undertake activities designed to confront and perhaps solve some of these problems. Along the way in the issue-grappling, problem-solving process, the humanity of the members will have been sustained and reinforced. They see they are not alone; others are in the same boat. Strength is gained in that each individual's struggle is not one's alone but is part of a larger common struggle. People learn from each other in such groups; they help each other out through babysitting, car pooling, and listening and attending to each other's private troubles and joys. Empathy, understanding, and sensitivity are gained through a sharing process that culminates in the construction of a heightened social consciousness, a more finely honed understanding of a common social reality. What happens in this kind of a small group is what C. Wright Mills advocated for people in becoming citizens: the transformation of private problems into public issues. If and when single parents in various groups begin to link their groups together through a more extensive networking process, they can become a formidable political force in a city, a state, a region, or perhaps the nation.

This description of group process presents a highly idealistic picture by leaving out the strains and tensions, the hostilities, angers, and rivalries that are also part of the story. Nevertheless, the benefits that derive from working together in facing and solving some common difficulties will more often than not surmount or transcend the negative aspects of group life. In social work with groups there are no inevitable positive outcomes, but rather a statistical probability of relative success more often than failure.

RECENT TRENDS RELATING TO SOCIAL SUPPORT IN SOCIAL WORK

Although social work has traditionally blended into practice the various supportive aspects discussed so far in this chapter, currently several trends invite more extensive use of supportive modalities. As social work has embraced a more ecological perspective, returning to a person-in-environment emphasis, there has been more readiness to identify and tap the pool of human support awaiting discovery in that environment. Concurrently, as professionals have recognized the existence of natural helpers and helping networks within communities, an appreciation has grown for the power of mutual aid; as a result, society has witnessed an upsurge in the self-help movement. These trends will be discussed in the context of their implications for social work.

The Ecological Viewpoint

The recent development of an ecological perspective in social work has reintroduced the issue of the environment, particularly the human environment, with its various informal and formal social interactions (Germain, 1979). This ecological school acknowledges the impact of the physical environment on people's health and functioning. It recognizes the health-producing effects of decent housing and convenient and efficient transportation systems; the human need for open spaces such as public parks; the constructive role of community meeting places; and so on. Yet social work's primary interest encompasses more than these concrete, environmental services; social work focuses on the ''fit'' between the person and his human environment. A good fit between people and their environment allows them to affect each other in constructive ways, namely by promoting mental and physical health. The human environment offers individuals educational and social facilities, safe and friendly neighborhoods, and an array of growth-producing stimuli. When people are under stress or in crisis, a good environment is one that can be responsive to that painful situation because it has helpers already in place. These include facilitators/enablers, professional and ''natural'' helpers, and natural or devised support systems—in brief, a host of formal and informal social structures that are ready to go into action when needed.

What has been problematic in social work since at least the end of World War II has been the question of how to create a profession that can attend to the fit between person and environment in a more holistic way, by not neglecting conceptually or in practice either the person or the environment. The social work literature, particularly the clinical social work (casework) literature, has emphasized the bio-psychosocial perspective in understanding human development and functioning. Clinical social work theorists constantly refer to the person-in-situation and the psychosocial approach to assessment (diagnosis) and strategy of interventions (treatment). Ortega y Gasset's formulation that ''I am myself plus my circumstances'' could be a clinical social work motto. The rhetoric of social work has traditionally acknowledged the importance of the environment, but the issue has been how to incorporate this belief into practice.

The historical downgrading of the neighborhood settlement house and its multi service, activist stance, along with the ascendancy of a clinical social practice designed along the lines of a psychiatric, psychotherapeutic practice, has had the effect of downgrading the importance of the human environment that surrounds the individual. Some social workers would argue that family therapy, which sometimes (infrequently) includes extended family members, and various forms of group treatment have provided a corrective force. These ''innovations'' are important advances in ways of working with the problems of a given client, but in themselves they do not expand sufficiently the social worker's theoretical and observational lens. The human environment cannot be restricted to the intimate nuclear family or even the extended family. The ecological perspective widens the lens to include all of those people who currently or potentially interact with a focal person on an informal or formal level. In brief, a focal person's social network and the actual and/or potential support system that might be formed from it constitute a significant part of the human environment. Thus, from the ecological viewpoint, every assessment and every treatment strategy should include (1) an analysis of a client's actual or potential support system and (2) a plan that indicates how, if at all, interventions might employ that support system. While there may be very good reasons for seeing a client alone in individual treatment, this arrangement should be justified by an analysis of her support system and other factors.

Natural Helping Networks

With the publication of *Natural Helping Networks* in 1974 by Collins and Pancoast, the field of social work became resensitized to a basic fact of life: People do get help from other people, natural helpers who do not have a professional education and may even be poorly educated in a formal sense. Natural helpers are in neighborhoods and in everyday places like beauty salons and bars, helping people in ways similar to and different from professional workers. Collins and Pancoast see social workers' roles vis-à-vis natural helpers as unobtrusive consultants who accept the existence of natural helpers and identify these individuals in the environment, thereby enhancing their own services and skills.

The general thrust of all professions, including social work, is to emphasize the esoteric nature of their ministrations. Rein and White (1981) however, offer this formulation of social work skills: "We ordinarily speak of this specialized training as forming the basis of the 'skills' of the social worker. In actual work, the skill of the social worker might more reasonably be regarded as a special combination of the natural and the trained, the ordinary and the esoteric" (p. 4). Social work and certainly social work education tend to emphasize the "trained" and the "esoteric." The special languages of clinical social work in its various forms (psychoanalytic, behavioral, cognitive, problem-solving, functional) can only be understood by their own adepts and professionals in cognate fields and thereby exclude the understanding of laypeople. Perhaps human service professionals might learn a great deal from especially gifted natural helpers, particularly in the ways they relate to troubled people.

Following Gisela Konopka's (1978) writing about working with groups, Papell and Rothman (1980) note that: "the naturalness of group process and the nonsynthetic qualities of the activities of the group predetermine that the professional posture shall be warm, informal and free of remote authoritarianism'' (p. 11). Papell and Rothman continue, in respect to working with all kinds of groups,

> Indeed the style of the worker in the mainstream model is characterized by authenticity, forthrightness, and abrogation of the mystique of professionalism in order to lessen social distance between the worker and the members. The therapeutic potential of worker-member relationships in this framework relates to expectations of diminishing defensiveness and increasing trust and intimacy on the part of the members. An informal style of interaction adopted by the mainstream worker is intended to heighten identification and role modeling processes in the group. [pp. 11-12]

Thus, social workers leading groups might do well to approximate more closely the qualities of natural helpers—naturalness, warmth, informality, authenticity, and forthrightness—in order to diminish the social distance between workers and members.

Mutual Aid

Peter Kropotkin's (1916) great classic, *Mutual Aid,* is a paean to the principle of social cooperation in collective life, offering a historical appreciation of the mutual-aid concept. Kropotkin records a number of impressive facts from history, biology, and anthropology to emphasize the power of mutual aid as a factor in cultural and social evolution. It is noteworthy that most of Kropotkin's examples of mutual aid among people are taken from what are thought of as primitive societies and from cultures of the Middle Ages where there were (1) highly structured relationships of mutual obligation among social classes and (2) mutual-aid activities within the guilds of skilled artisans. It is believed that William Schwartz in 1961 was the first social worker to advance the notion that mutual aid was a fundamental, basic concept, a high-level value which social workers should foster among their clients and themselves, and within the general society. Schwartz (1961) advanced the mutual-aid concept as follows:

> The group is an enterprise in mutual aid, an alliance of individuals who need each other, in varying degrees, to work on certain common problems. The important fact is that this is a helping system in which the clients need each other as well as the worker. This need to use each other, to create not one but many helping relationships, is a vital ingredient of the group process and constitutes a common need over and above the specific tasks for which the group was formed. [p. 18]

In the most current literature on social work with groups, the concept of *mutual support* has been introduced by theorists who recognize the healing quality of such emotional support and conceptualize the group as a potential mutual-aid system. This emphasis on mutual aid, social networks, and support systems provides the predominant clinical social work community with some useful conceptual foundations, applicable in working with clients. Historically, however, the differentiation between "social group work" and "casework" has emphasized particular splits in theoretical orientation. Despite social group work's commitment to the concept of mutual aid, casework was reluctant to follow suit.

How was it that an enabling concept such as mutual aid lay more or less dormant within the ranks of social casework for over 20 years, particularly when colleagues in social group work were promoting it as their most hallowed value? There are probably many reasons for this particular lacuna, but perhaps the principal one is the narrow, technocratic orientation fostered unwittingly in social work education. What workers think of as higher values, such as mutual aid, are not internalized by either social work teachers or students if they are not immediately applicable to working with individuals and families. Their relevance is not grasped in the same way as are such concepts as *relationship, transference,* or *acceptance,* which lend themselves immediately to direct work with people. This is not to suggest that such concepts are easily apprehended or profoundly understood, but rather that the surface connection to individual treatment is seen quite easily.

Another reason is that clinical social workers interested primarily in individual treatment see themselves essentially as psychotherapists and are drawn to those theories, ideas, and formulations that pertain to their work. Their orientation demands a commitment to the study of psychotherapeutic process and interventions, sometimes at the risk of becoming highly technocratic. At times, this search for psychotherapeutic skill and technique can distance the clinician from the humanistic and social context of the work, creating blindness to the power of the mutual-aid process.

Another formidable resistance to the concept of mutual aid lies in its naturalness. People helping each other through mutual exchanges of services and/or social support is probably as old as the presence of humankind on Earth. Its disappearance among groups of people is rare and difficult to imagine, and it apparently only happens when a people suffer from utter hopelessness and despair, as in the case of the Ethiopian Ik (Turnbull, 1972). Put very simply, people depend upon others for survival needs and an improved quality of life. While the history of cooperative effort and mutual help do not fill up the pages of history as do those of war, violence, and destruction, it is not too farfetched to conjecture that, to some considerable extent, the struggle against human barbarism and for human decency has relied upon humanity's capacity to cooperate and to give and receive (Katz & Bender, 1976).

Yet it is the very naturalness of the mutual-aid "methods" that raises doubt in professionals. Social workers, like all professionals, want very badly to distinguish their domain and expertise from others', particularly in the acquisition of esoteric knowledge and skills. Unfortunately, the acquisition of esoterica inherently signifies both symbolic and actual distancing from the very people social workers are supposed to help. The use of a symbolic professional jargon, with its intended and unintended effects, along with the assumption of a professional demeanor, convey a message of superiority and separateness from clients, marking a sharp social differentiation between helper and helped. While professionalism is an important facet of the effective clinician, the understanding and integration of mutual-aid theory provides a balance between the expert role and humanistic and egalitarian values. Whether or not social workers directly run mutual-aid groups, approaching their work with an appreciation for mutual aid's potential healing aspects lends a renewed dignity and empowerment to the client role. Social workers engaged in forming and leading mutual-aid groups appreciate the fact that the social and psychological distance between themselves and their clients must be shortened. Workers in groups are both physically and psychologically closer to their clients' everyday struggles, so workers can allow their genuine emotions to come through somewhat more than they might in regular clinical social work, where they are careful to guard their feelings in a highly controlled way. For instance, involvement in a mutual-aid group might allow for more social worker self-disclosure than might be permissible in a one-to-one casework relationship.

Often social workers who remain their natural selves and are by nature helping persons are effective agents. Their professional education and training will assist them in refining and shaping values, knowledge, and skills; but fundamentally their capacity to relate to a fairly wide range of people and be helpful stems from the natural baggage they bring to the professional process. Thus, as Rein and White (1981) point out, social work helping is composed of both esoteric and natural methods. Unfortunately, the disparagement and shedding of natural helping processes in social work is professionally detrimental and represents a loss to clients.

A final point to be made involves the misguided interchanging of the terms *mutual aid* and *self-help,* which are intended to indicate two different concepts. The former emphasizes human connection and cooperation, while the latter, taken by itself, has a definite connotation of the individual gaining something without any human connection. Although *self-help* has come to be the American term for mutual aid, such usage is rejected in this book. We favor the term *mutual aid,* a concept whose connotations and resonances are replete with ideas of people helping each other.

The concept of mutual aid has been relatively unknown in clinical social work, and understandably so. Typically, social work clients experience conflict with their support network, frequently masking the potential for mutual aid. Recognizing, however, that mutual aid is *the* fundamental theoretical principle of social work with groups, all social work groups could potentially become either temporary or permanent mutual-aid groups. Support groups are founded on the notion that people draw strength from each other when they recognize their commonality and where mutual empathy provides the basis for a cohesive effort.

Self-Help Groups

Fortunately, despite the professionals' difficulty in utilizing the mutual-aid concept, laypeople have recognized the strength in mutual aid, providing a clear experiential demonstration of the support process through self-help groups. While we reject the term "self-help" since it does not clearly connote the nature of the mutual aid process, we do not in any way abjure the purposes and workings of the self-help movement. We support it wholeheartedly.

The self-help movement began in the 1930s with the advent of Alcoholics Anonymous and has spread steadily in many forms since that time. Katz and Bender (1976) describe them as follows:

> Self-help groups are voluntary, small group structures for mutual aid and the accomplishment of a special purpose. They are usually formed by peers who have come together for mutual assistance in satisfying a common need, overcoming a common handicap or life-disrupting problem, and bringing about desired social and/or personal change. The initiators and members of such groups perceive that their needs are not, or cannot be, met by or through existing social institutions. Self-help groups emphasize face-to-face social interactions and the assumption of personal responsibility by members. They often provide material assistance, as well as emotional support; they are frequently "cause" oriented, and promulgate an ideology or values through which members may attain an enhanced sense of personal identity. [p. 9]

A reading of the self-help literature (Caplan & Killilea, 1976; Gartner & Reissman, 1977) indicates that the great majority of Americans do not seek help from mental health professionals (Cowen, 1982), but from a wide array of "natural helpers" or from self-help groups created by laypersons, who themselves suffer from self-defined or socially assigned deficiencies. These people come together to contend with a common set of negative circumstances for two primary reasons. First and foremost is the battle against isolation, depression, and often enough, self-hatred—all outcomes of the social stigmatization process. By coming together, they can fortify themselves and each other against psychic pain, which cannot always be resolved by the individual alone. By joining others, these "victims" can see that they are not alone, that others are "in the same boat," and that together they can learn from each other. They give each other emotional support while actively struggling against stigmatization and for a greater acceptance within the larger community.

A second potent reason for the formation of self-help groups is the failure of mental health professionals either to address the needs and concerns of a particular population (alcoholics, child abusers, single parents, the families of cancer patients) or to help people overcome their social-psychological difficulties. For example, the parents of severely disturbed children, such as autistic children and adolescent schizophrenics, complain that professionals are quite adept in pointing out the psychopathological interactions within their families but are almost totally uninformative on how parents might handle everyday conflictual situations that arise between them and their disturbed children. Apparently, they can learn more from listening to each other in their own support groups. It is this kind of help they need, but the profession has failed to offer assistance with specific life situations by failing to provide the information people desperately need to make life more bearable.

Levy (1973) classified self-help groups into four types: (1) groups that aim to help people control and finally subdue their socially unacceptable and self-destructive behavior, such as Alcoholics Anonymous or Parents Anonymous; (2) groups designed to enhance personal growth, such as women's consciousness-raising groups; (3) groups of people undergoing a common life stress and predicament, such as single-parent and divorce groups; and (4) groups formed at once to defend an embattled minority and to normalize the minority's status, such as gay and lesbian groups.

The proliferation of self-help groups has been astounding but not really surprising, given the social dynamics heretofore discussed. Social workers' attitudes toward the self-help movements have ranged from highly positive to highly negative. An example of the highly positive is that of Leonard Lieber, a social worker who was one of the founders of Parents Anonymous, for parents of abused children. On the highly negative side is the attitude held by many that only professional intervention can be helpful in a definitive way. For social workers, two major insights should be extracted from the self-help movement. First, people will continue to attempt to help each other in a way that has been historically validated, namely, coming together in groups and facing a common life circumstance. Second, the formation of social support groups that are of a mutual-aid or self-help nature ought to be a part of every social work agency's armamentarium of interventions.

PROFESSIONALLY INITIATED SUPPORT GROUPS

Within the last 10 years, social workers, sometimes in conjunction with professionals from other disciplines, have actively created support groups for clients. There is an increasing number of articles in the social work literature on the use of support groups in practice. These professionally initiated support groups are formal in nature because they do not spontaneously arise out of people's voluntary actions. Professional workers not only create them but lead them. Their formation and composition and, to some extent, their "process" depend upon professional leadership and guidance. If, upon termination, a professionally conducted social support group evolves into a lay self-help group, it becomes an informal social support system, for, at the point of termination with professional helpers, the members of the group have voluntarily decided to continue their relationship.

Every field of social work has introduced professionally initiated groups—including gerontology, health, mental health, family and childrens' services, and school social work. As a mode of agency, clinic, and hospital practice, support groups have become quite popular, despite feelings among a minority of group workers that it is not "the real thing" since it is "not really therapy."

The support group idea has taken root at this time in social work practice as a result of a synergy of forces. The social and behavioral sciences have produced a barrage of theoretical papers and research studies on social support and its connections to mental health. The rise of the self-help movement, the recognition of mutual aid as the central concept in social work with groups, and the continued quest to recapture the social aspects of clinical social work have all, singly and together, given impetus to the growing acceptance of social support as a powerful treatment concept.

Unquestionably for the field of social work, the support group concept represents the most imaginative attempt in our contemporary history to bring the "social" back into clinical social work. The support group carries the potential of initiating social ties among people and of becoming a source of advocacy for people who suffer from either a lack of resources (single parents and their children) or stigmatized status (the victims of violence). It is also a remarkable social phenomenon, not to mention a testament to effectiveness, that the professional formation of support groups for a victimized population, such as battered women, has led to the establishment of similar groups for the perpetrators, battering men.

Social work has the potential to play a critical role in these efforts. Sidney Cobb (1976) of the Community Health and Psychiatry Program at Brown University concludes his review article, "Social Support as a Moderator of Life Stress," as follows:

> There appears to be enough evidence on the importance of social support to warrant action, although, of course, all the details as to the circumstances under which it is effective are not yet worked out. Following the behest of Stephen Smith . . . we should start now to teach all our patients, both well and sick, how to give and receive social support. Only in rare instances of psychiatric disability should this instruction require a psychiatrist. It seems to me that this is the real function of which Richard Cabot designed the profession of medical social work. [p. 312]

Dr. Cobb has not only thrown down a challenge to medical social work, but to social work in all fields of practice.

More recently, Benjamin Gottlieb (1985), in an article entitled "Assessing and Strengthening the Impact of Social Support on Mental Health," encourages social workers to organize support groups and promote workshops for assessing their own social networks and support systems, eventually transferring this strategy to their work with clients.

Social work is the sole mental health profession that historically has organized itself as a "socialized" profession, that is, one practiced in agencies, clinics, hospitals, schools, community centers, and the like, rather than along the lines of private practice. Social work with groups, from its beginnings in the settlement house movement, has promoted the democratic principles of citizen participation, underpinned by a collective effort. Thus, social work is the sole discipline possessing both the historical tradition and the appropriate organization of services to become *the* profession whose main purpose is the creation, maintenance, and strengthening of support systems for people. Nevertheless, there is a truism in social work that begs for resolution. While the ethos of social work testifies to the salience of the concept of interdependence, there also is a very strong attitude in social work which follows the form and contours of most human services professional practice. The worker viewed as *the* source of knowledge, the expert giver of help, and the client as the more or less unknowing, passive recipient (Lenrow & Burch, 1981). What this indicates is a less optimistic view of the possibilities of developing interdependent relationships between professional and self-help organizations. However, Froland, Pancoast, Chapman, and Kimboko (1981) declare:

> Combining formal and informal services of support is certainly not an easy process, nor may it be desirable or possible in many instances. But it does provide a perspective and a direction that can be pursued in providing more comprehensive services. It also provides a new opportunity to forge a more equal partnership with informal, voluntary sources of caring, one that is in sharp contrast to traditional perspectives that at times have seen informal caregivers as handmaidens of professionals or as unruly nuisances. [p. 274]

Whether or not social workers will begin to view themselves and their clients as potential givers and receivers of social support and mutual aid, only time will tell. What we can see is that there is a stream in social work history that may be adaptable to contemporary practice.

CONCLUSIONS

There is a confluence of ideas that comprise a possible new/old thrust in social work practice. For those interested in putting the "social" back into social work, the support group concept represents an important development in providing a service for people who can benefit from sharing their ideas and feelings with others who occupy similar circumstances. In no way does the formation of support groups under agency auspices negate the importance of individual and family counseling. Unquestionably, some clients want and need only individual casework; others require only a support group; and still others can benefit from a combination of both. Social work's historical emphasis upon cooperation and mutual aid in the quest for individual and collective well-being, as well as its focus on stigmatized populations, make it the logical profession to promote the social support "technique" as a critical method of intervention.

REFERENCES

Abels, S.L., & Abels, P. (1980). Social group work's contextual purposes. *Social Work with Groups, 3*(3), 25–37.

Bandler, B. (1963). The concept of ego-supportive psychotherapy. In H.J. Parad and R.R. Miller (Eds.), *Ego psychology and dynamic casework* (pp. 27–44). New York: Family Service Association of America.

Barnes, J.A. (1972). *Social networks: Module in Anthropology, No. 26,* 1–29. Reading, MA: Addison-Wesley.

Barrera, M., Jr. (1981). Social support in the adjustment of pregnant adolescents: Assessment issues. In B.H. Gottlieb (Ed.), *Social networks and social support* (pp. 69–96). Beverly Hills: Sage.

Bloom, J.R. (1982). Social support systems and cancer: A conceptual view. In J. Cohen, J. Cullen, & L.R. Martin (Eds.), *Psychosocial aspects of cancer* (pp. 129–149). New York: Raven Press.

Bott, E. (1971). *Family and social network: Roles, norms and external relationships* (2nd ed.). London: Tavistock.

Caplan, G., & Killilea, M. (Eds.). (1976). *Support systems and mutual help.* New York: Grune and Stratton.

Caplan, G. (1974). *Support systems and community mental health.* New York: Behavioral Publications.

Cassel, J.C. (1974). Psychiatric epidimology. In G. Caplan (Ed.), *American Handbook of Psychiatry* (2nd Ed., 2nd Vol.) (pp. 401–410). New York: Basic Books.

Cobb, S. (1976). Social support as a moderator of life stress. *Psychosomatic Medicine, 38,* 300–313.

Collins, A.H., & Pancoast, D.L. (1974). *Natural helping networks.* Washington, DC: National Association of Social Workers.

Compton, B.R. (1979). An attempt to examine the use of support in social work practice. In B.R. Compton & B. Galaway (Eds.), *Social work processes* (pp. 378–386). Homewood, IL: Dorsey Press.

Cowen, E.L. (1982). Help is where you find it. *American Psychologist, 37*(4), 385–395.

Coyle, G.L. (1948). *Group work with American youth.* New York: Harper and Row.

Craven, P., & Wellman, B. (1973). The network city. *Sociological Inquiry, 43*(3/4), 57–88.

DiMatteo, M.R., & Hays, R. (1981). Social support and serious illness. In B.H. Gottlieb (Ed.), *Social Networks and Social Support* (pp. 117–148). Beverly Hills, CA: Sage Publications.

Durkheim, E. (1951). *Suicide.* Glencoe, IL: The Free Press.

Farris, R.E., & Dunham, W.H. (1939). *Mental Disorders in Urban Areas.* Chicago: University of Chicago Press.

Froland, C., Pancoast, D.L., Chapman, N.J., & Kimboko, P. J. (1981). Linking formal and informal support systems. In B.H. Gottlieb (Ed.), *Social networks and social support* (pp. 259–276). Beverly Hills, CA: Sage.

Gartner, A., & Riessman, F. (1977). *Self-help in the human services.* San Francisco: Jossey-Bass.

Germain, C.B. (Ed.). (1979). *Social work practice: People and environments.* New York: Columbia University Press.

Gore, S. (1978). The effect of social support in moderating the health consequences of unemployment. *Journal of Health and Social Behavior, 19,* 157-165.

Gottlieb, B.H. (1981). Preventive intervention involving social networks and social support. In B.H. Gottlieb (Ed.), *Social networks and social support* (pp. 201-232). Beverly Hills: Sage.

Gottlieb, B.H. (1985). Assessing and strengthening the impact of social support in mental health. *Social Work, 30*(4), 293-300.

Hartford, M.E. (1976). Group methods and generic practice. In R.W. Roberts & H. Northen (Eds.), *Theories of social work with groups.* New York: Columbia University Press.

Kahn, R.L., & Antonucci, T.C. (1980). Convoys over the life course. In P.B. Baltes & O.G. Brim, Jr. (Eds.), *Life-span development and behavior.* New York: Academic Press.

Katz, A.H., & Bender, E.I. (1976). *The strength in us: Self-help groups in the modern world.* New York: New Viewpoints.

Konopka, G. (1978). The significance of social group work based on ethical values. *Social Work with Groups, 1*(1), 123-131. New York: National Association of Social Workers.

Kropotkin, P. (1916). *Mutual aid.* New York: Alfred Knopf.

Lambert, M.J., & DeJulio, S.S. (1978, March). *The relative importance of client, therapist and technique variables as predictors of psychotherapy outcomes: the place of therapist "non-specific" factors.* Paper presented at the annual mid-winter meeting of the Division of Psychotherapy, American Psychological Association, Scottsdale, AZ.

Langer, T.S., & Michael, S.T. (1963). *The mid-town Manhattan study: Life stress and mental health.* New York: McGraw-Hill.

Leighton, A.H. (1959). *My name is legion.* New York: Basic Books.

Lenrow, P.B., & Burch, R.W. (1981). Mutual aid and professional services: Opposing or complementary? In B.H. Gottlieb (Ed.), *Social networks and social support* (pp. 233-258). Beverly Hills: Sage.

Levy, L.H. (1973). *Self-help groups as mental health resources.* Bloomington: Indiana University Press.

Lieberman, M.A., & Borman, L. (1979). *Self-help groups for coping with crisis.* San Francisco: Jossey-Bass.

McBroom, E. (1976). Socialization through small groups. In R.W. Roberts & H. Northen (Eds.), *Theories of social work with groups* (pp. 268-303). New York: Columbia University Press.

Mitchell, J.C. (1969). The concept and use of social networks. In J.C. Mitchell (Ed.), *Social networks in urban situations* (pp. 1-50). Manchester, England: Manchester University Press.

Nelsen, J.C. (1980). Support: A necessary condition for change. *Social Work, 25*(5) 388-392.

Papell, C.P., & Rothman, B. (1966). Social group work models: Possession and heritage. *Education for Social Work, 2*(2), 67–77.

Papell, C.P., & Rothman, B. (1980). Relating the mainstream model of social work with groups to group psychotherapy and the structured group approach. *Social Work with Groups, 3*(5), 5–23.

Rein, M., & White, S.H. (1981). Knowledge for practice. *Social Service Review, 55*(1) 1–41.

Rogers, C. (1957). The necessary and sufficient conditions of therapeutic personality change. *Journal of Consulting Psychology, 21,* 95–103.

Selby, L.G. (1956). Supportive treatment: The development of a concept and a helping method. *Social Service Review, 30*(1) 400–414.

Selby, L.G. (1979). Support revisited. *Social Service Review, 53*(4) 573–585.

Srole, L. (1962). Mental health in the metropolis: *The midtown Manhattan study.* New York: McGraw-Hill.

Turnbull, C.M. (1972). *The mountain people.* New York: Simon and Schuster.

Wilson, G., & Ryland, G. (1949). *Social group work practice.* Boston, MA: Houghton-Mifflin.

2 Stress and Support Systems

Chapter 1 referred to Cassel's (1976) work, which linked people's resilience to stress with the presence of social supports. This chapter will further interrelate the concepts of stress and social support as well as their significance in determining people's physical and mental health. This analysis utilizes the conceptual framework for the stress process developed by Pearlin, Lieberman, Menaghan, and Mullan (1981) and the ecological analysis as applied to social work practice by Germain and Gitterman (1980).

STRESS AND LIFE EVENTS: THE STRESS PROCESS

One can think of stress as an organism's potentially positive or negative response to a particular life event or a series of life events. Pearlin et al. (1981) write that there is "probably a general agreement that stress refers to a response of the organism to conditions that, either consciously or unconsciously, are experienced as noxious" (p. 341). However, Bartlett (1961) notes, "Stress is not always bad or painful. Life is full of stressful experiences which, when sucessfully integrated by the individual, produce stimulation, satisfaction, and growth" (p. 138). Thus, situations that are perceived as stressful and pregnant with negative possibilities for some people are viewed by others as challenging, stimulating in a positive sense, and, in the current parlance, potentially growth-producing. Therefore, the meaning attached to events is crucial in determining the nature of the person's response. Of course, above and beyond individual differences in subjective interpretation, undoubtedly some circumstances universally create harmful results, such as concentration camps.

In their conceptual framework, Pearlin et al. (1981) have abstracted "a process of stress," which is formed by combinations of "life events, chronic life strains, self-concepts, coping, and social supports" (p. 337). They view these five circumstances as components of a stress *process*, rather than limiting their conceptualization of stress to a single life event. In examining the stress process, they broadly categorize sources of stress into two areas: discrete life events and chronic life strains. Pearlin et al. recognize, however, that, given these two sources of stress, other factors will affect the intensity and outcome. Specifically, they suggest that life events and life strains have greater potential to result in stress if they produce a loss of self-esteem. They go on to elucidate how two types of mediating resources—social supports and coping—further affect the impact of life events, life strains, and diminishment of self. As they develop this paradigm, these theorist-researchers, like all of the investigators in this field, are guided by what might be called "Cassel's Dictum": There is a linkage between stress and susceptibility to physical illness and emotional disorder.

Sources of Stress

Life Events (acute stress)

The great bulk of research relating to the stress process has been done around the connections between stress and life events. This encompasses both expected and unexpected events, including those that are unique and transitional in nature. Typically these events do not yield a pervasive change in the individual's attitudes or behavior, unless the occurrence promotes an unresolved crisis culminating in a chronic stress response. Most of these events are expectable and connected with tasks involved in life transitions, such as a child entering school, a person getting married, or a first child born to a couple. Because they involve developmental and transitional stages, successful outcome depends on a relatively smooth articulation between the individual's capacities and motivations and her environment's resources and opportunities. If the individual has good coping capacities and the environment is responsive and nutritive, the life event culminates in increased well-being. Most people come through these events, such as entering school at age five or six, without great emotional scarrings or sequelae of isolation, loneliness, and stigmatization.

Pearlin et al. (1981) point out that, in respect to life events, "adverse consequences, at least those involving psychological stress, depend not only on the number of events and the magnitude of the changes they entail, but on the quality of eventful change as well'' (p. 339). Thus, a child dealing with a parental divorce after many years of strained relations is at greater risk for an emotional or physical upset when he goes to school for the first time than a child who does not have to cope with such untoward circumstances.

Another example would be a move to an unfamiliar environment—a new neighborhood, a strange city, a new job. These ''migrations'' often entail the loss of family, friends, neighbors, or work associates. The people ''at risk'' have the task of rebuilding new social networks and support systems in order to assure their healthy, adaptive, psychosocial functioning.

In both instances—the performance of tasks associated with developmental life stages and the adaptation to new environments—there is a certain amount of role strain. This suggests a ''stretching'' or ''overtaxing'' or, in the other direction, a ''contraction'' of the threatened role. In the case of the migratory family, its members may well be deprived of their basic roles as work associates, friends, neighbors, church members, or relatives of an extended family. While some of these roles will be regained, there is nothing automatic about the process, and the factor of time is inevitably important.

Pearlin et al. (1981) point out that undesirable and unscheduled life events are the most damaging, again indicating that the quality of events represents an important aspect of understanding profound psychosocial stress.

Life events, whether expected or unexpected, tend to encompass a discrete period of time, evoking an acute period of stress. For this reason, this text will refer to stressful life events as incidents of acute stress.

Life Strains (chronic stress)

Historically, social workers have been involved with individuals, groups, and families suffering from chronic life strains—what Fried (1982) calls ''endemic stress.'' Germain and Gitterman (1980) elaborate this theme as follows:

> There are also changes to less-valued and to stigmatized statuses when one becomes a foster child, a mental patient, a parolee or probationer, a welfare client, or a physically handicapped person. The tasks associated with these changes, however, are of a different order. In some instances, they are directed toward escaping the status, although the more stigmatized statuses have lim-

ited legitimized exits in our society. In other instances, these changes place heavy coping demands in maintaining a positive self-image, controlling anxiety and depression, and taking effective action to escape the boundaries of these statuses. Moreover, occupants of these statuses are also dealing with the same developmental, status, and crisis tasks as other citizens. Hence, they carry an enormous adaptive burden, but with far less environmental nutriment. [p. 604]

Typically, the informal support systems of those in our society looked upon as losers are fragmented or nonexistent, while formal social supports are usually quantitatively insufficient and qualitatively unresponsive and punitive. Often they have depleted their support systems' material and emotional capital.

Fried (1982) has written one of the most powerful pieces on life strains in the professional literature. It is entitled "Endemic Stress: The Psychology of Resignation and Politics of Scarcity." He defines *endemic stress* (or what we and others have called chronic stress) as:

a condition of continuous and manifold changes, demands, threats, or deprivations, frequently overall in scale and embedded in daily life events. These forces may be widespread and affect much of the population, or they may be discrete and personal; they have diverse origins in economic, political, social, physical-environmental, psychological, or physiological conditions and events. Such events readily summate or cumulate to produce a measurable increase in psycho-social strain and a measurable alteration in social behavior. [p. 5]

People caught up in lives of endemic stress are not always attractive, winning human beings. On the level of behavior, particularly in the realm of relationship to other people, they rely on such defensive avoidance mechanisms as withdrawal and flight, or they tend toward an automatic reliance on impulsive behaviors. They have a poor capacity to cope with feelings of anxiety and depression. Some, especially those who suffered from severe early deprivations, live lives of excessive dependency or much violence, such as parents who neglect or physically abuse their children. It is a cliché in the social sciences and in social work that the brutal have been brutalized as children, and that people who neglect their children have themselves been the victims of neglect.

The psychoanalyst, Heinz Hartmann (1951), suggested that most people are reared in what he called an "average, expectable environment." In this kind of normal environment, an infant is attended to, cared for, held lovingly, fed properly, played with, cooed and sung to—in brief, brought up in an environment of parental love and care. Not all, certainly, but large numbers of people who are seen by social workers in social agencies, mental health clinics, hospitals, and schools did not grow up in "average, expectable environments," having suffered early ruptures in relationships to parents or parent surrogates. This type of long-standing deprivation exemplifies the self-perpetuating endemic or chronic stress that concerns the social sciences today.

Acute versus Chronic Stress

To provide greater clarity when researching and discussing acute versus chronic stress, several points should be kept in mind. First, the great bulk of the research on stress and its consequences has focused on the acute stressors, that is, discrete life events (Fried, 1982). There is relatively little on the chronic stressors, particularly of the type on which social work focuses: the stress situations of child maltreatment; mental illness and its effects on mental patients and their families; and chronic, severe, organic illness and its stressful effects. It should be noted that researchers interested in the prevention of bodily illness or psychiatric disorder tend to focus either on (1) populations where there is no discernible pathology, such as first-time parents, or (2) populations where the possibility of harmful outcomes is expected on the basis of past research (e.g., those suffering painful separation, such as divorce). These kinds of human conditions are relatively understandable and researchable in comparison with, say, the prevention of severe child abuse or neglect.

A second aspect of the acute and chronic categorizations is that they are not mutually exclusive and discrete. They should be viewed as covering a continuum. That is to say, a discrete life event such as divorce or the death of a loved one can unfold in such a manner that it becomes a chronic, severe, stressful response. This explains the development throughout the country of Widow-to-Widow groups and groups for people recently separated and divorced. One of their functions is to prevent a time-limited, discrete, stressful event from evolving into a chronic stress response.

While recognizing that acute and chronic stress frequently "flow into one another so that attributing effects to one or the other becomes difficult," Fried (1982, p. 6) maintains that, under conditions that differentiate between the two, their effects are strikingly distinct. Concerning endemic stress, he states, "Its most striking effects emerge in the subtle, ominous, subclinical manifestations of apathy, alienation, withdrawal, affective denial, decreased productivity and resignation" (p. 6). He contrasts this with acute stress, which "generally invokes a sense of shock, followed by anxiety and grief. These, in turn, lead to a gradual process of marshaling adaptive resources'' (p. 6–7).

Fried (1982) employs role concepts that help us discern the difference in behavioral adaptation to the two kinds of stress. The principal behavioral adaptation to endemic stress is role contraction, the presence of which is critical in discerning the differential reactions to acute and chronic stress. Role contraction occurs gradually as a result of the pervasive and persistent nature of the stress. It refers to a reduction in the number of social roles in which an individual is engaged, indicating a marked decrease not only in social interaction but in different environments of interaction. The person's range narrows as an actor in different social worlds. Isolation, insularity, and stigmatization are the social correlates of chronic stress, and role contraction is one of the consequences. A closer reading of these social-psychological processes would attest more to their simultaneity and circularity rather than to a linear explanation of cause and effect. In contradistinction to the paucity of adaptive role behaviors in the endemic stress situation, acute stress often brings about positive role responses such as role adoption and expansion (taking on new tasks, engaging in information gathering activities, seeking sources of emotional and material support), and assuming obligations heretofore carried out by others.

It is a remarkable and harsh social phenomenon that individuals and families suffering from endemic stress tend to be beset with continuous crises or acute stressors. These individuals and families seem to be crisis prone as a function of the pervasive stress. This phenomenon typically is seen in what Minuchin, Montalvo, Guerney, Rosman, and Schumer (1967) have labeled *disorganized families,* where there is little or no family leadership, where the ''executive,'' parental authority is virtually nonexistent, and where the lack of environmental supports is due to the family's isolation and its unattractiveness as a group of people.

Thinking about social work practice and what it should attend to, it becomes clear that professionals must address both acute and chronic stress responses. The profession has begun to recede from the latter, but not because of a preference for preventing pathology stemming from acute stressors. Rather, social workers have moved steadily into remedial treatment of what used to be considered the milder psychiatric disorders, those that form the heart of a private psychotherapeutic practice. While it would be a distortion to say social work has abandoned the severe, chronic situations, the greater the movement into full-time and part-time private practice, the less time, energy, and effort can be extended to these doleful human conditions.

To some considerable extent, situations like child neglect and abuse and sexual molestation represent the generational playing out of the victim-become-perpetrator nexus. The children are victims of the parents, and when these same children become adults they victimize their own children. Victimization passed on from one generation to another is not always precisely the same, but it often takes an equally dangerous form. A sequence of pathological states may not be inevitable, but one ought to assume a very high probability of generational transmission, at least until solid research indicates otherwise. On the basis of child development theory, clearly in family situations where a child is not respected as a human being who deserves love, proper care, and understanding, there lies the basis for a persecutor-victim outcome with the concomitant disastrous results (Miller, 1981, 1983).

Social work cannot morally afford to abandon families or children situated in cycles of generational dysfunction, such as those in child maltreatment. This does not speak of those even more hidden situations of vague but very real emotional abuse and neglect, absent of visible physical evidence. Assuming for a moment that social work does not run away from these extreme situations, service delivery systems must be created that provide perpetrator-victims with an opportunity to break the chains holding them in moral bondage.

Bloom (1979) has delineated the current research paradigm which is based on prevention of mental illness and emphasizes acute stressful situations and the construction of effective coping behaviors. It is difficult to oppose this trend because it makes good sense, and social work should play a significant role in supporting this thrust in practice and research. However, social work must not turn away from the great numbers of people currently suffering from the hardships of chronic stress. Vulnerable populations—people at risk—are both acute and chronic stress victims, but they are primarily the latter because their lives are already devastated or soon will be, as in the case of children who are born to families caught in a web of social pathology.

Factors Interacting with Stress

Self-Concept

As discussed earlier, Pearlin et al. (1981) suggest that factors other than the quality of the life event or life strain will impact the stress response. While much of the sociological literature on the stress process overlooks the central fact of the impact on self-concept, Pearlin et al. recognize that it is always a particular individual who is undergoing stress. Reactions to stressful situations are essentially a function of (1) how a person evaluates his capacity to control the particular events affecting him—what is called mastery in psychological terms, and (2) whether or not a person thinks of himself as being of worth—the quality and strength of a person's self-esteem. An individual's decline or breakdown signals that the self-concept is undergoing or has undergone a process of diminishment.

Wasserman and Sadoff (1984) have described their work with unemployed Jewish professionals who had joined their combined agencies' support groups. This social-worker/vocational-counselor team was very moved by the epidemic of demoralization (diminished self-concept) among those unemployed for two months or more. While the self-esteem for the majority of the unemployed numbers did not continue to recede during the life of the support groups, there were some members of the group who overcame moderate to severe depressions as a consequence of support from the group process. Improved self-concept is simply not a function of making the "right" human connections, but it is an integral part of an individual's basic strength prior to the advent of a crisis.

Just as the amount of self-diminishment experienced as a result of the stressor affects one's reaction to the situation, it is suggested here that three other factors play a significant role: isolation and loneliness, stigma, and shame and guilt. These three factors are discussed in expansion of Pearlin et al.'s (1981) paradigm.

Isolation and Loneliness

Social work clients who have weak, overburdened, fragmented, or nonexistent support systems suffer from common psychosocial situations: They are besieged by isolation and loneliness, accompanied by feelings of guilt and shame. These emotions encompass their existential worlds and must be considered when looking at the impact of stress. These painful mixtures are the primary data, the ineluctable facts of their lives, and a viable social work assessment and intervention scheme must necessarily address itself to these bedrock feelings and social situations.

According to Weiss (1973) there are two kinds of isolation/loneliness: emotional and social isolation. In a commentary on Weiss' distinction, David Riesman writes: "loss or lack of a truly intimate tie (usually a spouse, lover, parent, or child) and social isolation [is] the consequence of lacking a network of involvements with peers of some sort, be they fellow workers, kinfolk, neighbors, hobbyists, or friends" (p. 7). The purpose of differentiating social and emotional isolation and their attendant states of loneliness is more heuristic than reflective of real-life situations. Usually the two forms of loneliness accompany each other, although one type may predominate in any individual or group situation. For instance, a recently widowed woman may suffer mostly from feelings of emotional isolation accompanied by an attenuated sense of her normal social ties. On the other hand, a woman (in this case a homemaker) who has recently moved with her family, despite a very solid relationship with her husband, may find herself suffering from social isolation. She has not yet found any social groups—in the form of friends, neighbors, fellow parishioners, or voluntary organization members—into which she fits. In ordinary circumstances this is a temporary situation and this woman will soon meet people and begin to feel once again the bonds of social connection out of which she and possibly her family will build a support system.

There is a type of emotional loneliness that apparently inhabits the being and lives of people diagnosed as schizophrenics, a loneliness so experientially devastating and despairing that recovered patients, according to Fromm-Reichman, actively reject its recall. R.S. Weiss (1973) quotes Fromm Reichman as follows, "It is so frightening and uncanny in character that they try to dissociate the memory of what it was like and even the fear of it" (p. 10). Perhaps this form of emotional loneliness is an extreme example of the isolation/loneliness spectrum. The frozen bodily position of the catatonic patient is perhaps the most notable, dramatic symbol of the person cut off and unresponsive to others. But there are others, too, whose suffering is less dramatic and in a way less known to the public; people whose everyday lives come close to the emotional isolation and loneliness of the schizophrenic, namely, neglectful or abusive parents, and fathers and stepfathers who sexually molest their daughters. Social workers and psychotherapists who have treated abusive parents have observed and commented upon the encapsulated, closeted nature of their lives. They tend to cut themselves off from all relationship outside the family. Weiss (1973) believes that

> the complex of symptoms associated with the loneliness of emotional isolation is strongly reminiscent of the distress of the small child who fears that he has been abandoned by his parents. On the other hand, the symptoms associated with the loneliness of social isolation are like the boredom, feelings of exclusion, and feelings of marginality of the small child whose friends are all away. [p. 20]

In brief, the loneliness of social isolation is usually a less noxious state of affairs. It is unpleasant and wearisome, but it is less suggestive of a deep, intrapsychic turmoil in both its temporary and more permanent forms. It is the kind of loneliness that is a universal experience, a more or less transient desolation caused by a dislocation or break in one's relationships. Reparation of old ties or the creation of new ones or a combination of both are the usual prescriptions for a good outcome.

Stigma

Stigmatization is a social process that affects the ability to face stress. As Spitzer and Denzin (1968) describe it, "a stigmatized person is one with a deeply discrediting identity" (p. 385). The stigmatized person is constantly apprehensive about how she will be received by others, experiencing a feeling of dread which she carries with herself as if it were a biological appendage. People become stigmatized as a consequence of other people's perceptions and definitions. So, like shame, stigma possesses both subjective and objective characteristics: "I feel the stigma of being a crippled person because people who come in contact with me see me (or look away from me) as not being a whole person." The stigma that attends social work clients runs on a continuum from none or hardly any to what might be called massive. A widow who seeks counseling in response to her loss suffers from little or no stigma, as there is generally no pejorative social definition attached to widowhood. A parent who neglects a child is highly stigmatized and carries that feeling within. In between these two poles are people who seek marriage and family counseling, people going through divorce, children who go into foster or adoptive homes, adolescents released from reformatories, and so on.

Stigma, which usually appears in combination with other components of chronic life strain discussed in this section, is an endemic stress syndrome that necessitates comprehensive programs of human support.

Shame and Guilt

Feelings of shame and guilt are linked to the isolation/loneliness complex and are universal human experiences woven into the texture of social life. There are guilt cultures and shame cultures, and it is difficult, if not impossible, to determine which of the two types is predominant in American life. One thing is certain: The psychoanalytic literature reflects a much greater attention to the psychodynamics of guilt than it does to those of shame. Yet it seems that, while the great bulk of social work clients, like the rest of humanity, are beset by an intricate combination of both guilt and shame, the latter is the stronger and the most vexing, particularly in situations where clients are either alienated from or bereft of support systems.

These feelings of guilt and shame must be addressed when looking at the impact of stress. The principal affects that form the basis of shame are a sense of inadequacy or inferiority and, beyond these, a fear of abandonment (Lynd, 1961; Piers & Singer, 1953; Wurmser, 1981). Guilt, on the other hand, in both its conscious and unconscious forms, suggests an actual or fantasized breaking of social and moral codes by acts of commission and omission. The social and moral codes are delineated in the forms of "thou shalts," and "thou shalt nots." Feelings of guilt arise in people capable of empathy toward others when one of these codes is violated or where the fantasies of such violations permeate the psyche of the individual.

In Erikson's (1953) scheme of psychosocial development, the child's first stage of growth and crisis is that of *trust versus mistrust,* which takes place during the first year of life. The second stage is *autonomy versus shame and doubt* (during the second year of life), and the third is *initiative versus guilt.* Thus, according to Eriksonian theory, feelings of shame precede those of guilt in human development. On the practical level of working with clients, it is noteworthy that feelings of shame are much more difficult for clients to express in terms of past or present events than those of guilt. Both shame and guilt, particularly guilt in the psychoanalytic sense of unconscious guilt (feeling guilt without knowing the source of that nagging, overpowering feeling) are destructive to one's sense of self-control and self-esteem.

Feelings of isolation and loneliness among neglectful mothers are noted by Polansky (1980). In talking with his associates, he said, "I asked my case workers to sum up their impression of forty-six neglectful families we had studied; the reply was, 'They're such lonesome people' " (p. 89). Polansky went on to propose that "we make the understanding and treatment of loneliness the major focus of our field" (p. 109).

Isolation, loneliness, and the sense of shame are prototypical of all social work clients who have been locked into a chronic personal and interpersonal matrix marked by feelings of inferiority and inadequacy, and into relationships characterized by a lack or absence of empathy. Their distress is manifested in narcissistic withdrawal or excessive violence. When these people who perpetrate harm on their victims are publicly exposed, the feelings of shame are often overpowering. That which has been hidden has now been brought out in the open. It may be a relief to some, but it is a humiliation to all.

Returning to the theme of loneliness and Polansky's (1980) notion that social work's mission is *"easing loneliness,"* we find that he has indirectly touched upon a critical oversight in much of social work assessment, namely, the overlooking or disregard of clients' social support systems. Loneliness and the lack of a felt connection with others are synonymous. Thus, treatment working on the maintenance, rebuilding, or creation of support systems points toward a strategy of connecting people under the temporary leadership of caring, accepting leaders. Such interpersonal connecting can best be initiated by bringing together people caught in the same set of difficult and often painful circumstances. At that critical point of their lives, they must talk to each other about their collective situation, their virtues and defects, strengths and weaknesses, the good and the bad in themselves. Ultimately, they must make choices about some current dilemmas and about the future direction of their lives.

The essence of this experience is captured in this line from "Holiday," a story by Katherin Anne Porter: "They wept away the hard core of secret trouble . . . secure in a communal grief" (Howe, 1983, pp. 42–43). The support group, as a small community, is a locus of solace.

MEDIATORS OF THE STRESS PROCESS

There are two primary mediators of stress: individual coping and social support. We will discuss each in turn.

Individual Coping as a Mediator of Stress

This discussion begins with a caveat on coping and social support, quoting from Lazarus and De Longis (1983). While their specific interest is in the relationship between psychological stress and coping in the aging process, their remarks are quite appropos to our discussion.

> First, we must be far more thoughtful and systematic than we have been in measuring stress and coping processes. For example, we must abandon the simplistic notion that stress is adequately described by life events, however psychometrically sophisticated, and that it is sufficient to treat coping as a stable, overarching style with which people address the myriad sources of stress in their lives.
>
> Second, stress and coping theory must take into account that variability in processes of aging, sources of stress, and problems of coping arise not only

> from the environmental conditions of living, but also from the personal agendas and characteristics that shape stressful encounters and are shaped by them.
>
> Third, throughout life, people struggle to make sense out of what happens to them and to provide themselves with a sense of order and continuity (Butler, 1975). This struggle is centered in divergent personal beliefs and commitments, shapes cognitive appraisals of stressful transactions and coping, and therefore has profound consequences for morale, social and work function, and somatic health. It is thus not age alone, but the significance of stressful events viewed within the continuity of a person's life that must be taken into account. [pp. 245–246]

We would add this observation to Lazarus and De Longis's admonition: The great bulk of social support literature and research generally disregards individual coping histories and capacities, including those coping strategies that seem to be stable and those that have undergone change as a function of personal development.

With respect to unemployment, Pearlin et al. (1981) indicate that successful coping entails two kinds of thinking or cognitive appraisal: (1) a philosophical stance in which the unemployed person compares her position with those who are worse off; and (2) an idealized posture, which denigrates the importance of money and material success. This kind of appraisal might be relevant and useful for a small group of professional and artistically minded people who have totally rejected the materialistic values trumpeted in our society. For everyday working people, however, a more adequate, effective way of coping is to make a shift from self-blame to blaming the system. Instead of anger being turned inward on the self, it is projected outward on an economic system which, often without warning, turns people who normally work and feel useful into people who feel useless and hopeless. However, getting stuck psychologically at the point of blaming the system does not help an unemployed person cope with a long-term loss of work. The issue still poses itself: How can depression be warded off sufficiently to avoid draining the psychic energy needed to maintain ego integrity?

In their article entitled "Models of Helping and Coping," Brickman and associates (1982) develop four models of coping, the most effective and health-producing of which is the compensatory model, in which "people are not responsible for problems but are responsible for solutions" (p. 371). Brickman et al. assert,

> The strength of the compensatory model for coping is that it allows people to direct their energies outward, working on trying to solve problems or trans-

> form their environment without berating themselves for their role in creating these problems, or permitting others to create them in the first place. [p. 372]

Brickman et al. (1982) think a potential deficiency of this model is the possibility that an individual might acquire "a rather negative or even paranoid view of the world" (p. 372). It would seem that much depends on the kinds of relationships, including personal and political social networks, they have maintained or acquired.

In the social work literature there are few references to how people actually do cope with their problems. Perlman (1975) is the only major social work theorist who has given much thought to the coping process and how social workers can help clients improve their coping abilities. She defines coping as follows:

> Coping is a person's effort to deal with some new and often problematic situations or encounters or to deal in some new way with an old problem. Its purpose is mastery or problem-solving at best; at least, it serves to reduce tension and ameliorate the problem. It is a process in which we are engaged from birth onward at levels of the unconscious, the preconscious, and in full consciousness. [p. 213]

This definition—and particularly an aspect she labels "conscious coping, . . . a person's conscious, volitional effort to deal with himself and his problem in their interdepenence" (p. 214)—still seems accurate. As a clinical social work theorist, Perlman is particularly sensitized to the cognitive work and the necessary actions one must undertake to cope with troubles.

A host of researchers, primarily clinical and social psychologists interested in cognitive processes, have developed coping inventories which seemingly aid people in effective adaptation to stressful situations. Some of these coping strategies are (1) logical analysis, (2) complex redefinition (in family therapy this mental activity is referred to as reframing), (3) information seeking, (4) problem-solving action, and (5) affective regulation (Moos & Billings, 1982).

Moos and Billings write, "We still know relatively little about the specific coping processes people use in adapting to stressful life circumstances" (p. 241). Even less is known about the coping processes of people who live in steady, unchanging, oppressive conditions (endemic stress) that must be endured on an everyday basis.

In her concluding remarks about the lives of low-income mothers, Belle's (1982) comments on a single item, the lack of money: "Money problems are particularly central to depression . . . and since many women regard decent paid employment as a potential route out of poverty and depression, programs which help women to find and keep such employment could have a powerful impact on mental health'' (p. 242). The question arises as to how these women *cope* day in and day out without enough money, in order to live decently in a material sense? How do they cope cognitively, affectively, and behaviorally? By what miracle do some women actually avoid becoming depressed under these conditions? Professionals have hardly begun to understand how this positive outcome is possible.

This discussion of coping processes proves important because much effort in clinical social work is helping people cope with everyday problems. While this book emphasizes the therapeutic effects of social support systems for the individual in trouble, the irrefutable fact is that the focal person engages in a process of internal problem solving. Much social network and social support literature leaves the reader with the impression that, while support systems are doing their therapeutic work, a person is not much involved in the struggle to gain mastery or ameliorate a problematic situation. It is as if there were a lot of interested, concerned, and caring people dancing around a person who is hardly involved in the choreography. Historical experience in clinical social work indicates that such is not the case. Possessing a functioning support system is an important component of the coping process, but the focal person's internal cognitive/affective/behavioral strategies and tactics cannot be ignored and are central to any human problem-solving effort.

Social Support as a Mediator of Stress

There are several reviews (Bloom, 1982; Cobb, 1976; Dean & Lin, 1976) of the research literature on the mediating or buffering effect of social support on the stress process. This literature is characterized by a rather typical but useful generalized ''scientific'' posture toward research findings: There are some rather solid indications that social support does buffer stress, but theorists and researchers are not at all sure how this phenomenon works. Furthermore, there is little agreement among them on the definition of social support. Definitional, conceptual, and methodological problems are very complicated.

Yet, with the obvious paucity of knowledge in a strictly scientific sense, too many studies point toward the helpful effects of social support in the face of stress to disregard the phenomenon. Quite the contrary, professionals ought to pay a great deal of attention to it. Much knowledge and skill are needed in order to assist people in coping with the problems of everyday life, some of which can be deadly in their effects if there are no "buffers."

A growing and now sizable literature exists on the relationship between stressful life events and the occurrence of organic and psychiatric illness and mortality (e.g., Antonovosky, 1972; Dohrenwend & Dohrenwend, 1974; Langer & Michael, 1963), but this evidence is not clear-cut.

In this brief review of the connections between social support and illness, total coverage of the literature is not the objective. The review that follows is a brief discussion of research findings in terms of specific stress situations and the effects of mediators or buffers when present or absent.

Antonovosky (1979) powerfully and incisively speculated that supportive ties to people serve as a source of resistance to the effects of social stress, particularly bodily and psychological illness. Everyday conventional wisdom confirms that this is true, but, as a scientific hypothesis, it beckons theorists and practitioners to search for facts that either confirm or deny it. We will discuss some of the many studies that tend to confirm Antonovosky's hypothesis.

Joan Bloom (1982) in her study of the connection between demographic factors and well-being, that, "contrary to general impressions, marital status is a stronger predictor of age-adjusted mortality ratios than are those for ethnicity (white/non-white) or gender" (p. 130). Married men have lower mortality rates for chronic health conditions (certain types of cardiac conditions and cancer) and score lower on social indicators such as suicide and homicide than do never-married, divorced, and widowed men. (Marriage is not as protective of health for women as it is for men.)

Berkman (1982) did a nine-year follow-up study of a sample of adults from Alameda County in California. She developed a weighted Social Network Index in which she included such variables as marriage, membership in formal organizations such as a church or synagogue, ties to relatives, and so on. Berkman found that "individuals with many social ties . . . and poor health habits had lower mortality than individuals with relatively better health habits and few social ties" (p. 133). What is an even more telling and powerful finding in this study is that the correlations between the factors in the Social Network Index and the mortality rates were independent of other important variables, including health practices, drinking, smoking, obesity, and socioeconomic status.

Another study (Bruhn, 1982) that speaks to the resistance factor of social support in regard to organic illness was conducted over a seven-year period in the town of Roseto, Pennsylvania, a small community settled by Italian immigrants in the early part of the 20th century. Of interest in this community was the low death rate from coronary disease, particularly among men, which was coupled with what are generally considered to be very poor, harmful eating habits. Food intake was high in calories, fats, and alcohol, and there was high incidence of obesity in the population. Bruhn did a comparative analysis of the lifestyle differences between the people of Roseto and those of neighboring communities. The people of Roseto engaged in less residential and social mobility, and they held more memberships in community organizations than their neighbors from comparable communities. During crises, they received more help from other nuclear family members and from extended family and friends. These close social ties seemed to have protected them from illness. These ties apparently were more powerful in determining health outcomes, at least for serious cardiac illness, than were dietary factors.

Several other researchers have investigated the hypothesis that social support buffers stress and reduces the risk of illness. Nuckolls, Cassel and Kaplan (reported in Cobb, 1976) did a study of 170 pregnant U.S. Army wives. The researchers correlated two factors, life-change scores and social-support scores. Among those wives who had high life-change and low social-support scores, 91% had complications during pregnancy, while only 39% of those with low life-change and high social-support scores suffered from complications. The most interesting finding, however, was that women with high life-change and high social-support scores had the best outcome. Only 33% of this group sustained complications in pregnancy.

Finlayson (1976) investigated the post-hospital adjustment of men recovering from a heart attack (mycardial infarction). The more emotional support these men received, the better the recovery they made. Perhaps a more significant finding is that the families of the heart attack victims who received material and emotional support during the man's illness and over the long term retained their social ties and thus had more favorable outcomes than those families where support was either absent, scanty, or inconsistent. Here we see another important aspect of the relationship between social support and stress, namely, the issue of who "supports the supporters," raised by Bronfenbrenner (1979) in relation to the education of children. He believes that parent education should focus not on "who cares for the children but on who cares for those who care" (p. 777). Finlayson's (1976) study illustrates something that social workers know from their practice: many clients' natural support systems undergo excessive stress and become overburdened, and some burn out. While the prevalence of clients' with overburdened or devastated support systems is unclear, it is probably true that a sizable number of people seek professional help when their own system can no longer serve them adequately.

Another study bears on Bronfenbrenner's (1979) question of who cares for those who care. Pless and Satterwhite (1972) recruited women who themselves had chronically ill children, to counsel some families whose children were chronically ill. These families were compared to a control group of families who received no counseling. After a year had passed, the two groups were assessed. The psychological health of the children whose families had received social support through counseling improved more than those children whose parents were in the control group.

Parkes (1969) found that loss of emotional support results in psychological decompensation and despair. As Bloom (1982), describes the findings, "while investigating psychiatric admissions in two hospitals in England, he discovered that 340 adult patients during a 2-year period had been widowed within 6 months prior to admission. This is six times the rate of newly bereaved individuals one would expect to be admitted" (p. 131).

Brown, Bhrolchaim, and Harris (1975) studied depressive reactions among women by dividing their sample into two groups. In one group of women, each had a confidante, while in the other they did not. Those women who lacked a confidante were 10 times more likely to be depressed than those who possessed one. In this study, a confidante was usually a man with whom the woman had "a close, intimate and confiding relationship" (p. 242).

In another study along the same lines, Lowenthal and Haven (1968) found, in studying the psychological adjustment among elderly women, that a confidante of either sex was protective of health. Women with confidantes were better able to deal with retirement and survive the loss of people close to them than were women who lacked confidantes.

In a doctoral dissertation on single, older, childless women, Rice (1982) corroborated Lowenthal and Haven's (1968) findings that a confidante was protective of well-being. Rice (1982) further found that the confidantes (other women) were long-term friends (mean time known = 51.7 years) and were seen frequently. Rice wrote, "Over 50% see their confidante once a week or more, almost 75% of them call each other once a week or more" (p. 96).

Belle (1982), in the book *Lives in Stress: Women and Depression,* wrote, "Among low income mothers, those with particularly low or unreliable income, those who have been unable to secure the kind of paid employment they have sought, those without confidante and child care help, and those with a history of change and loss in childhood appear to be at high risk [for depression]'' (p. 241). Belle prescribes for these women, including those who are depressed, ''decent paid employment'' and ''mutual help groups.'' She believes that the latter ''can be particularly powerful resources for women in emotional distress and in the midst of oppressive life conditions. In such groups, women meet with others who have similar experiences, provide and receive emotional support, and work together toward solutions to problems'' (p. 242).

Gore (1978) studied the effects of unemployment upon men who had been regular workers with previously stable work histories. She compared the health outcomes of these unemployed men with those who continued to work. The comparisons were made at intervals, the first being soon after loss of their jobs and then at 6, 12, and 24 months after the factory closing. Those who perceived their wives as supportive had fewer symptoms in general. They had lower cholesterol levels and blamed themselves less for their unemployment situation than men whose wives were not perceived as supportive.

There are some indications that social support is an important buffer in marital disruption. Many studies indicate that divorcing or recently divorced people who receive social support from family and friends cope more effectively than those who do not receive social support. Bloom, Hodges, and Caldwell (1982) found that in postdivorce situations, women's support systems were stronger than men's and that women reported more psychological and social benefits as a consequence of divorce than men.

In this brief review of the beneficial effects of social support on stressful life situations, it is a plausible hypothesis that people who can depend on others for material assistance and/or emotional care and nurturance fare better than those who are more or less deprived of these sources of sustenance. There is nothing surprising about this conclusion, yet it should be kept in mind that social support itself is only one component among the many protective factors in coping with stress. Segal (Seligman, 1983) of The National Institute of Mental Health lists four such protective categories:

1. An assumption that there is meaning or a rationale for the stress that is being experienced
2. A capacity to maintain a sense of control over one's environment
3. Identification with the larger society of which one is a part
4. Support ties to family and community

The protective factor that is most clearly intrapsychic in nature and provides the undergirding for a person's individual coping style is the first one. In order to cope with some modicum of success, the stressful situation has to make sense or has to fit into the logic of things, even though there may be great conflict and pain endured. Fitting into the logic of things does not mean that whatever is happening to the person can be justified as fair or deserved. It simply means that one can say, "Something has happened, I know what it is (or I hope I can find out), and that is why I am having all of this trouble."

In order to maintain a sense of control over his environment, a psychologically healthy individual must believe that some important things in his life are under his control. In this precarious world, some of the greatest danger seem to be out of individual and even collective control. But one aspect of maintaining an internal locus of control is the sense that people, particularly those who are closest to us, can be relied upon, and that we, in turn, are dependable. This mutuality, reliability, and dependability are critical to our capacity to feel that the world is not total chaos and that the intentions and actions of others are trustworthy. Beyond the factor of mutual dependability is each individual's sense of inner security, whether that competence resides in human relationships or in work or in playing the piano—or in any intricate combination of factors that help him to maintain a sense of coherence.

Segal's (1983) last two protective factors in coping with stress involve a person's social identity and affiliations and her more personal social ties. Identification with the larger society does not mean a total acceptance of all of the values, beliefs, and norms of the society. What it does mean is some deep sense of identification with some aspects of a society's way of life and values; some sense of ongoing connectedness with the people of a town, region, or a country; some pervasive feeling that one belongs to a larger whole of which one is part. This describes a state of being that is quite the opposite of the anomic person, whose sense of belonging is utterly deficient and whose ties with others are marginal. As Cassel (1976) notes,

> A remarkably similar set of social circumstances characterizes people who develop tuberculosis and schizophrenia, become alcoholics, are victims of multiple accidents, or commit suicide. *Common to all these people is a marginal status in society.* They are individuals who for a variety of reasons (e.g., ethnic minorities rejected by the dominant majority in their neighborhood; high sustained rates of residential and occupational mobility; broken homes or isolated living circumstances) have been deprived of meaningful social contact. [p. 110]

Finally, the more abstract aspect of social identity in regard to the larger society is reinforced and energized by Segal's (1983) fourth factor, supportive ties to family and community. People's personal social networks and support systems are central to their sense of identity and their capacity to deal with the problems of everyday life, including those that border on the unimaginable. We recently listened to some people who belong to an organization called The Parents of Murdered Children. Is there anything worse that can happen than for parents to bury their own murdered children? By their collective testimony, it was clear to them that they were fortunate to find each other. All said that without each other they didn't know how they could make it. All of these people were to a greater or lesser degree depressed, yet, without the support group, the severity of their difficulties would have been infinitely greater.

As a closing note to this chapter, consider that only the first of Segal's (1983) protective categories in coping with stress is truly intrapsychic, while the other three are clearly interpersonal or more broadly social in nature. This implies that bonds to others, particularly the quantity and quality of attachments, determine in some considerable measure our capacity to grapple with the less noxious, more expectable, and more normal transitional changes, as well as the unpredictable and (sometimes) unimaginable events. Without other people, what would we be? Yet, without an inner sense of integrity, there is little moral courage with which to grapple with the troubles and difficulties of life.

REFERENCES

Antonovsky, A. (1972). Breakdown: A needed fourth step in the conceptual armamentarium of modern medicine. *Social Science and Medicine, 6*(5), 537–544.

Antonovsky, A. (1979). *Health stress and coping*. San Francisco: Jossey-Bass.

Bartlett, H.M. (1961). *Social work practice in the health field*. New York: National Association of Social Workers.

Belle, D. (1982). *Lives in stress: Women and depression*. Beverly Hills, CA: Sage.

Berkman, L. (1977). *Social networks, host resistance and mortality: A follow-up study of Alameda County residents*. Unpublished dissertation, University of California, Berkeley.

Bloom, B. (1979). Prevention of mental disorders: Recent advances in theory and practice. *Community Mental Health Journal, 15*(3), 179–191.

Bloom, B., Hodges, W.F., & Caldwell, R.A. (1982). A preventive program for the newly separated: Initial evaluation. *Journal of Community Psychology, 10*(3), 251–264.

Bloom, J.R. (1982). Social support systems and cancer: A conceptual view. In J. Cohen, J.W. Cullen, & R.L. Martin (Eds.), *Psychosocial aspects in cancer* (pp. 129–150). New York: Raven Press.

Brickman, P., Rabinowitz, V.C., Karuza, J.J., Coates, D., Cohn, E., & Kidder, L. (1982). Models of helping and coping. *American Psychologist, 37*(4), 368-384.

Brown, G.W., Bhrolchaim, M.N., & Harris, T. (1975). Social class and psychiatric disturbance among women in an urban population. *Sociology, 9*(2), 223-254.

Bronfenbrenner, U. (1979). *The Ecology of Human Development.* Cambridge, MA: Harvard University Press.

Bruhn, J.G. (1965). An epidemiological study of myocardial infarctions in an Italian-American community. *Journal of Chronic Diseases, 18,* 353-365.

Butler, R.N. (1975). The facade of chronological age: An interpretive summary. In B.L. Neugarten (Ed.), *Middle age and aging.* Chicago, IL: University of Chicago Press.

Cassel, J. (1976). The contribution of the social environment to host resistance. *Journal of Epidemiology, 104*(2), 107-123.

Cobb, S. (1976). Social support as a conductor of life stress. *Psychosomatic Medicine, 38*(5), 300-313.

Dean, A., & Lin, N. (1976, September). *The stress buffering role of social support on occupational stresses and strains.* Paper presented at the 84th annual convention of the American Psychological Association, Washington, DC.

Dohrenwend, B.S., & Dohrenwend, B.P. (1974). *Stressful life events: Their nature and effects.* New York: John Wiley.

Erikson, E.H. (1953). Growth and crises of the healthy personality. In C. Kluckhohn & H.A. Murray (Eds.), *Personality in nature, society and culture* (2nd ed.) (pp. 185-225). New York: Alfred A. Knopf.

Finlayson, A. (1976). Social networks as coping resources. *Social Science and Medicine, 10*(2), 97-103.

Fried, M. (1982). Endemic stress: The psychology of resignation and the politics of scarcity. *American Journal of Orthopsychiatry, 52*(1), 4-19.

Germain, C.B., & Gitterman, A. (1980). *The life model of social work practice.* New York: Columbia University Press.

Gitterman, A., & Germain, C.B. (1976). Social work practice: A life model. *Social Service Review, 50*(4), 601-610.

Gore, S. (1978). The effects of social support in moderating the health consequence of unemployment. *Journal of Health and Social Behavior, 19,* 157-165.

Hartmann, H. (1951). *Ego psychology and the problem of adaptation.* New York: International University Press.

Howe, I. (1983, September 11). Stories of our loneliness. [Review of *Cathedral* by Raymond Carver.] *The New York Times Book Review,* pp. 42-43.

Langer, T.S., & Michael S.T. (1963). *Life stress and mental health.* New York: Free Press.

Lazarus, R.S., & De Longis, A. (1983). Psychological stress and coping in aging. *American Psychologist, 38*(3), 245-246.

Lowenthal, M., & Haven, C. (1968). Interaction and adaptation: Intimacy as a critical variable. *American Sociological Review, 33*(1), 20–30.

Lynd, H.M. (1961). *On shame and the search for the identity.* New York: Science Editions.

Miller, A. (1981). *Prisoners of childhood.* New York: Basic Books.

Miller, A. (1983). *For your own good: Hidden cruelty in child rearing and the roots of violence.* New York: Farrar, Straus, Giroux.

Minuchin, S., Montalvo, B., Guerney, B., Rosman, B.L., & Schumer, F. (1967). *Families of the slums.* New York: Basic Books.

Moos, R.H., & Billings, A.G. (1982). Conceptualizing and measuring coping resources and processes. In L. Goldberger & S. Breznitz (Eds.), *Handbook of stress: Theoretical and clinical aspects* (pp. 212–230). New York: Free Press.

Nuckolls, K.B., Cassel, J., & Kaplan, B.H. (1972). Psychosocial assets, life crises and the prognosis of pregnancy. *American Journal of Epidemiology, 95*(5), 431-441.

Parkes, C.M., Benjamin, B., & Fitzgerald, B.G. (1969). Broken heart. A statistical study of increased mortality among widowers. *British Medical Journal, 4,* 740–743.

Pearlin, L.I., Lieberman, M.A., Menaghan, E.G., & Mullan, J.T. (1981). The stress process. *Journal of Health and Social Behavior, 22,* 337–356.

Perlman, H.H. (1975). In quest of coping. *Social Casework, 56,* 213–225.

Piers, G., & Singer, M.B. (1953). *Shame and guilt.* Homewood, IL: Charles C Thomas.

Pless, I.B., & Satterwhite, B. (1972). Chronic illness in childhood: Selection, activities and evaluation of nonprofessional family counselors. *Clinical Pediatrics, 11*(7), 403–410.

Polansky, N.A. (1980). On loneliness: A program for social work. *Smith College Studies in Social Work, 50*(2), 85–113.

Rice, S. (1982). *Single older childless women: A study of social support and life satisfaction.* Unpublished doctoral dissertation, School of Social Welfare, University of California, Los Angeles.

Riesman, D. (1973). Foreward. In R.S. Weiss (Ed.), *Loneliness: The experience of emotional and social isolation* (p. ix). Cambridge, MA: MIT Press.

Seligman, R. (1983). Israel at 35: A stressful but healthy society. *Women's American ORT Reporter, 33*(3), 3–4.

Spitzer, S.P., & Denzin, N.K. (1968). *The mental patient: Studies in the sociology of deviance.* New York: McGraw-Hill.

Wasserman, D., & Sadoff, L. (1984, May 30). *Support groups for unemployed professional people.* Paper presented at the National Conference of Jewish Communal Service Workers, Los Angeles, CA.

Weiss, R.S. (1973) (Ed.). *Loneliness: The experience of emotional and social isolation.* Cambridge, MA: MIT Press.

Weiss, R.S. (1973). The study of loneliness. In R.S. Weiss (Ed.), *Loneliness: The experience of emotional and social isolation* (pp. 9–29). Cambridge, MA: MIT Press.

Wurmser, L. (1981). *The mask of shame.* Baltimore, MD: John Hopkins University Press.

3 Why Do We Need Support Groups?

NORMALIZING THE SEARCH FOR HELP

There is now a formidable literature that indicates that stress is a ubiquitous phenomenon and that mental and physical breakdowns are often the consequences of unrelieved, unmediated stress. All stress reactions, it should be noted, are expressed in varying intensities of psychological distress.

The societal reaction to stress has been the proliferation of a bewildering variety of remedies designed to mitigate the baneful effects of stress—physical exercises including yoga; meditation and relaxation therapies; nutritional regimens; the "group-think" of cults; off-the-shelf and prescribed medicines; legal and illegal drugs; alcoholism; holistic therapies; individual, group, and family psychotherapies; and self-help and professionally led support groups. Some wag has remarked that if the 1950s were the Age of Anxiety, the 1980s are the Age of Stress.

The search for relief from stress very often generates desperation and frenzy which lead people astray. The cure for stress can be infinitely worse than the pain and malaise that accompany stress itself. The point need not be belabored. It is evident that many lives have been destroyed in the frantic search for relief. The exploitation of psychic and physical pain has always been and is today a flourishing enterprise.

Note also that, with the exception of the groups, the relief of stress is sought through the path of individual "salvation." Whether one turns to EST or relies upon drugs, it is the individual seeking his own relief, unconnected to others who face the same or a similar situation.

The tremendous popularity of self-help groups can be explained because actual and prospective members view them as relatively nonstigmatized, less threatening, natural ways of getting help for a problem. This is of enormous importance to human service workers interested in extending their therapies to populations who are fearful, disrespectful, or rejecting of professional help.

Social work, especially among the professions, has been identified with stigmatized populations and organizations whose purposes are ambivalently ameliorative and restrictive. Social workers find themselves in county and state hospitals, protective services for abused and neglected children, probation agencies, and so on. The wider public identifies social work with "welfare." As a result, in those agencies and programs where social work has traditionally served stigmatized populations, the search for a normalized helping modality has met with little success. Stigmatization and the attribution of normality cannot be joined, either conceptually or in practice.

Social work's search for a normalized modality of giving help has found a resolution in the emergence of the professionally led support group. What is important is the creation of a helpful modality that is therapeutic but is not publicized as therapy, a term that imputes illness and/or deviance to wide segments of the public.

The traditional recipients of social work services, those people who are counted among disadvantaged populations, frequently are not voluntary seekers of psychotherapy. Unlike some members of the upper-middle and middle classes, who think of psychotherapy as a more or less natural way of resolving problems and conflicts, many members of the lower socioeconomic groupings are not drawn to agencies and clinics that are reputed to offer psychotherapeutic services. People do not want to view themselves as being crazy, nor do they want to be defined as such by others. A very large, potential "mental health" clientele exists who reject the idea of therapy because to them it means mental illness, a sign of deviance or weakness, and/or a mark of abnormality.

Current evidence from self-help groups demonstrates that people will seek assistance and accept referrals for help if it is not initially viewed as humiliating and threatening. Since social workers extend their services to a wide range of voluntary and involuntary clients, it would seem logical that a treatment modality such as the professionally led support group might well be an effective and potentially attractive way of reaching both sets of clients. This appears to be true, judging by the increasing number of articles in the social work journals in which support groups—although they are not always called that—are either a principal or ancillary treatment modality.

Social workers and other human service professionals have organized support groups for voluntary clients, including prospective first-time parents; first-time mothers; people either going through or recently divorced; unemployed blue-collar and white-collar workers; the aged; adult children of aged parents; single parents; parents of retarded children; parents of autistic children; foster home parents, and so on. Support groups for involuntary clients have also been conducted, with a modicum of effectiveness and success. Involuntary clients are ordered by an official authority, such as a judge, to attend group sessions. Men who batter their wives, fathers and stepfathers who sexually molest their children, and people caught up in substance abuse are among the populations of involuntary clients who have been members of support groups.

Thus, through professionally led support groups, social work has magnified its capacity to reach populations who (1) such as previously had not been viewed as potential clients, such as first-time parents, adults having difficulties with their aged parents, or other cases of "life cycle transitional" problems, or (2) were viewed as untreatable either by virtue of poor motivation or by the inherent intractability of the problem, such as child molesters and wife batterers. In effect, social work had been wittingly or unwittingly ignoring many classes of people with particular social problems ranging from the normal crises of everyday life to those suffering from severe, chronic stress which rendered them and their families susceptible to bodily disease and/or psychiatric disturbances. In reaching out to these populations, social work is working toward normalizing the search for help and support.

THE IMPETUS BEHIND GROUP TREATMENT

Social work's major treatment perspective in the United States revolves around a basic fact: Clinical social workers make up the majority of the profession, with their principal treatment modality being the dyadic arrangements—an individual client and a social worker engaged in a problem solving process. While early social work history shows that there was much interest in family influences on shaping the individual's attitudes and behavior, this interest did not translate into what might be thought of as family treatment. Quite the contrary, the impact of psychoanalytic thinking in social work practice solidified the trend of working almost exclusively in dyads or what the profession calls, in a more homely way, individual treatment. Beyond the influence of psychoanalysis in determining the predominant treatment modality for helping people, there is a yet more powerful social value in American life—the right to privacy. According to that belief, a person has the right to withhold her feelings and thoughts about anything or anyone or to disclose them as she sees fit to those who carry the authority of legitimation through either religious or secular sanctions. Once disclosed to authorized parties, the content remains only with them. The right to privacy is central in the American lexicon of rights and, understandably, is a primary social work value. While there are increasing threats to privacy or confidentiality, social workers are in agreement with the great majority of Americans in believing this right is inviolate.

Dyadic treatment has come to be viewed as the modality par excellence for assuring a client's privacy, and in contrast to it, group work is "public." One-to-one confidentiality is not possible in a group; therefore, maintaining group confidentiality becomes more complicated to insure. In support group work, all members of the group share the same basic problematic situation, so to some extent this is a binding force among them. However, this bond does not prevent the possibility of unfair behavior that compromises the privacy of group members. As a result, social work with groups inherently presents an increased and somewhat uncomfortable risk for breaches of confidentiality. Rather than face this challenge of actively reinforcing and discussing the value of confidentiality in groups, many social workers and potential members have avoided the group modality.

Individual treatment, increasingly in the form of psychotherapy, has become social work's most important way of rendering help to people. This emphasis and the extension of services to populations other than those defined as being at risk, vulnerable, or disadvantaged go hand in hand. The ascendancy of individual treatment during social work's history from approximately 1918 to the present has beclouded the slow but steady rise of the family therapy movement since approximately 1955 and the continuing presence of social work with groups during this entire period.

This method of working with people has generally taken place in such locales as community centers, settlement houses, YMCAs and YWCAs, residential treatment centers, psychiatric facilities, and so on. Clinical social workers have also used the group method in their work, although they favor calling it "group therapy." A great deal of confusion exists in all the human service professions, including social work, as to the similarities and differences between group psychotherapy and other forms of helping in groups. Later in this chapter, a differentiation among group psychotherapy, support groups, and self-help groups is essayed.

Social group work's original perspective was generally but not wholly confined to working with people who were viewed as "normal." The people who make up groups under social group work auspices are neither patients nor clients; they are members. The professionally led support group represents the most recent version of social work with groups, and clinical social workers make up the bulk of professionals conducting these groups.

The question arises as to why some social work agencies and other human service organizations are increasingly using the support group method. There is no simple or single answer to this question.

First, there is a growing realization that many actual and potential social work clients, for one reason or another, cannot benefit from individual treatment. This is especially true of the client whose lifestyle is characterized by too little reflective thinking and too few super-ego inhibitions. Lack of impulse control is often at the center of their troubled and troubling lives. Few schools of psychotherapy make claims of success with such clients or patients. On the other end of the scale are people whose needs are as much educational as they are psychological. First-time parents, foster parents, parents of disabled children, and so on can benefit from short-term (of 6 to 12 weeks' duration) support groups of an educational-experiential type. The group method is both more powerful in its effects and more economical for both clients and agencies.

Second, there is a growing public and professional awareness of the seriousness of family violence in all of its forms: spouse battering, elder abuse, child abuse and neglect, and child molestation. No one knows the true numbers of people involved in these inhumane and psychologically damaging practices, yet the growing sensitivity to these violent behaviors has alerted some human service workers to devise methods of intervention that promise beneficial outcomes.

Another generating force toward the creation of support groups for a wide range of human problems is connected with the first two points, namely, that the group method is the method par excellence for dealing with disaffected and deviant individuals. Beyond the current popularity and apparent success of self-help groups such as Alcoholics Anonymous, helping in traditional societies has been mainly situated in the group. Without invoking the Jungian collective unconscious as the source of current interest in group helping, it may be that contemporary social support theorists and practitioners have begun to sense the limits of individual therapy, particularly where isolation, stigma, and powerlessness dominate people's lives and render them increasingly purposeless and helpless. Taken together, these elements are the negative conditions describing the very opposite of the concept of belonging. The human being, as a social animal, needs to maintain some group membership in order to feel a sense of security. The support group, as compared to the individual psychotherapist, offers a greater sense of belonging for the individual who has lost the human connection, either temporarily or for longer periods of time. It may be that the human services professions are once again beginning to discern the meaning of this ancient wisdom.

What the group offers people who share a common publicly disapproved situation is a ritual akin to religious practice, namely, a small community among equals where the confession of wrongdoings is accepted by fellow sufferers. This religious language of confessions is undoubtedly jarring to the ears of social workers and other human services workers who eschew language that is not "scientific" in nature, with the exception of concepts dealing with professional values and ethical matters. One may speak of clients disclosing their feelings or hidden thoughts, but confession of misdeeds ("sins," in religious language) is acknowledged as the first step in the healing process by clinicians who work with people suffering from socially disapproved behaviors. The pervasive feeling in support groups is that "we are all in the same boat" regarding the feeling of universal moral culpability in respect to the particular misdeed. This reduces the feeling that "I'm the only one in the world who has to contend with this situation." Freud believed that, regardless of the nature of misfortune, people tend to blame themselves. But self-blame, whether it is hardly felt by the person or, on the contrary, floods a person's everyday consciousness, cannot be relieved or overcome unless there is a "significant other or others" to hear the confessions. All helping groups, to greater or lesser degrees, serve this function.

Lakin (1985), who is one of the outstanding theorists on helping groups, writes as follows:

> The group confession is clearly an enduring psychotherapeutic form. Although it may have originated in religious practice, it persists in contemporary psychotherapeutic and self-help or support groups. Confession in helping groups (i.e., disclosure) is taken as a sign of readiness to be helped and as a token of the seriousness with which the sufferer asks for help. In traditional societies it implies a determination to modify previous maladaptive and socially injurious patterns of behavior. It is interpreted in similar fashion by members of a therapy group. [p. 12]

The group can offer a person who has engaged in socially disapproved behavior a feeling of acceptance or, in religious language, forgiveness. In a psychological sense, acceptance and forgiveness are very close to each other in their meaning and effect.

According to one religious perspective, there are three major barriers to inner healing: failure to forgive others, failure to receive forgiveness for ourselves, and failure to accept ourselves (Payne, 1984). The support group at its very best does provide an experience in acceptance that individual treatment cannot provide, particularly for people who feel ashamed or guilty about what they have done. There is a growing understanding in the professional community of this phenomenon.

COMPARING THREE KINDS OF HELPING GROUPS

There are many different kinds of helping groups, and they cater to people seeking remedies for a large variety of problems and troubles. In this section, psychotherapy groups, support groups, and self-help groups are analyzed. These three represent the modalities most commonly employed in the treatment of mental health problems and those of physical health with accompanying psychological difficulties.

These modalities of working with people in groups resemble each other in some ways and differ in others. All three function as support systems in that they promote

> an enduring pattern of continuous or intermittent ties that play a significant part in maintaining the psychic and physical integrity over time. . . . [They] are attachments among individuals or between individuals and groups that serve to improve adaptive competence in dealing with short-term crises and life transitions as well as long-term challenges, stresses, and privations. [Caplan 1974, p. 7]

Sources of Support

Since the self-help group is not led by a professional person, the members of the group are the sole sources of support. In therapy and support groups, the group leaders as well as the group members act as supportive persons throughout the group life. In all three, "the fundamental function . . . is to be an organizer and disseminator of information about the world—a feedback guidance system" (Rosenberg, 1984, p. 174). This feedback guidance system provides members with observations about each other's behavior in a receptive, nonpunitive atmosphere. Thus a well-functioning, affective support system (which includes all three of the modalities) heightens self-esteem and advances social competence. In all of the modalities, the feedback guidance system promotes the positive reinforcement of prosocial trends and exercises negative pressure (disapproval, criticism) against asocial or antisocial kinds of behavior.

Promotion of Social Norms

All three support systems promote value-laden social norms, according to Sherif (1966), who comments, "[People] cannot help producing rules, customs, values and other sorts of norms whenever they come together in a situation that lasts for any considerable time" (p. 3). In these support systems—particularly those that endure from several months to many, many years, such as some chapters of Alcoholics Anonymous—there is a value-laden push toward "appropriate" behaviors. "Appropriate" means, at the least, those behaviors that neither harm oneself nor others and, at their best, are manifestations of mutual aid.

Commenting on the construction of norms in therapy groups (and the same holds true for support and self-help groups), Yalom (1975) writes,

> Norms of a group are constructed both from expectations of the members for their group and from the explicit and implicit directions of the leader and more influential members. If the members' expectations are not firm, then the leader has even more opportunity to design a group culture which, in his view, will be optimally therapeutic. Obviously, he is the initial seat of influence in the group and the members look to him for direction. [p. 109]

In brief, the three group modalities are engaged in the building of "minicultures," where *culture* signifies a way of life, a set of habits, customs, values, and rules.

A good example is provided by Barbara Star (1983) who writes about the goals and philosophy of a program called the Counseling/Educational Domestic Abuse Project:

> The goals of the men's therapy program are to end the violent behavior and the threat of violence, to change attitudes that lead to violence, and to deal with other issues which are indirectly related to the violence . . . [According] to the men's therapy coordinator, "The techniques we use are not unique, but the combination and way we structure them probably are. They reflect our view of aggression which is based on a social learning theory model . . . This is not an instinctual or inherited trait; it is not something that results from frustration-aggression drive theory. We believe we have to teach them new ways of responding to conflict. That is why we adopted it as a teaching model as opposed to an insight model." [p. 160]

Here one sees an echo of Yalom's (1975) assertion that a group leader, as "the initial seat of influence in the group," forms and shapes the possibilities of a new culture—in this example, a nonviolent culture. It is clear, however, that this possibility can only come into fruition if one or more of the most active participants (member-leaders) in the group subscribe to the new "way of life" through word and deed. They become active agents of a mutual-help process by assisting each other in many ways, supporting each other through crises via the telephone, visiting one another's homes, and so on.

Underlying Ideologies

There are certain ideologies (belief systems, basic assumptions) that underpin the three modalities. In the case of some self-help groups, particularly those involved with aberrant behavior (Recovery, Inc.; Alcoholics Anonymous), there is an explicit set of beliefs for the members to adopt, which promises not simply an improvement in psychological and physical well-being, but offers a strategy that "provides opportunities to join together in an effort to cease disruptive and deviant behavior in order to set the stage for the resumption of normal, occupational, marital, and community roles" (Killilea, 1976, p. 58). In brief, there is a *way* for a person to become a decent person again.

Therapy and support groups, too, are undergirded ideologically, but in less explicit ways and perhaps with less authoritarian undertones and rigid agendas. They abjure religious orientations but cloud over their ideological underpinnings by appealing to scientific theories, conceptual frameworks, and so on. For instance, Star (1983) quotes a psychotherapist in reference to a battering men's group as follows: "We believe that aggression is a learned response to conflict. It is learned principally through the family of origin and is maintained by cultural norms" (p. 160). This view of aggression can be interpreted as an ideological stance because it is one among many "scientific" perspectives about the nature of aggression. There is no universally agreed upon theory about the source(s) of aggression.

Kind of Help Offered: Approaches, Interventions, and Goals

Support and self-help groups do not offer therapy but claim to be therapeutic without using that specific term, which has medical and psychological connotations. Therapy and self-help groups both claim curative powers, that is, that by joining the group one can change for the better in one or many ways. Support groups do not emphasize the therapeutic aspect of their workings. The possibility of individual change is implicit rather than explicit, and the emphasis is on the amelioration of stress through the helping group. The accent is as much on the helpfulness of the group as it is on the benefits the participant might derive from membership. In this respect, support groups may appeal to a sizable number of actual and potential clients who desire relief from a wide variety of painful circumstances but do not seek therapy, that is, do not see themselves as wanting to undergo some profound internal change. Social work might entertain the hypothesis that people living with chronic stress (disadvantaged clients) do not set a high value on therapy but do want relief from stress. Thus the support group as a stress reducer, offered in conjunction with other social service or medical programs, can be an attractive resource for these potential participants.

Yalom (1975) divides the curative factors of group therapy into 11 categories:

1. Installation of hope
2. Universality
3. Imparting of information
4. Altruism
5. The corrective recapitulation of the primary family group
6. Development of socializing techniques
7. Imitative behavior
8. Interpersonal learning
9. Group cohesiveness
10. Catharsis
11. Existential factors [pp. 3–4]

It is difficult to know without the benefit of comparative research the precise differences in the personal reactions, sociodynamics, and group processes of these modalities. Surely there are some differences, if only in the degree to which certain aspects of the 11 categories are accentuated or not. The very fact that the self-help group does not have a professional leader, an expert who carries a certain psychological authority with her status and role, promotes a different kind of individual self-evaluation and group interaction. Rosenberg (1984) believes that the self-help movement tends to be antiprofessional and therefore antiintellectual. Furthermore, she thinks support group leaders encourage "cognitive learning," whereas self-help "lay" leaders dismiss it as "mental gymnastics."

Rosenberg (1984) makes an important discrimination between support groups (and presumably therapy groups) and self-help groups:

> Most self-help groups, however, have no designated leader, and therefore no one person is responsible for the efficient functioning of the group and for fostering the satisfaction of the needs of each of the members. A support group leader is a conscientious gatekeeper for the group, making sure everyone has an opportunity for participation, encouraging, sharing, guiding discussion, and ensuring its ambience as the prototype of the well-regulated family, the benign feedback system. While there are individuals in the self-help group who can take and do take this role, as the intensity of the problem situation increases, the objectivity of the spontaneous leader often is threatened, if not overwhelmed. [p. 183]

In reconsidering Yalom's (1975) curative factors, it can be presumed that generally in self-help groups the factors of the corrective recapitulation of the primary family group and interpersonal learning are not subject to the interventions of a group leader who makes interpretations about members' responses, including transference reactions. Psychodynamic group leaders emphasize bringing into consciousness those aspects of individual thinking, feeling, and behavior that have been repressed in preconscious and unconscious spheres.

The same difference between professionally led therapy and support groups and member-led self-help groups would obtain in regard to the factor of interpersonal learning. Here, too, the absence of the professional group leader in the self-help group would eliminate interventions of an interpretive nature or those that search for meaning. Even if a member-leader did act as a "therapist," his credentials might be questioned or, just as seriously, his role as "equal" member might be at stake.

There are undoubtedly some differences between therapy and support groups in terms of the group leaders' intervention strategies and techniques, the "depth" of interpretations, especially those comments directed toward "making the unconscious conscious." In therapy groups the group leaders, especially those influenced by psychoanalytic theory, see themselves mainly in the interpretive role. This would not be true for professional support group leaders, who view themselves essentially in the integrative role of facilitators or enablers who encourage group cohesion while maintaining, aiding, and abetting the growth of self-esteem.

Basically the differences between group therapy and support group work lie in their somewhat divergent purposes. Rosenberg (1984) comments that

> the main thrust of the support group constitutes the development of cohesion and the enhancement of self-esteem, which in turn produce better coping patterns in society at large. Group therapy . . . usually focuses on problem-solving, increased self-awareness, and individual self-awareness through generic insights with a deliberate attempt at personality change. [p. 181]

This analysis confirms the notion that personality change is a goal in therapy groups, whereas it is not an explicit goal in support groups. The question arises, however, as to whether or not it is an implicit goal in the support group process. Undoubtedly it is. Personality change can be thought of as an epiphenomenon (a secondary phenomenon accompanying another phenomenon and thought of as caused by it). The curative factors of the support group process in toto can be considered the primary phenomena. A paradox thus emerges: A helping process that is not conceptualized as therapeutic may be just as therapeutic, if not more so, than one that is. This may be the case of the support group vis-à-vis the therapy group.

The support group process potentially contains the power of experiential knowledge, which is an attribute of self-help groups, as well as the learning-informational benefits of professional knowledge, symbolized and expressed by the group leader (Borkman, 1976). This is not an inevitable synergy, but a combination of forces (professional and experiential) that can move people profoundly.

Rosenberg (1984, p.181) characterizes the activities of support group leaders (as compared with those of group psychotherapists) as follows:

- Support group leaders are more transparent (are more apt to engage in self-disclosure).
- They emphasize interpersonal rather than intrapsychic understandings.
- They tend to accentuate socially approved behavior through positive reinforcement and "strokes."
- They encourage increased control and the helping function among group members.
- They provide more direct guidance, advice, and information.
- They reinforce interdependence by pointing out the similarities and differences among members, in the service of increased group cohesion.

They consciously role-model an attitude of trust and confidence in people.

As to the issue of transparency, it is certain that the group leader discloses more about himself—his anxieties and uncertainties—than traditional group therapists, especially of the analytic school. The latter still hold to the notion that the analysis of the transference is the critical curative factor in group therapy, as it is in individual treatment. Yet, even in support groups, leaders must limit self-disclosure, using it judiciously and only when there is some rationale or justification for doing so.

While the social distance between a group leader and a support group is shorter than that between a group therapist and a group, there should be sufficient distance for the leader to guard the objectivity she needs to guide the group process when that is needed. If she becomes totally immersed in the group as another member, she will have destroyed her role as group leader.

To "focus on interpersonal rather than intrapsychic understandings" means that the support group leader generally avoids the kinds of "deep" interpretations that are designed to promote self-awareness in therapy group members. She may comment, for instance, on how some participants reacted one way to a given situation, while other members had a different view of the problem, and still others had a third response. She may then have the group discuss how their reactions affected them, the other members of the group, their family members, and so forth. In other words, the support group leader sustains the fundamental function of being a feedback guidance system, someone who positively reinforces prosocial behavior and also discourages antisocial and self-defeating behavior, through "negative" pressure, ignoring, questioning, challenging, posing alternatives, and criticizing.

Support group leaders "deliberately seek opportunities for positive strokes or reinforcement and focus on supportive rather than interpretive issues," according to Rosenberg (1984, p. 181). They do not abjure interpretation of members' behavior. They do engage in some interpretations, especially those that are meaningful for more than one member of the group and for the entire group itself. Such comments are also directed toward individuals. The difference, then, between the interpretive and supportive roles of the two group heads is primarily a matter of emphasis. Group therapists engage in a great deal of supportive work, but they see their critical professional role in the interpretive realm.

The course of a successful support group begins with a very active group leader and ends with the group members on the whole in control of the group process. Support group leaders strive for this kind of development, for it signifies the desired outcome of people dealing with their own problems with little or no professional intervention. In a successful therapy group a similar course may well take place. Members who, toward the end of the group, are functioning at higher levels than at the beginning of the group's formation will take leadership roles within the group, but the group therapist remains the most powerful voice, particularly in the interpretive role. No member of the group can challenge his leadership in this respect.

A support group leader does not behave as a blank screen or *tabula rasa* upon which members "project" fantasies. Therefore, she does not remain silent or throw questions back to members when they ask legitimate queries. She is willing to give information to members where this seems appropriate, including answering questions about herself. It is quite clear that people in support groups (depending upon their *raison d'être*) seek and need information about legal issues, medical problems, the operation of social agencies, and so on. There is no justification for withholding what is often critical information to members. The better informed people are, the better they can deal with their problems.

In a review of the research literature on the importance of group cohesiveness in group therapy, Yalom (1975) summarizes his findings as follows:

> We have cited evidence that patients in group therapy consider group cohesiveness to be a *prime* mode of help in their therapy experience. . . . Highly cohesive groups have an overall higher outcome. Although further controlled research is needed, these findings taken together do support the contention that group cohesiveness is an important determinant of positive therapeutic outcome. [p. 53, italics added]

A support group leader will extend every effort to build and increase group cohesiveness. As Rosenberg (1984) observes, this is done by "pointing out similarities and differences among [group members'] contributions to the discussions, showing how one statement builds on another, and reinforcing the interdependency among them" (p. 181). Although by definition the members of a support group suffer from the same stress and therefore share the same problem, various members react to their common plight in similar and dissimilar ways. It is through comparing their reactions that the process of cohesion takes place. Their common ground is in all being in the same boat. The differences in their reactions to the same stress are in themselves a source of learning for the members. A conflict-ridden husband and wife can "see" that another more cooperative couple is better able to deal with their child's asthmatic attack; the mother of a retarded child can "see" that her militant overprotectiveness is not helpful when she compares her behavior with that of a mother who can allow her child to be freer; and so on. At the same time, the "learners" are not ridiculed in the group; they are accepted. In learning from each other and the group leader, the members feel a strengthening of the bonds that tie them together.

Lastly, the support group leader acts as a role model for the members. He does not do this by displaying an attitude of detachment and "objectivity," but by demonstrating his confidence in the members' capacity to become a group of people who can help each other. Here he demonstrates his faith, based on his experience with many small groups, that every group member in some measure can contribute to her own and others' well-being.

While the three modalities—therapy groups, support groups, and self-help groups—are similar and different in many regards, each has its place. When they function at a high level, all serve an important integrative function in our society: They create and reinforce values that press toward keeping people connected to each other; in the dreadful circumstances of people suffering from isolation and stigma, they aim to get them started in rejoining the mainstream, so they can assume their roles as citizens. There is no higher calling in a democratic society.

THE HUMAN CONNECTION: THE FUNDAMENTAL BASIS FOR SUPPORT GROUPS

Whether acknowledged or not, social work has its roots centered firmly in the concept of humanity's interconnectedness. This is not to overlook the profession's attention to the value of individual dignity and the need for self-determination, but the profession recognizes, in Spinoza's (1908) words, that "man is a social animal" (p. 206). In confronting the pains and troubles of clients, social workers build upon humanity's natural predisposition to seek affiliation, which is an assumption underlying the helping process, even on the most basic and intimate level of the one-to-one therapeutic relationship. In such a private pairing, that of the social worker with the client, the bond stems from empathy, an intervention that requires the ability to find the human connection and the commonality of emotion. Working *with* the human condition of interdependence, social work fosters relationships. It would appear that, within the practice of support groups, workers amplify and emphasize the connection, forming a sustaining and healing sense of unification and belonging.

Thus, in discussing support groups as a modality often used to reduce isolation and stigma, it seems essential to recognize the pivotal role of connection.

Social work, with its integrative, interactionist, and sometimes eclectic style, blends theories from various thinkers, weaving the human connection into its foundations. With respect to growth and personality development, the importance of connection is clear although the mechanism has been given various labels. Among these is Murray's (1938) early reference to the human need for "affiliation." Likewise, Mahler (1975) based her object-relations theory on the mother-child connection, which critically affects the child's psychic structure and forms the prototype of future social relationships. Her emphasis on healthy mother-infant bonding has received extensive attention and expansion in theory (e.g., Klaus & Kennel, 1976).

Also acknowledging the primary foundation left by a child's first relationship, Bowlby (1969) viewed the need for attachment to be a function of a process akin to an instinctive behavior. He addressed humanity's natural, lifelong search for attachment, especially in times of stress:

> That attachment behaviour in adult life is a straightforward continuation of attachment behaviour in childhood is shown by the circumstances that lead an adult's attachment behaviour to become more readily elicited. In sickness and calamity, sudden danger or disaster a person will almost certainly seek proximity to another known and trusted person. In such circumstances an increase of attachment behaviour is recognized by all as natural. . . . To dub attachment behaviour in adult life regressive is indeed to overlook the vital role that it plays in the life of man from the cradle to the grave.[pp. 207–208]

Shor and Sanville (1978) discuss this need for attachment or connection in terms of an individual's lifelong challenge to achieve some balance between the innate struggle for intimacy versus the desire for independence. They speak of a myth of "primary illusion," an unattainable state of complete intimacy or connectedness that people desperately seek:

> The source of the myth lies in the fact that each human being has indeed had an experience of blissful fusion with another. Every infant begins life in a sort of dream state in which he experiences an illusion of oneness with the mother, not yet able or needing to distinguish "me" from "not me." . . . Inevitably each child must awaken from that dream, and he awakens to a potential dissonance between self and other. [pp. 12–13]

Viewing humanity's connectedness from a different perspective, yet still as affecting personality development, Jung (1964) proposed the existence of the collective unconscious. This sharing of common archetypal images among all people speaks to another form of connectedness that pervades psychological theory.

From a developmental orientation, Erikson (1980) discussed the progression of the human connection from that consisting of the infant-parental bond to age-appropriate allegiances to one's group or society. He stressed the importance the influence of others has on identity formation, thus indirectly accenting the crucial role of the child's interconnection with society: "Identity formation finally begins where the usefulness of identification ends. It arises from the selective repudiation and mutual assimilation of childhood identifications, and their absorption in a new configuration, which, in turn is dependent on the process by which a society identifies the young individual" (p. 68). Thus Erikson articulates the essential connection between the individual and society.

It would appear that the recognition of this need provided a foundation for the concept of group intervention itself. Sociologists have long postulated the integral and powerful role of the group, specifically what Cooley (1956) identified as the "primary group." The primary group offers its members intimate, face-to-face relationships which result in a collective identity and sense of belonging, and therefore have a considerable impact on individual development. By establishing a formal group setting, such as a support group, the worker thus creates a ready-made primary group, a social microcosm, where the member can experience the healing qualities of the human connection.

Referring to Yalom's (1975) curative factors, listed earlier, one sees that several depend directly on the element of human bonding. The concept of universality, which unquestionably serves as a primary factor in the support group modality, depends on humanity's commonality. Yalom's emphasis on the role of interpersonal learning within the group speaks to the human connection: "Man's interpersonal behavior has been clearly adaptive in an evolutionary sense; without intense, positive reciprocal interpersonal bonds, both individual and species survival would not have been possible" (pp. 19–20). In his discussion of group cohesiveness, he makes reference to the importance of the members' commonality: "It is not the sheer process of ventilation that is important, it is not only the discovery of others' problems similar to our own and the ensuing disconfirmation of our wretched uniqueness that is important; it is the affective sharing of one's inner world and *then* the acceptance by others that seems of paramount importance" (p. 47). He goes on to summarize, "Group membership, acceptance, and approval are of utmost importance in the development of the individual" (p. 48).

As a clinician more directly associated with social work with groups, Konopka (1983) echoes the fundamental importance of human connectedness and the group experience: "Human beings are not only related to each other, but are intertwined with other people and their physical, economic, and human environment. No human being can live separated from others. . . . Most important are therefore small groups, including the family, friendship, and other face-to-face groups" (p. xvii).

Despite the imperative need for connectedness with fellow beings, as represented in all of the theories just cited, theorists have observed a disintegration of society's sense of unity. In fact, Bronfenbrenner (1974) provides this phenomenon with a label: "This feeling, and fact, of disconnectedness from people and activities has a name that has become familiar: alienation" (p. 53). Lasch (1979) attributes this growing sense of alienation to the individualistic and narcissistic emphasis of our technological age. In looking to the future trends of society, Naisbitt (1982) contends that the level of alienation will have to change and that people will need to acknowledge their interdependence and seek mechanisms of greater self-help. Perhaps then it will be time to consider George Bernard Shaw's (1941) wisdom when he wrote, "Independence? That's middle class blasphemy. We are all dependent on one another, every soul of us on earth" (p. 279).

The following conclusion by Bronfenbrenner (1974) might be taken by social work as a challenge:

> It may be fitting to end this discussion with a proposal for nothing more radical than providing a setting in which young and old can simply sit and talk. The fact that such settings are disappearing and have to be recreated deliberately points both to the roots of the problem and to its remedy. The evil and the cure lie not in the victims of alienation but in the social institutions that produce alienation, and in their failure to be responsible to the most human needs and values of a democratic society. [p. 61]

It would appear that the support group modality, with its ability to foster connectedness and mutuality amidst isolation, stigma, and despair, provides a building block in countering the faltering sense of community. Support groups offer a reparative potential by tapping a universal human resource—the need for and the strength of interconnection.

SUPPORT GROUPS IN A "CASEWORK" AGENCY: AN EXAMPLE

During the past 10 years the Jewish Family Service (JFS) of Los Angeles has instituted a wide variety of groups for its different populations, speaking to the need for human connectedness in treatment.[1] This is a large agency in a large city, with satellite offices throughout the urban area. Support and therapy groups have been formed for the following special populations:

Aged persons
Adult children of the aged
Divorcees
Married couples
Parents
Unemployed workers
Parents of children in cults
Ex-members of cults
Blended families needing multiple-family therapy
Holocaust survivors
Children of holocaust survivors
Holocaust survivors and children (not necessarily their own) together
People of different generations
Teenagers
Parents whose adult children have committed suicide
Parents whose adult children are schizophrenic
Women seeking careers

The last decade has seen the JFS transformed from an almost wholly casework agency, featuring individual treatment, to an agency in which individual and group methods are used according to the needs of each case and the needs of an identifiable population with a common problem. Critical in this particular transformation was the vision of the agency leaders, who believed in the power and efficacy of the group method. While the agency was not oblivious to the economic advantages of the group (a worker can see eight clients instead of one), this was not the primary incentive. It was, rather, the professional knowledge that the

[1]Rama Weizmann, Director of Professional Services of the Jewish Family Service of Los Angeles, is the source of information about the various groups that the agency has created during the past 10 years.

group was the treatment of choice for people sharing the same situations or conditions, with the proviso that some group members might benefit simultaneously from individual treatment.

The groups that had the greatest influence on the agency's policy of encouraging the group method were those composed of children (mostly late adolescents and young adults) of holocaust survivors. These groups proved to be the context in which these "children" were able to view themselves and their parents in changed ways. Acceptance, forgiveness, and deeper understanding formed the crucible of inner change and improved relationships with parents. Also having a strong impact on the course of the agency's transformation were the groups for the aged at the Freda Mohr Center.

The JFS's development provides some good answers to the question posed at the beginning of this chapter: Why do we need support groups? As this case shows, the main reason is the recognition that social work often is not serving the populations who most need what it has to offer: agency resources, a dignified way of working on personal problems, and a link to other social services. The support group is a relatively non-threatening way in which people can get help for their difficulties and at the same time be helpers of others, as members of the group.

Social work is particularly concerned about the most vulnerable people of our society. They are in the most need of help and often are the least willing to seek it out or accept it. For them, too, the support group is a more acceptable medium of help than individual treatment.

The support group offers the sense of belonging that so many people lack today. To feel connected with others, through one's own and others' pain and confusion, is part of the group process. That sense of belonging cannot be felt or achieved as powerfully in individual treatment.

Even where help is available, such as at JFS, it should not be assumed that it is easy for people to come to agencies for group-work treatment. People resist taking the risk of seeking help, because that initial step implies they are flawed. The agency must keep reaching out and offering encouragement. These steps, plus not taking the first or second no for the final answer, are still indispensable means for getting people to join a support group.

PREVENTION AND SUPPORT GROUPS

The mental health professions, including social work, have traditionally acclaimed the prevention of severe psychological disturbances as a noble cause. Yet there is little in terms of historical evidence that the mental health professions have seriously undertaken the tasks associated with preventive work.

Broskowski and Baker (1974) have identified a phalanx of barriers to doing preventive work. They categorize these impediments as definitional problems, systemic complexity, difficulties of demonstration, and lack of constituent demands. Another barrier is the mind-set of the professionals in the field, who are primarily psychotherapists specializing in individual (dyadic, one-to-one) psychotherapy. While it is true that family and group psychotherapy have recently come into greater use, they still lag behind the dyadic form.

What seems to happen in individual therapy, including that conducted by social workers, is the disappearance of social factors as the foci of treatment. The client's or patient's psychological life, and what goes on between the client and worker, become the primary emphases. There is nothing startling about this, because the individual case does not lend itself to an understanding of social factors. There are only two people in the room. When the client talks about his "social" life (work, relationships to people, role functioning), the worker gets some understanding of the client's interactional style, but it is still a secondhand experience. He has to depend on the client's perceptions and understandings, although he may not agree with the client's conclusions.

While workers generally have unclear, vague notions about their clients as social beings, their understanding of their clients' psychology is generally constructed upon much more data, including, of course, their own interactions in the consulting room. Yet it is clear that the social and psychological factors of common stressful situations can be weighed, discussed among people, and, perhaps, worked through. This is not to say that the group method is superior to the individual method in terms of treatment outcome, but that support group work and prevention coalesce conceptually and in a much smoother way than the individual treatment model. Moreover, because social workers intervene with the widest range of people among all of the mental health professions, the group support modality should be a form of intervention par excellence.

Bloom has sketched out a new paradigm for understanding the development and prevention of mental disorders. It fits very well with notions about stressful events and situations, their variable effects upon people, and the effectiveness of support systems, including professionally devised support groups, in maintaining and improving mental health and social functioning. Bloom (1979) writes "[Preventive] intervention programs can be organized around facilitating the mastery or reducing the incidence of particular stressful life events without undue regard for the prior specification of which forms of disability might therefore be prevented'' (p. 183). He goes on to state, ''[We] would be well advised to identify a stress producing critical precipitating events in our environments and develop systematic and multidimensional interventions to help in the mastery of these stresses. Included among these strategies might well be the development of social support systems where needed and the increasing of both individual and collective competencies for their resolution'' (p. 186).

As shown throughout this book, support groups are one among many interventions designed to help people suffering from stress. In social work, the application of support groups can become—perhaps for the first time in the profession's history, with the exception of the settlement houses—an important large-scale means of doing preventive work. Support group work is a natural way of bringing people together who can help each other overcome their common suffering.

ADVANTAGES AND DISADVANTAGES OF SUPPORT GROUPS

There are two basic assumptions that we make here about support groups and, for that matter, any form of helping. First, all strategies, modalities, and interventions of a potentially helpful nature are also potentially harmful, at least to some people. There is no universal ''all-good'' helping procedure for people who are trying to cope with psychosocial stress. Just as penicillin and aspirin are effective healing agents for the majority of the population, they are extremely dangerous for a minority. Likewise, while professionally led support groups are helpful to many participants, they are undoubtedly not helpful, and perhaps harmful, to others. Believing as we do in the effectiveness of this modality, we have reason to hope that those who are harmed represent a small minority. But even a small number (either in real numbers or percentages) is unacceptable.

Our second assumption has already been alluded to, namely, that the lack of research about support group process and outcomes means that our ideas and even our conclusions are simply speculations or hypotheses to be investigated. A great deal is known about small-group behavior, including support groups. Yet is is surprising to learn from a recent investigation of ''125 naturally functioning groups'' that ''to date, no researchers have described the categories and frequencies of problems to be anticipated in the field'' (Weinberg, Rovinski, & Beitman, 1981, p. 81). This lack means that, while we are not completely in the dark, we are still to some extent groping our way through an unknown region.

Another cautionary note arises as we reflect on the social work literature on support groups. There is a lack of clarity in the labeling of support versus other types of groups. In some cases, the authors may not have *referred* to their group as a support group; however, if the primary focus was on mutual aid, they *thought* of it as a support group. For example, Lee and Park (1978) do not refer to their services for depressed adolescents in foster care as support groups, although they describe them as ''developmentally-oriented mutual aid groups focused on depression and coping.'' Later they state that ''one cannot underestimate the group's importance or the worker's role in facilitating mutual aid and influencing the development of norms within the group'' (p. 525). Another instance is the work done by Cahners (1970) for families of burned children. She refers to her group work as ''group meetings'' but goes on to describe them very much in terms of the essential qualities of a support group:

> Group members bring to the meetings their guilt (which most parents feel after a child's accident), their depression, fears, rage, resentment, helplessness, and feelings of isolation. At meetings they share their defenses against being overwhelmed by these emotions. They reach out to each other, supported by the feeling that only another parent of a burned child really understands.[pp.169–170]

Further, it is possible that some therapy groups are essentially support groups. But, as suggested, the defining boundaries between the two modalities are fuzzy.

Advantages

Reaching Underserved Populations

The use of support groups at times enables workers to serve populations that traditionally are neglected or underserved. Often these populations involve ''nonidentified patients'' (Bloom, 1979) such as parents of psychiatrically hospitalized children and significant others of rape victims. In other cases, these populations are people whose problems fall through the cracks of routine service delivery, such as Vietnam veterans, the recently bereaved, "mature" adult students, adult victims of childhood incest, young children from alcoholic families, and the siblings of handicapped children.

Support groups, with their minimal amount of associated stigma, can be more attractive to populations that are characteristically difficult to involve in treatment, as Giarretto (1982) has shown in his work with incest families and as Breton (1979, 1981) has illustrated with her groups for abusive mothers. As discussed earlier, the focus of support groups is not on changing the individual, but on providing support, mutual aid, and possibly increased effectiveness in dealing with a shared event.

In brief, support groups, with their less stigmatized nature, provide the opportunity for people who would not ordinarily seek a therapeutic setting to experience the healing qualities of their curative factors, as conceptualized by Yalom (1975). At times it seems unreasonable to ask a person already facing a stigmatized life to embark on something that in his own eyes increases stigma, namely, therapy. Support groups provide an alternative to that dilemma.

Flexibility for Members and Leaders

Support groups often lend greater flexibility to their members and leaders, in areas ranging from goal setting to where the meetings will be held. Since support group members share a common problem, maintenance issues of the group members may frequently be similar and thus more easily solved. In their descriptive study various sorts of naturally functioning groups, Weinberg et al. (1981) found that the most frequently encountered problem was that of cohesiveness. It may well be that the support group has an advantage over all other mental-health-related groups in that the sharing of a common problem facilitates the cohesive process. It does not assure it, but is an inherent building block.

Because of the interactive nature of stressors, emphasized earlier, flexibility is required with regard to the content of sessions. As Mitchell, Billings and Moos (1982) describe it, "Support programs may also need to plan for content changes over time because the relevance of certain types of support may vary as the nature of the stressful circumstances change" (p. 92). The support group format lends itself to this type of flexibility.

Assessment and Screening

The support group setting can also serve as an excellent assessment tool for the clinical social worker. In the group's normative, peer-interactive atmosphere the worker can assess and screen individuals who may have to seek additional help. This seems especially true in medical settings where high patient turnover forces group supportive effort to consist of one or two sessions. Brown, Glazer and Higgins (1983) found the chance to conduct this type of observational assessment paramount to their work with open-heart-surgery patients.

Prevention

By nature, support groups frequently allow for a preventive emphasis which is often lost in current practice (especially since many consultation and educational services have lost financial backing in the mental health field). Perhaps this advantage should be the most cherished in a time when profuse social problems create impossible demands on time from the profession, as well as in a time of increased awareness of the cyclical nature of many social maladies of our era. Often preventive emphasis in support groups is most evident in areas involving children. Gitterman (1979) stressed prevention in her groups for learning-disabled children and their parents, as did Massenzio (1977) in her work with mothers of severely retarded children. In her doctoral dissertation, Massenzio shows the value not only of support but *early* intervention. Wandersman (1982) illustrates the preventive value of supportive intervention with new parents of infants. She quotes a new mother:

> I think I have been able to adjust to parenthood more readily and comfortably simply by knowing that other new parents share the same problems in adjusting to their new roles. I also feel that it has helped my husband and I discuss our feelings more openly because I have had a reason to share them with this group experience. It has made us both feel less isolated in this business of parenting. [p. 113]

Allocation of Resources

As with any type of group work, as opposed to individual work, a support group is economical in terms of the worker's time and the agency's financial possibilities. Frequently, this point will be listed as a major factor in the decision to use a support group. Yet it must be immediately added that substituting group work for individual treatment simply for "practical" or "opportunistic" reasons—such as saving agency funds or maximizing workers' caseloads—is a misuse of the group-work method in any of its forms. Efficiency cannot be the highest priority in professional social work practice. The choice of treatment modalities in respect to clients' problems is a diagnostic issue and not a matter, for instance, of promoting flattering statistics about "the large numbers of cases we handle in this agency."

Disadvantages

Group Casualties

In an article entitled, "Warning: Groups May Be Dangerous," Galinsky and Schopler (1977) have constructed a set of "strategies for the prevention and treatment of group casualties" (p. 91). It should be noted at the outset that the authors' research on the issue of group casualties was based mainly on work relating to encounter groups. Nevertheless, their analysis can be useful in conducting all helping groups, including professionally led support groups. Galinsky and Schopler have created a "blueprint" that illuminates the primary sources of casualties in groups and at the same time indicates strategies for prevention and treatment.

Group casualties arise from both personal and interpersonal sources. Personal sources refer to the individual personalities and behaviors of leaders and members, while interpersonal sources refer to group structure and process—the ways in which people relate to each other and the explicit and implicit rules and norms that have evolved from the beginning of a group's existence.

Galinsky and Schopler's (1977) findings are to some considerable extent supported by Weinberg et al.'s (1981) findings on problem identification in naturally functioning groups. As previously noted, the most important problem, by far, was that of cohesion. The next two in importance were those of leadership and personality. Cohesion is such a complex variable, containing personal and interpersonal elements, whereas the factors of leadership and personality stem more clearly from personal sources.

These authors advise agencies and others interested in the promotion of support groups to read the Galinsky and Schopler (1977) piece carefully and to use it as a constant guide in the formation and running of groups.

Support Versus Therapy

Another difficulty or disadvantage in leading support groups appears to be the delicate task of conducting a support group and not a therapy group. This is a fine line to walk, and the problem presents a challenge to workers and a potential risk to the members. Two potential risks seem clear when social workers and their group members proceed in a support group with a poor understanding of the meaning of support as opposed to therapy. First, without clear definition of the group's intention in using support, both workers and members may build false, overzealous expectations of the group's intervening power. Wandersman (1982) describes this possibility well in her discussion of the effectiveness of parent-infant support groups:

> Few program designers, however, have clearly defined and operationalized what they mean by support in their programs or the mechanisms by which support can facilitate specific areas of adjustment. Ambiguity in the use of the support concept may have contributed to the development of unrealistic expectations about the potential of support programs to enrich family functioning. [p. 101]

Second, forming a support group without a solid distinction between its functions and the workings of a therapy group yields the potential risk of the members being exposed to therapeutic techniques or workings for which they did not offer their consent. This risk is especially seen in the "psychologically naive" client and with children whose parents have given consent for group participation, not therapy. Dincin, Sellek, and Striecker (1978), in their support group work with the parents of several psychiatrically ill adolescents and young adults, emphasize some of the following "principles," which militate against the notion of parents receiving therapy: "A general theme engendered in the group is that of looking toward improvement rather than cure" (p. 601). Further, "we indicate to them that the greatest assistance they can offer at this moment is not to change their own personalities, but rather to learn new ways of relating to their adult child" (p. 601). Finally, they state their group "offers an opportunity for the parent's view to be taken seriously and legitimized" (p. 602).

There is quite a different emphasis in such a support group, as contrasted with a group of parents whose principal goal is personality change. While in these instances the departure from use of support would clearly be unethical, it is not meant to imply that social workers would intentionally deceive their members. Rather, recognizing the fine line between therapy and support, it is conceivable that such unethical intervention could occur if the worker were not clear on the purpose and meaning of support. This possibility is most likely to occur with the inexperienced worker, but seasoned workers also face the difficult question as to what an appropriate intervention is, when they first begin support group facilitation.

Increased Conflict

The third disadvantage, already alluded to in the section on the prevention and treatment of group casualties, involves the well-known risk of the group triggering increased conflicts for members, who thereby suffer potential harmful results in the group. For example, a member may become a group scapegoat and the group leader may not be able to reverse this process. Or a member may be asked to leave a group for persistently disruptive behavior. Sometimes external conflicts are aroused, such as in the case of a new mother, for whom the added burden on her time schedule created by going to a support group may be more troublesome than helpful. Or an individual may face internal conflicts with the group norms and values, thus creating more rather than less difficulty. In these instances, support groups offer a distinct advantage over self-help groups, as they have a professional worker in a leadership role who can troubleshoot and avoid such casualties.

Worsened Depression

The fourth disadvantage does not seem to be entirely supported by the literature on support groups, but it is occasionally mentioned and is a serious issue. Thus, it deserves some discussion. Some professionals have expressed concerns that support groups, especially those involving victims, are potentially detrimental to some members. The allegation is that the exposure of already despondent people to the problems of others in a group setting may be overwhelming and not beneficial. The most extensive article on this possibility is "Counteracting the Deviance of Depression: Peer Support Groups for Victims" (Coates & Winston, 1983). The authors studied three support groups for rape victims, involving a combined total of 15 women. The groups met for eight weekly sessions conducted by two female social work students. The authors found a significant drop in the women's depression in relation to their perceived self-deviance; however, they found no significant change in the women's overall reported depression. They offer this explanation:

> One interesting possibility for what could be happening in support groups is that many of the positive functions they serve for members may have simulta-

> neous negative effects. For example, if they meet similarly affected others who are as distressed or more distressed than they are, they are likely to feel that their own sadness and anxiety are appropriate and normal. But this same social encounter could also lead unhappy individuals to feel that their common problems are more horrible than they had realized, since others in the same situation appear to be so devastated by it. [Coates & Winston, 1983, p. 188]

One wonders immediately if eight weeks are long enough for a rape victim to work through that devastating traumatic experience. It may be time enough to reduce the feeling of self-deviance but not to alleviate all the other affective experiences that accompany rape. In addition, the authors do not address the amount of experience the social work students had in working with the rape-victim population, nor do they comment on the students' familiarity with support group work. However, the authors conclude, "Clearly, the important task for researchers is to develop a better understanding of how victims can help one another without hurting each other" (Coates & Winston, 1983, p. 189). Despite the problems in their study, they have opened the door on an area in need of exploration.

CONCLUSION

The proliferation of support groups in social work, along with the increasing popularity of self-help groups, suggests that people are relearning an ancient piece of wisdom, namely, that human beings are social animals. In acknowledging and absorbing that belief, there is no rejection or denial of individualism and individuality. Where people can help each other through mutual support and aid, the dignity and integrity of the person are enhanced. Social work and the other mental health professions have begun to act upon that premise through the use of support groups.

REFERENCES

Bloom, B. (1979). Prevention of mental disorders: Recent advances in theory and practice. *Community Mental Health Journal, 15*(3), 179–191.

Borkman, T. (1976). Experiential knowledge: A new concept for the analysis of self-help groups. *Social Service Review, 50*(3), 445–456.

Bowlby, J. (1969). *Attachment*. New York: Basic Books.

Breton, M. (1979). Nurturing abused and abusive mothers. *Social Work With Groups, 2*(2), 161–174.

Breton, M. (1981). Resocialization of abusive parents. *Social Work with Groups, 26*(2), 119–122.
Bronfenbrenner, U. (1974). The origins of alienation. *Scientific American, 231*(2), 53–61.
Broskowsky, A., & Baker, F. (1974). Professional, organizational and social barriers to primary prevention. *American Journal of Orthopsychiatry, 44*(1), 707–719.
Brown, D. G., Glazer, H., & Higgins, M. (1983). Group intervention: A psychosocial and educational approach to open heart surgery patients and their families. *Social Work in Health Care, 9*(2), 47–59.
Cahners, S. S. (1970). Group meetings for families of burned children. *Health and Social Work, 3*(3), 165–172.
Caplan, G. (1974). *Support systems and community mental health.* New York: Behavioral Publications.
Coates, D., & Winston, T. (1983). Counteracting the deviance of depression: Peer support groups for victims. *Journal of Social Issues, 39*(2), 169–194.
Cooley, C. H. (1956). *Social organization.* Glencoe, IL: Free Press.
Dincin, J., Selleck, V., & Streicker, S. (1978). Restructuring parental attitudes—working with parents of the adult mentally ill. *Schizophrenia Bulletin, 4*(4), 597–608.
Erikson, E. (1980). *Identity and the life cycle.* New York: Norton.
Galinsky, M. J., & Schopler, J. H. (1977). Warning: Groups may be dangerous. *Social Work, 22*(2), 89–94.
Gitterman, N. P. (1979). Group services for learning disabled children and their parents. *Social Casework, 60*(4), 217–226.
Jung, C. G. (1964). *Man and his symbols.* Garden City, NY: Doubleday.
Killilea, M. (1976). Mutual help organizations: Interpretations in the literature. In G. Caplan & M. Killilea (Eds.), *Support systems and mutual help* (pp. 37–93). New York: Grune & Stratton.
Klaus, M. A., & Kennel, J. H. (1976). *Maternal-infant bonding.* St. Louis: Mosby.
Konopka, G. (1983). *Social group work: A helping process.* Englewood Cliffs, NJ: Prentice-Hall.
Giarretto, H. (1982). *Integrated treatment of child sexual abuse.* Palo Alto, CA: Science and Behavior Books, Inc.
Lakin, M. (1985). *The helping group: Therapeutic principles and issues.* Reading, MA: Addison-Wesley.
Lasch, C. (1979). *The culture of narcissism.* New York: Warner Books.
Lee, J. A., & Park, D. N. (1978). A group approach to the depressed adolescent girl in foster care. *American Journal of Orthopsychiatry, 48*(3), 516–527.
Mahler, M. S. (1975). *The psychological birth of the human infant: Symbiosis and individuation.* New York: Basic Books.
Massenzio, S. E. (1977). A supportive group experience for mothers of severely retarded children. *Dissertation Abstracts International, 37*(11–A), 6954–A.
Mitchell, R. E., Billings, A. G., & Moos, R. H. (1982). Social support and well-

being: Implications for prevention programs. *Journal of Primary Prevention, 3*(2), 77–98.

Murray, H. A. (1938). *Explorations in personality*. New York: Oxford University Press.

Naisbitt, J. (1982). *Megatrends*. New York: Warner Books.

Payne, L. (1984). *The healing of the homosexual*. Westchester, IL: Good News Publications.

Rosenberg, P. P. (1984). Support groups: A special therapeutic entity. *Small Group Behavior, 15*(2), 173–186.

Shaw, G. B. (1941). *Pygmalion*. In *Six Plays* (Act V, p. 279). New York: Dodd, Mead & Co.

Sherif, M. (1966). *The psychology of social norms*. New York: Harper & Row.

Shor, J., & Sanville, J. (1978). *Illusion in loving: Balancing intimacy and independence*. New York: Penguin Books.

Spinoza, B. (1908). *Ethics* (p. 206). New York: Macmillan & Co.

Star, B. (1983). *Helping the abuser: Intervening effectively in family violence*. New York: Family Service Association of America.

Wandersman, L. P. (1982). An analysis of the effectiveness of parent-infant support groups. *Journal of Primary Prevention, 3*(2), 99–115.

Weinberg, S. B., Rovinski, S. H., & Beitman, M. (1981). Common group problems: A field study. *Small Group Behavior, 12*(1), 81–92.

Yalom, I. D. (1975). *The theory and practice of group psychotherapy* (2nd ed.). New York: Basic Books.

4 Understanding Stress: Implications For Support Groups

This chapter will extend the discussion on the linkage between acute and chronic stress and social support, as it relates to needs assessment. The high-risk factors confronting people will be identified, as well as how these risk factors contribute to the development of a hierarchy of priorities for social support, particularly in the form of professionally led support groups.

A professional practice worthy of its name must be underpinned by some basic formulation(s) that link the mental constructions of the mind (concepts) with the actual performance of a skilled activity. While this material does not represent a full-blown theory in the strict sense of the word, *theory* here is used to connote what Carl Rogers (1949) had in mind—"a fallible changing attempt to construct a network of gossamer threads which will contain solid facts" (p. 9).

TYPES OF PSYCHOSOCIAL STRESS

As mentioned in Chapter 2, Fried (1982) classified stress under two categories: acute stress and endemic stress. Howcvcr, this framework proposes three types: (1) acute, (2) ameliorable chronic, and (3) permanent chronic. The concept of acute stress is well known to clinicians as an immediate, intense, disrupting force, commonly seen in crisis states like a recent death of a loved one. An ameliorable chronic stress is a condition of long-standing difficulty that has at least some potential for eventual alleviation, even if intervention is required. An example is the condition of poverty. A permanent chronic stress, however, represents an enduring, incurable problem, as would be experienced by an irreversibly deaf child.

The main factor differentiating permanent chronic stress from ameliorable chronic stress is the necessity of a permanent support network for those afflicted by either bodily illnesses or mental states which, at this time, either promise little or no improvement or in which remissions are likely as a consequence of susceptibility to further stress. Fountain House in New York City and Project Return in Los Angeles, for example, represent "total programs" (housing, employment, recreation, support groups, professional care) for chronic schizophrenics who need a permanent support network.

Ameliorable chronic stress and permanent chronic stress break down the larger concept of endemic stress, thus broadening the understanding of the various possible forms of stress. At first glance, one might conceptualize stress on a continuum running from "nonexistent or minimal stress" to "permanent stress," as illustrated in Figure 4-1. On this continuum, every stress condition would have the potential to advance to the next stage to the right. In actuality, cases where acute stress finally culminates in ameliorable or permanent chronic stress do happen, but how frequently stress progresses along this linear continuum is unknown. For example, unresolved grief from the loss of a spouse or reactions to unemployment may culminate in chronic stress. It is important to recognize, however, that acute stress responses do not necessarily (and as far as we know do not very often) follow a linear pattern.

There also exists the potential for circularity, from acute or chronic to minimal stress and back to acute, a pattern observed in people whose lives are filled with what Lazarus and De Longis (1963) call *daily hassles,* their term for the "irritating, frustrating, distressing demands and troubled relationships that plague us day in and day out. Some of these hassles are transient, others are repeated or even chronic. These hassles should be distinguished from dramatic, change-centered life events" (p. 247).

In addition, stressors may have an interactive quality. As Fried (1982) writes, "Frequently acute and endemic stress flow into one another so that attributing effects to one or the other becomes difficult. . . . Cer-

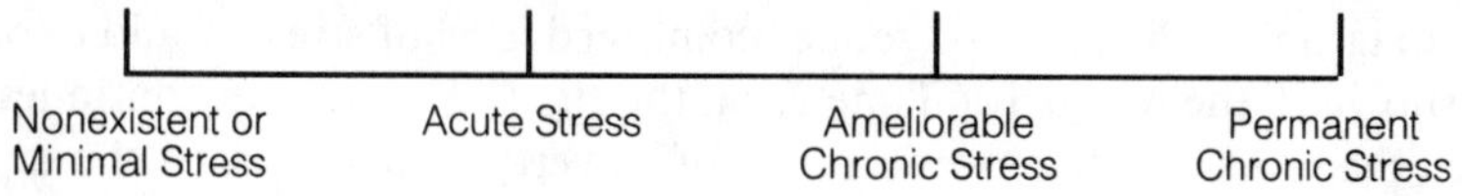

FIGURE 4–1 Stress continum.

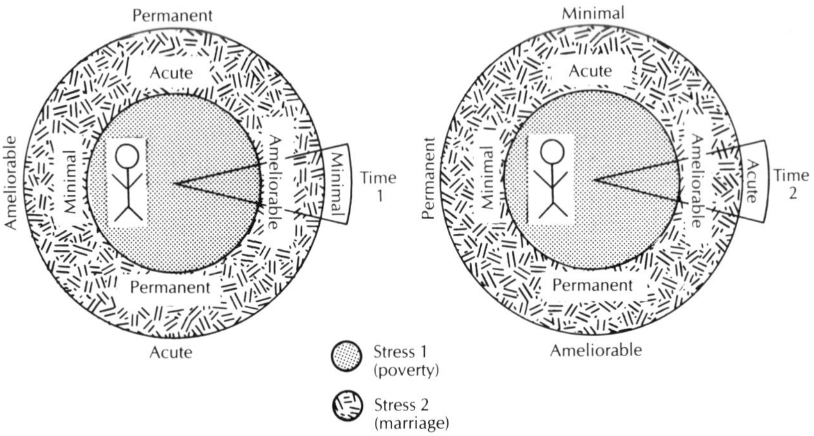

FIGURE 4–2 Circular and interactive nature of stressors, with rotation showing changes over time.

tainly acute stress can be superimposed on conditions of endemic stress [and] . . . other combinations of, or interactions between, acute and endemic stress can also occur'' (p. 49).

Thus, to evaluate an individual's stress level requires careful assessment, and one must abandon the linear model of stress. Instead, this linear form must be bent into a circular representation, as shown in Figure 4–2, with each stressor affecting an individual represented by its own circle and all stressors resting together to show potential interaction. The subject in the figure is a woman, and two stressors in her life are shown: poverty and marriage.

Let's look first at Time 1, on the left. In regard to poverty (Stress 1), as a mother of two living below the poverty level she experiences an ameliorable chronic stress. In regard to Stress 2, she enjoys an intact marriage, an experience of nonexistent or minimal stress. In the diagram, the pie-shaped slice captures her stress levels at Time 1: She faces an ameliorable chronic problem of poverty but has little or no stress in relation to her marriage. However, if we suppose that there develops a crisis in her marriage, resulting in the rotation of the marriage circle on the diagram to the acute stage, her combined level of stress would appear as shown in the wedge for Time 2, on the right. The woman continues to face the ameliorable chronic stress of poverty in addition to the acute stress of a sudden separation from her husband.

Figure 4–2 reflects Fried's (1982) conceptualization of the interactive nature of stressors, which should be considered when assessing the stress level of any individual. Clearly, the woman in this example may be in need of support services at Time 1, but she may be in greater need at Time 2. This model uses a stimulus-based definition of stress similar to the standard life-events scale of stress of Holmes and Masuda (1974). If the model presented here is expanded to include all of an individual's stressors (such as a recent move, a job change, a death in the family, and so forth), as does a life-events scale, it even more dramatically illustrates the interactive and cumulative effects of stress as well as the potential need for support.

PSYCHOSOCIAL CORRELATES OF STRESS

In assessing a person's stress level and resultant need for support, it proves valuable to be familiar with the frequent and expected responses to stress. There appear to be relatively predictable psychosocial correlates to the three types of stress—acute, ameliorable chronic, and permanent chronic—discussed earlier. Specifically, these responses are evident in three areas of the individual's psychosocial functioning: (1) the wider social sphere, (2) the more intimate interpersonal domain, and (3) the intrapersonal or intrapsychic realm.

With respect to an individual's social functioning as a citizen, friend, acquaintance, worker, church member, and so forth, it is found that stress most often makes an impact upon these social roles as well as in the availability of social contacts. In addition, relationship disorders, frequently in the form of a decrease in interaction, appear in the person's interpersonal functioning. In their severest form, these changes result in the social isolation of the individual. In the person's intrapsychic workings, one frequently observes an increase in negative affective manifestations (increased feelings of guilt, shame, and so forth) and evidence of a threatened or injured self-concept. Table 4–1 offers detailed descriptions of the social, interpersonal, and intrapsychic correlates to acute, ameliorable chronic, and permanent chronic stress. Using this table in examining, for instance, the acute stress category, one can identify the common correlates to stress. The example given is the recent death of a spouse, following which the surviving spouse might experience (1) a social role response of adaptation, finding a new identity after the spouse's death; (2) an interpersonal response of increased dependency on others; and (3) an intrapsychic manifestation of depression and anger.

TABLE 4–1 Common Psychosocial Correlates of Stress

	Acute stress	Ameliorable chronic stress	Permanent chronic stress
Type of Stressor:	Life event Life transition	Serious life event	Serious life event
(Example)	(Recent death of spouse)	(Life-threatening illness)	(Severe, chronic disabling mental illness)
	Social correlates		
Social role Response:	Role strain Role confusion Role expansion Role adoption Role adaptation	Role contraction Severe role disruption Role failure Role loss	Role contraction Severe role disruption Role failure Role loss
Availability of social contacts:	If present, intense and short-lived: Isolation Stigma	Moderate to severe Isolation Stigma	Often severe Isolation Stigma
	Interpersonal correlates		
Relationship disorders:	Short-lived Withdrawal/flight Increased dependency Fight/violence Impulsivity Dominating/ authoritarian	Moderate to severe Withdrawal/flight Excessive dependency Fight/violence Impulsivity Dominating/ authoritarian	Often severe Withdrawal/flight Excessive dependency Fight/violence Impulsivity
Decreased Interactions:	If present, intense and short-lived Loneliness	Moderate to severe Loneliness	Often severe Loneliness
	Intrapsychic correlates		
Threatened self-concept:	Temporary disruption of sense of self-esteem, mastery, and competence	Diminished sense of self-esteem, mastery, and competence	Usually quite low sense of self-esteem, mastery, and compentence
Affective manifestations:	Intense and short-lived Anxiety Depression Sense of loss Helplessness Guilt Shame Somatic complaints Anger	Moderate to severe Anxiety Depression Sense of loss Helplessness Guilt Shame Somatic complaints Anger Weakened sense of hope	Often severe Anxiety Depression Sense of loss Helplessness Guilt Shame Somatic complaints Anger Weakened sense of hope

In the case of an ameliorable chronic stressor, such as a middle-aged man's battle with cancer, he may suffer (1) severe role loss as he needs to discontinue employment, (2) increased withdrawal from relationships, and (3) a moderate sense of depression and hopelessness.

Finally, looking at a permanent chronic stressor, such as chronic paranoid schizophrenia, the person so afflicted may experience (1) repeated role failure; (2) recurrent interpersonal conflict, at times culminating in complete withdrawal; and (3) intense anger and anxiety.

Chapter 2 already cited Fried (1982) on the major differences between acute and endemic stress. Table 4–1 does so in more detail, breaking down Fried's endemic stress category into the two we use: ameliorable and permanent chronic stress. Given the existence of a healing art, such as medicine, or of effective social legislation, such as an act providing for job retraining or for day care for children, an ameliorable chronic stress situation, whether a physical illness or disability or painful psychosocial conflict, contains a kernel of hope for remission or improvement. The permanent chronic stress situation for a person suffering, for instance, from paranoid schizophrenia first manifested at age 15 suggests, on the basis of current knowledge and treatment possibilities, little hope for change. But it may be that in the days to come this terrible scourge may be rendered less damaging to its victims or, in the best of all worlds, yield to a treatment as powerful as the Salk vaccine for polio. In the latter case, a permanent chronic stress would have been rendered minimal or nonexistent.

It may well be that the social forms of permanent chronic stress will be the least amenable to change. Racism, sexism, homophobia, poverty, poor education—in brief, the whole tissue of social pathology that crushes so many people early in their lives—will not yield to any measures short of long-term societal investment in social and human resources. This possibility is mentioned because examination of the social, interpersonal, and intrapsychic correlates of permanent chronic stress illustrates that society's not-so-benign neglect condemns people to lives of much physical and mental pain and suffering, the manifestations of which take multifarious forms. As Fried (1982) points out, a considerable amount of endemic stress is due to the injustices and inequalities of our economic and social systems.

Thus, the categories of acute, ameliorable chronic, and permanent chronic stress are not rigidly fixed but do suggest a set of sequelae indicative of the intensity and duration of reaction, and the kinds of support needed.

ASSESSING STRESS AND THE NEED FOR SOCIAL SUPPORT

Having identified the three types of stress and their resultant psychosocial correlates, we will discuss the connection between stress and social supports. It does not necessarily follow that the presence of stress requires intervention with formal supports; rather, there are variables or factors that seem to impinge upon the individual, influencing the need for support. These fall into two major categories: (1) duration and intensity and (2) risk factors.

Duration and Intensity

The two most obvious factors have been addressed in the delineation of the continuum of stress. The conceptualization of stress into acute, ameliorable chronic, and permanent chronic types inherently encompasses the variables of intensity and duration. Someone facing acute stress, such as a broken ankle incurred from a ski accident, will need a different set of supports in terms of intensity and duration than a person facing permanent chronic stress, such as irreversible kidney damage. In the former, the intensity of both professional and personal assistance will be the greatest at the beginning of the disability, and it will diminish in the latter stages as his condition improves. In the later case the supports, both material and emotional, have to be of an enduring nature, in the form of dialysis, a steady attendant capable of carrying out nursing activities, and a faithful family. Similarly, a person unemployed for six weeks generally needs a different, less complex set of supports than one who is unemployed for six months.

Risk Factors

Beyond the intensity and duration of a stressor, there are six risk factors that clearly affect the individual's need for additional support, specifically formal support, including professionally created support groups. These are (1) the strength of the existing informal support system, (2) the social acceptability of the stressor, (3) the person's subjective definition of the stressor, (4) the effectiveness of the individual's coping skills, (5) the normality of the stressor, and (6) the objective effects of needs blocked by the stressor.

Strength of Existing Informal Supports

Unquestionably, the strength of one's existing social network and informal support system directly affects the need for formal intervention. It follows that an isolated, nonsupported individual may need more sustainment than the person with an extensive, multidimensional, functioning support system. For example, a husband and a wife with their first newborn may require greater support if they have recently relocated to a new city and thus have minimal informal supports, than will a couple raising their first child in their hometown where they have an extensive social network.

Social Acceptability of Stressor

As Mitchell, Billings, and Moos (1982) point out, the acceptability of the stressor may affect not only the social response to an individual's call for support but also the person's willingness to seek support. They write, "Stresses may directly affect the availability of support, thereby indirectly influencing health outcomes" (p. 83). Imagine the difference in availability of supports to the father whose child died of leukemia and the father who lost contact with his child due to his incestuous behavior. Thinking of this example, one can see that the moral judgment and social stigma associated with a stressor will impinge on the need for formal support. The isolation and stigma suffered by the AIDS victim in today's society epitomizes this truth. One can anticipate that the greater the social disapproval associated with a stressor, the more urgent may be the need for provision of formal supports.

Subjective Definition of Stressor

In addition, the individual's subjective definition or judgment of the stressor initially affects support needs. A women defining her unemployment as a personal failure and weakness may be more vulnerable than the woman who perceives her unemployment to be the result of an economic recession. An interpretation that induces guilt, shame, or self-punitive feelings may require greater outside supportive intervention than an interpretation with more self-accepting qualities.

Effectiveness of Coping Skills

A person's coping armamentarium in the face of stress often includes a mixture of adaptive and maladaptive, task-oriented and defense-oriented behaviors. When the coping fails to help the person deal with the stress, especially when causing neurotic or psychotic reactions, more support would be needed. According to Jacobson (1974), the failure of coping skills brings on a crisis state. To illustrate, imagine the teenage girl with an unplanned pregnancy who is able to solve problems and seek assistance, as compared to a pregnant teenager who becomes immobilized and is unable to cope with her situation. While both may benefit from support, the latter may be in greater need of formal support services. In assessing the effectiveness of the person's coping mechanisms, it is helpful to remember that problems may occur in three component areas, namely, cognitive, affective, and behavioral responses.

Normality of Stressor

Another essential factor to consider is the relative normalcy of the stressor. A life event that falls within the average expected experience may require less formal support than a non-normative, traumatic, unexpected event. In their description of their support group with parents of homicide victims, Getzel and Masters (1983) offer a dramatic example:

> When a murder is committed, the survivor's major social supports change or weaken and the survivor has an altered perception of the availability and the security provided by the larger community. A positive balanced view of the world may be replaced by the one of unpredictability, hypocrisy, and moral bankruptcy. In this bleak context, estrangement escalates and signs of helplessness appear. [p. 83]

This distrustful, anomic view of the world common to the victim of unexpected life events may call for more extensive formal supports than are needed by the widower adjusting to the death of his aged spouse, a painful but "average expected" life event.

Needs Blocked by Stressor

Finally, the objective or concrete results of the stressor will affect the extent of support needed. Using Maslow's (1970) hierarchy of needs helps us to conceptualize this perspective most effectively. His hierarchy ranges from very basic needs to less crucial, higher-level needs, as follows:

1. Physiological

2. Safety
3. Belongingness and love
4. Esteem
5. Self-actualization
6. Cognitive
7. Aesthetic

Frequently, a particular stress will reduce a person's ability to fulfill one or more of these needs. While frustration of any need satisfaction might benefit from supportive efforts, the more basic the need the more imperative the availability of formal supports. Thus, by pairing Maslow's needs hierarchy with our conceptualization of the duration of stress, we can establish priorities for service. These are presented as a matrix in Table 4–2. The probable need for support services is represented numerically on a scale of one to five, with one being the lowest priority and five indicating the highest priority group for service delivery.

Using the table as a model, imagine a college student receiving notification that she needs to wait three months to establish residency before entering school. This circumstance appears to be an acute, short-term stressor which temporarily blocks the cognitive needs of the student; it would be rated "one" in our matrix. A second woman, unemployed and needing a job to sustain herself and her children, is experiencing an ameliorable chronic stress that blocks her physiological needs, a situation that would rate a "four" in the matrix. She is in greater need of support services than the first woman.

With regard to these six risk factors, it becomes clear that people may face greater difficulty if they experience:

TABLE 4–2 Stress and Unmet Needs[a]

		DURATION OF STRESS		
		Acute	Ameliorable chronic	Permanent chronic
HIERARCHY OF NEEDS	Aesthetic cognitive	1	2	3
	Self actualization Esteem Belongingness & love	2	3	4
	Safety Physiological	3	4	5

[a]1 = lowest priority for service; 5 = highest priority.

1. A weak existing social network
2. A stressor with high social unacceptability
3. A negative or self-punitive definition of the stressor
4. Failing coping skills
5. A stressor outside the expected range of events
6. Barriers to the fulfillment of basic human needs.

Applying these factors in the evaluation of an individual's need for formal support services, it can be said that a person is at risk and in high need of support services when one or a combination of these six factors exists. It may be that in some cases an individual is at risk when only one or two of the factors are involved. In no way does this imply that an individual who does not meet these criteria could not benefit from formal support groups. Quite the contrary, preventive support groups are seemingly quite successful. These risk factors are merely a guide for determining the extent of an individual's need for a support group when evaluating his acute, ameliorable chronic, or permanent chronic stress.

FLOW CHARTS FOR USE IN ASSESSMENT

The following flow charts (Figures 4–3, 4–4, and 4–5) will further assist in the decision making as to when a support group appears needed, by synthesizing the previously discussed material. Again, even when the chart indicates a support group may not be needed, this does not imply that it could not be in some way valuable to its members. Due to the flexible nature of support groups, they can be formed around any common issue or problem, regardless of its severity or seeming lack of importance. These charts indicate, rather, the *need* for support groups and their comparative service delivery priorities.

CONCLUSION

It is crucial to understand the connection between stress levels and the need for support. The concepts presented in this chapter can be used as a theoretical base in the assessment of support group need. By identifying the stressor as well as classifying its type, its psychosocial correlates, and its associated risk factors, one can decide if a support group format is a needed and appropriate form of intervention.

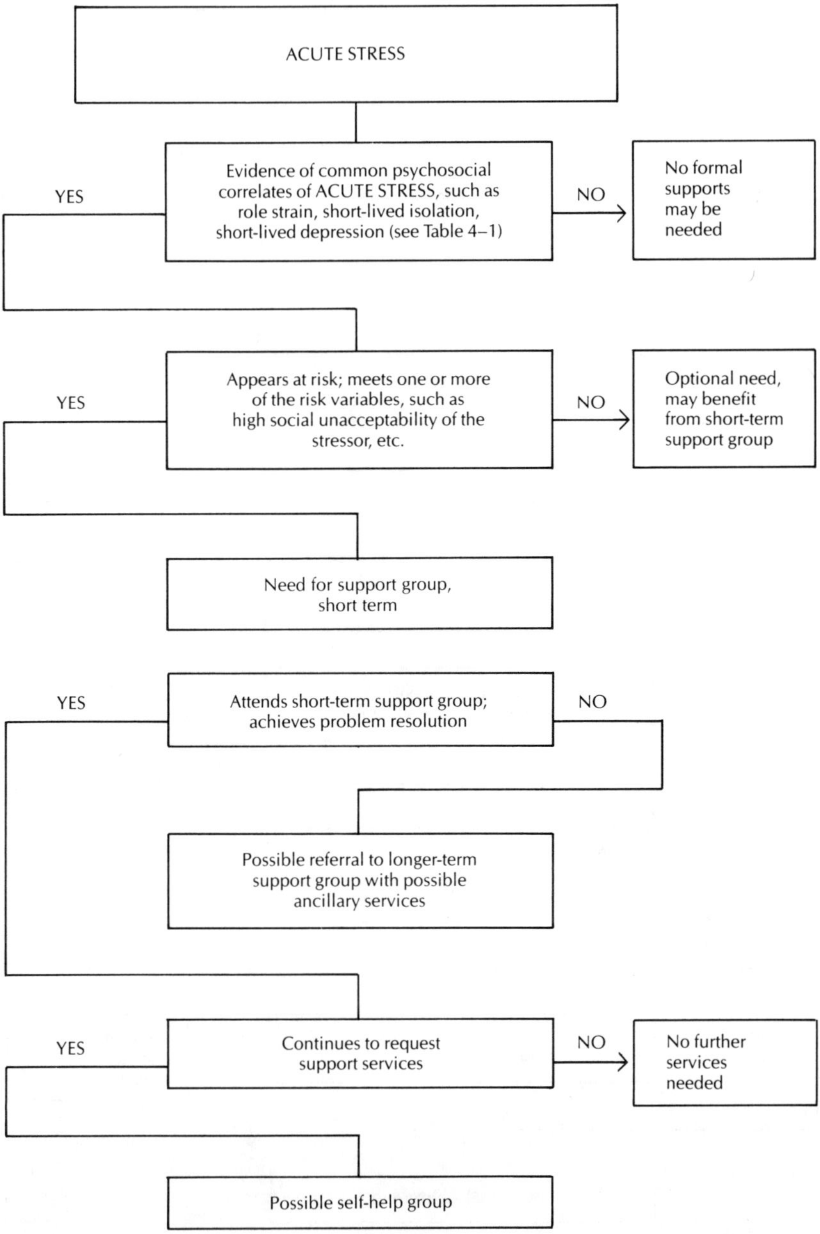

FIGURE 4–3 Flow chart for assessing need in cases of acute stress.

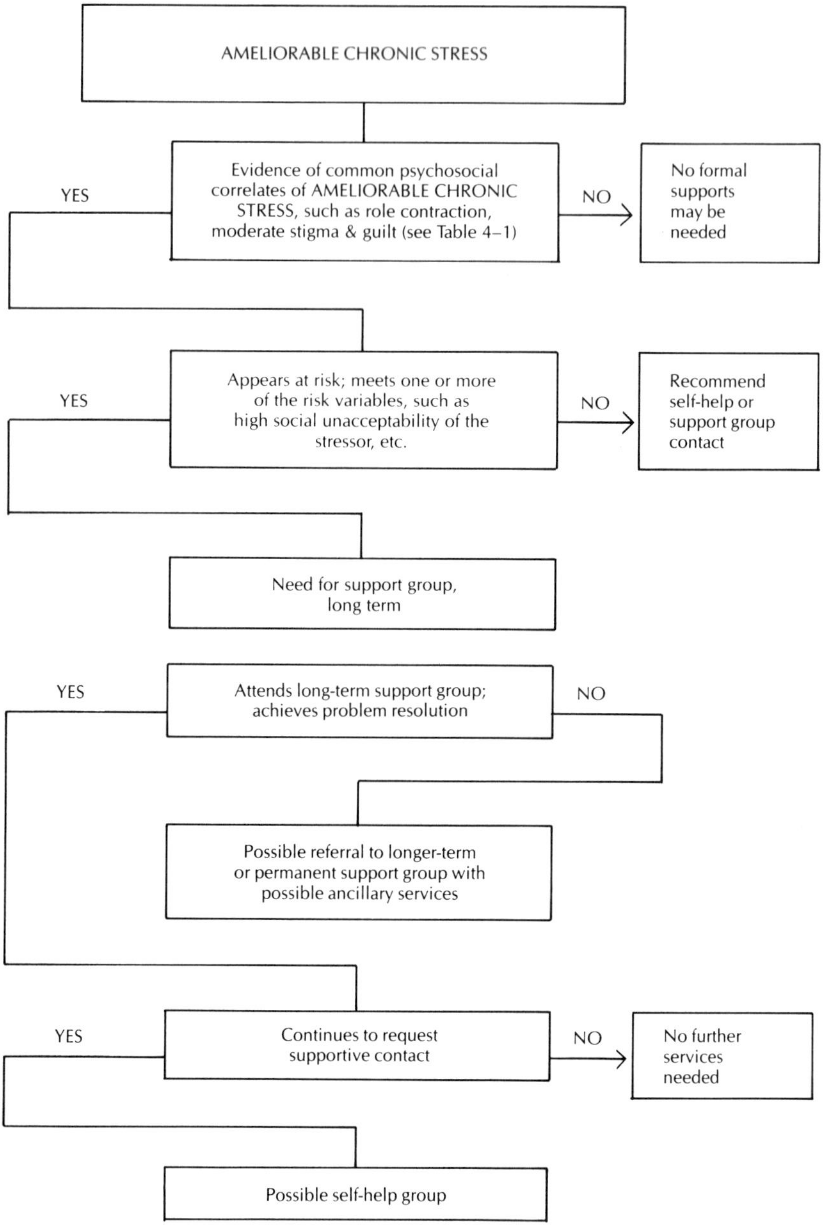

FIGURE 4–4 Flow chart for assessing need in cases of ameliorable chronic stress.

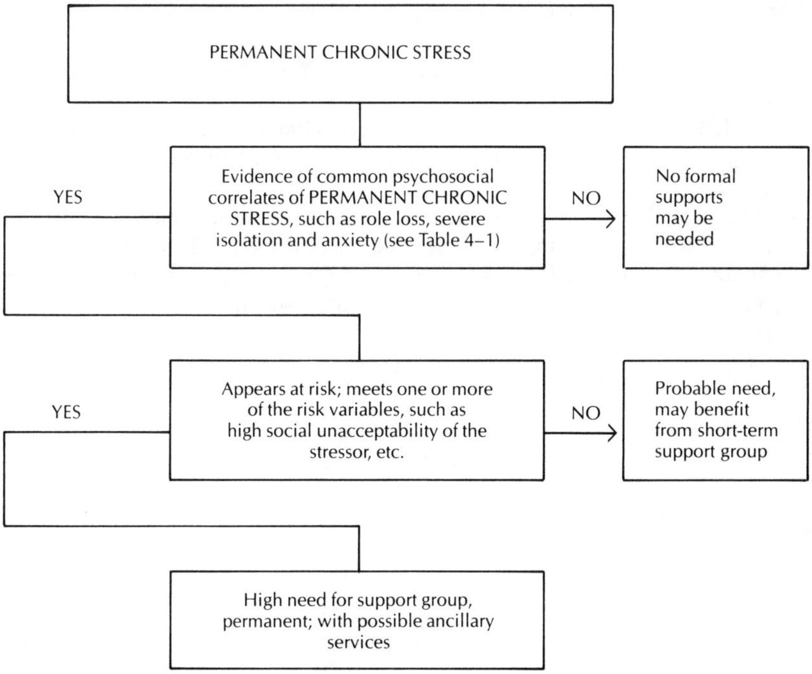

FIGURE 4–5 Flow chart for assessing need in cases of permanent chronic stress.

REFERENCES

Fried, M. (1982). Endemic stress: The psychology of resignation and the politics of scarcity. *American Journal of Orthopsychiatry, 52*(1), 4–19.

Getzel, G.S., & Masters, R. (1983). Group work with parents of homicide victims. *Social Work with Groups, 6*(2), 81–92.

Holmes, T.H., & Masuda, M. (1974). Life changes and illness susceptibility. In B.S. Dohrenwend & B.P. Dohrenwend (Eds.), *Stressful life events* (pp. 45–72). New York: John Wiley.

Holmes, T.H., & Rahe, R.H. (1967). The social readjustment rating scale. *Journal of Psychosomatic Research, 11,* 213–218.

Jacobson, G.F. (1974). Programs and techniques of crisis intervention. In G. Caplan (Ed.), *American handbook of psychiatry* (2nd ed.) (pp. 810–825). New York: Basic Books.

Lazarus, R.S., & De Longis, A. (1963). Psychological stress and coping in aging. *American Psychologist, 38,* 245–254.

Maslow, A. (1970). *Motivation and personality* (2nd ed.). New York: Harper & Row.

Mitchell, R.E., Billings, A.G., & Moos, R.H. (1982). Social support and well being: Implications for prevention programs. *Journal of Primary Prevention, 3*(2), 77–98.

Rogers, C. (1949). A theory for therapy, personality and interpersonal relationships as developed in the client-centered framework. In S. Koch (Ed.), *Psychology: A study of science, Vol. 2: General systematic formulations, learning and special processes* (pp. 184–256). New York: McGraw-Hill.

II Working with Support Groups

5 Planning a Support Group

THE IMPORTANCE OF PLANNING

A support group is formed around an existential fact: People share common, difficult, often painful, life situations, and it is this very commonality that makes the formation of support groups a relatively easy task to accomplish. When creating a support group, if one keeps in mind this philosophical intention undergirding the support group concept, formation will go more smoothly.

A support group is primarily focused on enabling members to cope more effectively with a common, shared problem. Wandersman (1982) lists four purposes of support with respect to parent-infant groups. Slightly modified to fit the intentions of support groups in general, they may be stated as follows:

1. To provide positive reinforcement and encouragement to members
2. To respect individual styles, needs, and values
3. To share information that could enhance individual coping skills
4. To discuss the advantages and disadvantages of the various coping methods the members of the group or the social workers offer.

Wandersman explains that "this approach encouraged diversity [but] . . . did not promote a particular 'correct' way to bring up children nor attempt to change parents' behaviors" (p. 104). The support group organizer builds a program geared to these nurturing, positively focused goals, usually avoiding primary emphasis on behavior change or intrapsychic restructuring. With this orientation in the forefront, the worker can proceed to the next step—the planning stage.

Roselle Kurland's (1978) first sentence in her article entitled "Planning: The Neglected Component of Group Development" reads as follows: "Planning for group practice is one of the most neglected areas in social work with groups" (p. 173). She expands her theme in the next paragraph:

> The price for lack of thorough and thoughtful planning is high. Frequently, it is paid in groups that terminate prematurely, groups in which attendance of members is sporadic and irregular, and groups that are felt by practitioners and group members to have failed in meeting the needs of group members. It is paid also in lack of worker confidence that results in practitioners who shy away from working with groups because they see themselves as incapable of group leadership. [p. 173]

Therefore, as Kurland indicates, careful planning will encourage group success while avoiding unnecessary failures.

Perhaps one of the most overlooked steps in the planning process involves building professional support for the planned intervention. Assuming that most professionally created and led support groups will be located in community mental health clinics and social agencies, a major task will be enlisting full agency commitment for undertaking their development. In effect, the professional staff who advocate for the agency's formation of support groups will need to educate both the administrative heads and their peers about the philosophy, importance, and effectiveness of support groups. This may be a difficult and arduous task in some places where issues will arise as to the differences between therapy and support groups, the fear of deprofessionalization due to similarities between support groups and lay-led self-help groups, and clinical social workers' rather pervasive anxiety about working in formats other than individual and family treatment.

While agency support may not be essential to support group success, it certainly helps. A commitment to the group that goes beyond the individual motivation and efforts of the worker may yield increased availability of resources, as well as greater emotional and supervisory backing. In addition, without agency appreciation for a group's importance, the group may be at risk for eventual dissolution. All too frequently, a courageous, innovative worker builds a support group only to watch it die as that particular worker moves on professionally to a different position. Agency commitment assures greater likelihood that staff will be hired to replace the departing worker and enable group continuation.

For these reasons, agency commitment should not be taken for granted. The support group advocate in the agency needs to educate through disseminating literature, by organizing workshops on the theory and practice of support groups, and by asking the agency for funding to support social workers' training in leading support groups. It should also be understood that, realistically, support groups will receive different levels of agency backing, particularly since the modality is in the developing stage.

COMPONENTS OF CAREFUL PLANNING

When a worker proceeds to form a support group program, whether with extensive or sparse encouragement, Kurland's (1978) analysis of the planning process should prove helpful. She identifies six components that should be assessed: need, purpose, composition, structure, content, and pregroup contact.

Need

Kurland (1978) suggests using the following questions:

> What are the needs of potential group members as perceived by them? By the worker? By the agency? By other relevant persons? What is the need for the group as perceived by potential group members? The worker? The agency? The other relevant and/or knowledgeable persons? Can these needs best be met by the group modality? [p. 177]

The following statements from the literature represent brief analyses of the needs of specific populations that would benefit from a support group experience.

> The possibility for group service was originally recognized by the school psychologist because a significant number of Hispanic female students were individually seeking counseling on a weekly basis. Although each counselee was dealing with unique problems, there emerged common themes in the counseling sessions. These themes encompassed both general adolescent issues and specific Hispanic cultural issues. [Delgado & Siff, 1980, p. 74]

> The self-help support group is an effective way for Hispanic parents to address the problems and obstacles they encounter. This approach provides them with an opportunity to build personal relationships and mutual support systems with those who share the same interests and concerns, thereby reducing isolation. [Leon, Mazur, Montalvo, & Rodriguez, 1984, p. 262]

> The authors believed that caretaking spouses could adapt positively to their new way of life through a small group experience. They saw the need to help an elderly population break out of their increasing isolation and depression. [Beaulieu & Karpinski, 1981, p. 552]

> After some years of considering the parents of members to be impediments to the rehabilitation efforts at Thresholds, we decided that the process of members' independence might accelerate if parents were converted from enemy to ally. [Dincin, Selleck, & Streicker, 1978, p. 597]

In all of the examples cited, individual agency workers are the source of support group formation. The literature indicates that this is fairly typical of the process.

Thus, recognizing a need for a particular service may simply stem from a social worker's clinical sense. For example, as a component of a sexual assault unit, workers initiated a support group for significant others of rape victims. As Rodkin, Hunt, Cowan, & Dunstan (1982) describe it, "The underlying assumption for the formulation of the group was that supportiveness on the part of a significant other affects the adjustment process of rape victims, and that a group situation with mutual sharing of experience enhances the ability of a significant other to provide the rape victim with support" (p. 93). The support group idea extended to the spouses and boyfriends of the sexual assault victims. This principle of connecting the intimately related through the nexus of sharing a common trauma or difficult, hazardous life situations has been extended to prisoners' wives (Daniel & Barrett, 1981); siblings of handicapped children (Chinitz, 1981); parents of mentally ill and developmentally disabled children (Atwood & Williams, 1978; Dincin et al., 1978; Hill, Raley, & Snyder, 1982; Massenzio, 1977; Samit, Nash, & Meyers 1980; Thompson & Doll, 1982); foster parents of placed children (Jacobs, 1980; Lee, 1979; Park, 1979); parents of learning disabled children (Gitterman, 1979); parents of seriously medically ill children (Kornfeld & Siegel, 1980; Feldman, Manella, & Varni, 1983); families of burned children (Cahners, 1978); parents of homicide victims (Getzel & Masters, 1983); children of alcoholic families (Brown & Sunshine, 1982); natural parents of children placed in foster homes (Carbino, 1982; Hess & Williams, 1982; McFerran, 1958); and relatives of dependent older and/or ill adults (Beaulieu & Karpinski, 1981; Hartford & Parsons, 1982). Inherent in this extension of support group services to significant others is the recognition that those who ultimately do the supporting and caring must themselves be supported and cared for. The needs assessment process as applied to support groups comes equipped with a wide net; as a result, human connections are immediately highlighted by the support system idea.

In addition, social service councils and United Way groups and their research arms routinely evaluate the needs of the communities they serve. These types of data, however, are generally not mentioned in relation to support groups. If such needs assessment data were available, perhaps underserved populations could be considered as potential support group participants. *Any people who share a common problem, experience, or situation may be candidates for support group formation.* For example, mental health agencies frequently find in their service evaluation that a particular minority group in a poverty-stricken area is often neglected. Commonalities in this community may yield a specific population that could benefit from support group services effectively, conveniently, and economically.

Finally, the need for a support group may become apparent through the requests of clients or community members. Gordy (1983) describes her formation of a support group for adult victims of childhood incest, based on the desire of one of her clients to talk to other women who shared her painful experience. In the future, as clinicians utilize the concepts presented in Chapter 4, particularly the risk factors, the need for support groups may become clearer and be discovered in a more structured way, rather than the present haphazard process. This development would help identify those underserved populations the profession often overlooks.

Purpose

In this category, Kurland (1978) lists the following questions:

> What are the goals of potential group members as perceived by them? By the workers? What is the tentative conception of the group purpose as viewed by potential members? By the worker? By the agency? (p. 177)

As previously stated, it appears that initiation of a support group in an agency is usually on a social worker's initiative. Once the agency becomes committed to the idea, the administrators, in conjunction with the professional staff, should begin a process of education and training. As part of that process, the clarification of support group purposes becomes an important consideration. Purpose cannot be divorced, however, from knowledge of a social problem which includes the stress factors, the range of responses, and the psychosocial correlates—in brief, all of the criteria discussed in Chapter 4. This point must be emphasized because it is entirely erroneous to assume that only the group treatment method has to be learned. A professional endeavor in social work should always be based on a mix of knowledge, values, purpose, sanction, and skill. Knowledge of the psychosocial problem is fundamental to all professional activities.

When formulating the group purpose, first one should identify whether the stress facing the majority of the members is considered acute, ameliorable chronic, or permanent chronic. From this analysis one can identify the psychosocial correlates of the stressor that need to be reduced and the risk factors that are pertinent to the population in question. This analysis will provide an initial framework for the social worker, such as whether the group is to be a short-term group to facilitate adjustment to the new role of parenthood or a permanent group to alleviate the severe isolation of the chronically mentally ill. Such an assessment is the bedrock of any statement of purpose.

Some examples of particular purpose statements may offer the best educational tool in understanding this step in planning. Lee (1979) created the following objectives in the context of a foster parents' workshop:

1. To help foster parents, through examining their own experiences, to understand the history and background of the natural parents and the child; to help them explain this to the child as well
2. To help foster parents understand what is expected of them in terms of their relationships to the natural parents, i.e., respective roles and rights
3. To explore some of the myths and feelings around the role of the natural parent in the child's life, and the ways of handling this area with the child [p. 136]

A more generalized statement of purpose is exemplified by the following:

> The aim of the group was to provide a milieu that was health oriented rather than problem oriented—one in which mothers could learn to enjoy being with their children rather than one in which they or their children would be "treated for sickness." [Phillips, Gordon, & Bodenheimer, 1981, p. 158]

As is often the case, a needs assessment and statement of purpose are intertwined; the one implies or determines the other. Consider the following example:

> (What) is needed for these families is an immediate informative and supportive approach when confronting parents with the news that their newborn is developmentally disabled. These parents need to be provided with an opportu-

nity to confront, work through, and accept their feelings, as well as the informal counseling, the availability of community services, agencies, and parent groups. [Davidson & Dosser, 1982]

A succinct statement of purpose for another support group was formulated as follows:

The purpose of the group was to bring about interpersonal communication among a group of people sharing a common problem: how to understand and cope with the mental illness of their family member and its effect on the family unit. [Atwood & Williams, 1978, p. 418]

Davis and Shapiro (1979) have outlined highly specific objectives for the mentally retarded members of their support group:

1. Development of verbal and social skills
2. Effective expression of thoughts and feelings
3. Identification as a more autonomous person
4. Increased mutual support and acceptance
5. Improvement of grooming and hygiene. [p. 330]

It can be seen, then, that the purposes of professionally led support groups vary from a fairly narrow concentration on the aims of a particular group to the possibilities of a larger mission designed to have an impact upon institutional workings, such as the foster care system. In the main, the stated purposes of the group should be limited to its members' actual needs and possibilities. Examining, for instance, Davis and Shapiro's (1979) purpose statements, one is struck by the "ambitions" of their treatment goals. But one can guess that they saw the members of this group as people involved in a chronic but ameliorable stress situation, all of whom were in individual treatment, and for whom a long-term support group was projected in order to achieve those ambitious aims. The group lasted 2½ years, having met weekly in 2-hour sessions.

While the leader's purposes usually resemble one or more of these examples, members' statements of purpose are rarely formally articulated. Members' principal psychosocial problems revolve around isolation, stigma, and either a lack of information or the possession of faulty information. Thus their goals are inextricably tied to their psychosocial/educational circumstances. They hope the group experience will lead to problem relief and a rebuilding of self-esteem. This is what they seek, consciously and unconsciously, and what the support group can honestly promise for its members.

Composition

Kurland (1978) proposes the following questions be posed when planning group composition:

> How many group members will there be? What will be the characteristics of the group members in regard to sex? age? homogeneity/heterogeneity? educational, occupational, socioeconomic, racial, ethnic, and cultural background? previous group experience? What are the characteristics of a worker who would best work with this group? Will there be one worker or more than one? [p. 177]

There is little discussion in the support group literature per se in regard to planning group composition. Gitterman (1982) states that "groups composed of members with common backgrounds (i.e., age, sex, ethnic, social class) and common personality capacities and behavior (i.e., ego functioning, role skills, authority/intimacy orientations) tend to be stable and supportive, quickly developing a group identity" (p. 14). Somewhat later, he states that members who do not share the aforementioned commonalities "tend to be less stable and predictable. They may experience difficulty in developing a sense of group identity and cohesion. Differing life experiences, concerns, interests, or adaptive styles create internal obstacles to achieving a common agenda and open communication" (p. 14). Ideally, Gitterman writes, "groups require both stability (homogeneity) and diversity (heterogeneity)" (p. 15).

In regard to group composition, Shulman (1984) declares that "the crucial factor in selection of members is that there be some common ground between their individual needs and the purpose of the group. Whether this purpose has been defined broadly or narrowly, each member must be able to find some connection between a personal sense of urgency and the work involved" (p. 186). Thus Shulman's statement implies that heterogeneity relative to the factors of age, sex, ethnicity, and the like is desirable as long as group purpose is clear in the minds of the leaders.

In reference to the composition of psychotherapy groups, Yalom (1975) writes, "No rigorous study exists which investigates the relationship between group composition and the ultimate criterion—long-term therapy outcome" (p. 261). In general, Yalom believes that the most productive groups are organized around the principle "*heterogeneity for conflict areas, and homogeneity for ego strength*" (p. 261).

How might this principle be applied to the formation of support groups? Homogeneity as an organizing factor revolves around the commonality of the situation; that is, the people in the group are faced with the same problem or difficulty. This is the critical element, the potential binding force necessary for group cohesiveness, which Yalom (1975) specifies as "a necessary precondition for effective therapy" (p. 261). It is, in his words, "the attractiveness of a group for its members" (p. 261). Among all of the factors that Yalom signifies as "curative" in group psychotherapy, that of "universality"—people in the support group being in the same boat—undergirds the sense of "we-ness" or belonging. Universality is the glue of cohesiveness.

In regard to sociocultural variables such as race/ethnicity, social class, age, and so forth, the literature indicates that support groups are not composed with any particular emphasis of heterogeneity and homogeneity. For instance, if looking at the various formats designed to "train" foster parents, one observes that in some of the support groups (often designated as workshops and training sessions), homogeneous racial/ethnic groups were formed in some and in one of them the foster parents were of mixed backgrounds (Park, 1979). It may well be that the racial/ethnic factor in the composition of support groups reflects the segregation of our urban neighborhoods and, more specifically, agency location and the population it serves.

The age factor often shows greater heterogeneity than one might have thought possible. Much depends on the nature of the problem and the developmental period in which the particular psychosocial problem takes place.

Hill et al. (1982), over a period of two years, have seen about 50 parents come through their parents' group program. One surmises that the age range was not great, since these were parents of psychiatrically hospitalized children. Davis and Shapiro (1979), in their group work with retarded adults, selected people in an age range from 22 to 55 years. The support group was "racially balanced": 60% white and 40% black. They also note, "The group was heterogeneous in terms of degree of retardation, ranging from borderline to severe levels" (p. 331). Beaulieu and Karpinski (1981) formed a support group of older people with ill spouses. Their comment on the age and sex factor reads as follows: "The fact that the groups comprised both men and women in their seventies and eighties was gratifying, because it provided a wider range of attitudes and viewpoints" (p. 553). Thus the authors proclaim the importance of the diversity principle, which all of the cited group theorists strongly support.

Chinitz (1981) formed a support group of nine members, all of whom had handicapped siblings. The ages ranged from 7 to 14 years. What do 7-year-olds have in common with 14-year-olds? On the surface it would seem very little; yet this was a highly successful support group.

Perhaps in a majority of cases the most important factor in composition is the common bond or experience the members share. The literature seems to indicate that heterogeneity where there is the common bond of experience can be effective. Reports do exist, however, of the opposite. For example, Gitterman (1982) found that combining learning-disabled students exhibiting social but no academic problems with learning-disabled students showing academic but no social problems did not prove effective.

One other point can be extracted from the literature in regard to composition. It appears that it is important to separate the identified patient or victim from friends and relatives, by placing them in different support groups. This was demonstrated in respect to cancer patients (Wood, Milligan, Christ, & Liff, 1978), open-heart surgery patients (Brown, Glazer, & Higgins, 1983), and burned children (Cahners, 1978). In some cases it appears that the inclusion of family members in groups inhibits patients or victims from expressing themselves freely and from developing a relationship with the other members of the group.

Structure

Regarding structure, Kurland (1978) suggests asking the following questions:

> What will be the duration of each meeting? of the total work? When will the group meet? How will members get to sessions? What are the resources and supplies that are needed? What is the budget for the group? How will confidentiality be maintained? cooperation and communication with other relevant professionals? Will membership be open or closed? [p. 177]

Duration

The structural aspects of the group must correlate directly with the level of stress: acute, ameliorable chronic, or permanent chronic. Ideally, acute stress would be dealt with in a short-term group (6 to 12 weeks), ameliorable chronic stress in a long-term group (3 months to 2 years), and permanent chronic stress in a continuous, enduring social support network.

Those in typical acute-stress situations would include divorcing or recently divorced people (Bonkowski & Wanner-Westly, 1979), hospitalized children (Stephenson & Boler, 1981; Kessler, 1976, 1982), the spouses of hospitalized adults (Beaulieu & Karpinski, 1981; Brown et al.,

1983; Hartford & Parsons, 1982), and those who have unwanted pregnancies (Blythe, Gilchrist, & Schinke, 1981). There are short- and long-term bereavement groups (Roy & Simpter, 1983; Walker, McBride, & Vachon, 1977), short- and long-term support groups for maltreating and nonnurturing parents (Barth, Blythe, & Schinke, 1983; Breton, 1979; Kruger, Moore, Schmidt, & Wiens, 1979; McFerran, 1958; Moore, 1982; Oppenheimer, 1978; Park, et al., 1982; Watkins & Bradbard, 1982), and short- and long-term groups with adult victims of childhood incest (Giarretto, 1982; Gordy, 1983). As pointed out earlier, the delineation between acute and chronic stress situations is not always clear. There are acute-stress flare-ups within chronic situations (a chronically poor couple who divorce), and what may begin as an acute situation (the removal of a child from his home) may turn out to be a chronic stress for all of the actors in this situation.

Thus, in actual support group practice, many short-term groups need to be given the option to continue for a longer period of time. Abundant examples in the literature exist to verify our suspicion that groups often are not maintained for a long enough period of time. In these cases, while there are often acute elements to the stressful situation, the chronic aspects are predominant and the most troublesome. Note the following examples:

1. In a group established for borderline to severely mentally retarded adults (a permanent chronic stress), the group became "a viable, cohesive unit," and was terminated after 2½ years because of a funding problem (Davis & Shapiro, 1979).
2. In a group for adult victims of childhood incest (an ameliorable chronic stress), after formation, the members complained that the eight sessions were too few (Guerney & Jordon, 1979).
3. In a workshop/support group for foster mothers for special children (an ameliorable chronic stress), when the 7-week program ended, "those who attended expressed that they got a lot out of the group experience and would like to come back for an ongoing group with the same members" (Park, 1979, p. 175).
4. In a group for socially isolated widows (an ameliorable chronic stress), after the eight sessions ended the group wanted to continue and a self-help group was formed (Crosby, 1978).
5. In a group for children of divorced parents, held on the average 1½ years post-divorce (during the ameliorable chronic stage), the 9- to 13-year-old members stated that the format of meetings was either the right amount or requested more meetings. None said that there were too many meetings (Guerney & Jordon, 1979).

In the ameliorable chronic situations, the duration of the support group is not simply a function of some theoretical ideal. The life situations of the potential members have to be considered carefully with regard to the amount of time and psychic energy they can invest in a support group. For instance, Beaulieu and Karpinski (1981), who work with the elderly with ill spouses, comment as follows: "A short-term group was selected; because each member was in the transitional stage. A long-term commitment would have been difficult for members" (p. 553). Leon et al. (1984) structured 12 group sessions for Hispanic mothers with children being treated in an outpatient psychiatric clinic. While one might well argue that these children and their families were undergoing a chronically stressful situation and that the mothers of these children could have benefitted from a long-term support group, the social workers who formed the group reasoned as follows:

> It was found that many of the mothers who were involved in the treatment did not return after 6 to 8 sessions. Dropping out might be attributed to treatment not being oriented to the "here and now"—not focused on and perhaps not applicable to the clientele's concern—or by necessity, because of the many time-consuming appointments with outside agencies that provide the basic necessities for survival. With these issues in mind, 12 group sessions aimed at the "here and now" and conducted in Spanish were planned as the appropriate format. It was hoped that members would not see the program as a "forever" matter and could appreciate the accomplishments they made. [pp. 263–264]

Thus, the social workers' rationale and justification for a short-term rather than long-term support group experience are based on some knowledge of their clients prior experience in the clinic and, just as important, the existential facts of their lives.

The idea has been posited that, for people suffering from some permanent chronic stressor such as a chronic, severe psychiatric disorder (schizophrenia), a permanent support group should make up a component of an enduring devised social system. Project Return in Los Angeles, which is a program for posthospitalized mental patients, offers people a "lifetime membership card." The purpose is to provide its members with an assurance of "lifelong friendship and support." Friedlob (1984) explains the program's philosophy as follows:

> Project Return believes this philosophy is in accord with self-determination and independent living because most human beings pursue independent interests while maintaining ongoing friendships. Thus, some members move on to jobs and other friendships and still attend club meetings or volunteer in various capacities. Other members move in and out of the organization;

Project Return is readily available whenever friendship is needed. [p. 119]

It should be noted that people who are burdened with permanent chronic stress cannot benefit from support groups that stand alone, unconnected to a network of other potentially helpful services. Questions of jobs, housing, employment, and medical care are always at issue. The support group, while critically important, is not enough in itself. It must be linked to an array of social services and basic employment and training opportunities and social and health services; then the chances for the chronically stressed to live with greater dignity are quite good.

Another potential question is, How long should meetings last? Just as the 45- or 50-minute hour has become the rule in one-to-one casework and psychotherapy, it seems from a reading of the literature that the 90-minute group session has become standard in all forms of helping groups, support, psychotherapy, encounter, and so on. How this time frame came to be established is difficult to determine with any exactitude, but it is one that Yalom (1975), among others, believes in.

The same conclusion might reasonably be applied to the duration of support group sessions. They normally meet on a weekly basis. While there is a generally held belief that a less frequent scheduling of sessions—for instance, once every two weeks or even less—often impedes the building of group cohesiveness, McFerran (1958) and Cahners (1978) both report good results with less frequent sessions—once every two weeks in the former case and only at times of parental visits in the latter.

Open or Closed Membership

Will the membership be opened or closed? First, it needs to be stated that open groups—that is, groups with a changing membership—can be supportive in nature. In such cases, the people who begin with the group remain in it for varying lengths of time, and people join the group at different times. Schopler and Galinsky (1984) have found that "the dominant purpose pursued in open-ended groups is helping clients cope with transitions and crises" (p. 5). Cahners (1978) reports that in an open group for families of burned children, "normal practice is not possible . . . because the parents in the group came from great distances and with varying frequency" (p. 167). Harris (1979) conducted a 5-month, 20-session support group with an open-ended format, in a home for the aged. At one time or another, there were 28 persons who attended meetings, with an average attendance of 9 to 12. Thus the open-ended format was not a function of any particular crisis or transition, but was instituted in terms of what was physically and mentally possible for older people. In a children's hospital in Boston, children with serious organic illnesses are seen biweekly, one hour per week, in a support group context. They join the group on admission to the hospital and leave the group upon being discharged. From 8 to 15 children attend the group, and most of them attend 10 to 18 sessions during their hospital stay (Hughes, 1982).

Open-ended groups make up an increasing part of a social work practice in "general and psychiatric hospitals, social services departments, mental health centers and family service agencies, drug and alcohol rehabilitation centers, residential treatment facilities, nursing and maternity homes, and prisons" (Schopler & Galinsky, 1984, p. 3). In examining this list, one sees that some of the agencies are designated to provide custody and/or treatment (rehabilitation) for their members. Very often their populations are reluctant to join long-term psychotherapy groups. It may be that the open-ended support group is less threatening and less demanding of a commitment to therapy. In an open-ended group, one may or may not attend, even though regular attendance is hoped for.

The open-ended group is particularly used in hospitals, since patients' varying length of stay require accommodation. Lonergan (1982) found that groups that meet only once or twice in a hospital setting are very effective in rendering psychological help to both adults and children. As Beck, Lattimer, and Braun (1979) comment, "Though most of the children participated only once or twice, they all shared certain common problems which had a strongly cohesive effect within the group. We found that even one session could be helpful in reducing anxiety and improving the individual child's capacity to cope in the situation" (p. 276). While reluctant to characterize the single-meeting group as a support group, the literature does show that members of such groups do feel strongly the common bond of similar illness and circumstance, and that the factor of universality does help in reducing anxiety and improving coping abilities.

When possible, a closed membership is recommended in the acute, short-term support group. Given the relatively brief time the members spend together (6 to 12 sessions), and the critical element of group cohesiveness, it would seem that the closed group potentially carries within it a higher mutual-aid component than the open-ended group. A stable membership group process promotes the possibility of people continuing to meet together as a self-help group after terminating their sessions with a social worker. The open-ended group does not lend itself as easily to such an outcome.

In longer-term support groups for those with ameliorable chronic stress, it appears to be a toss-up whether an open or closed format is most effective. While most groups fitting this category tend to be open-ended, a significant number are closed. These involve mentally retarded adults (Davis & Shapiro, 1979), alcoholic, polydrug-abusing adolescents (Citron, 1978), nonnurturing mothers (Avery & Wayne, 1978), adolescent mothers (Erf, 1981), and abusive (Breton, 1979) and potentially maltreating mothers (Wayne, 1979).

In summary, whether or not a support group should be open-ended or closed depends essentially on three factors: the structure of the setting, the characteristics of the clients served, and the nature of the compact or the purpose of the group (Shulman, 1984). For example, a neighborhood mental health clinic may promote daily open-ended sessions for people in crisis. The clinic may be located in a crisis-ridden area of the city and may have adapted its structure to meet that reality. A community center, on the other hand, may be located in an area where there are many elderly people. The agency may mount several kinds of support groups, both closed and open-ended. There may be weekly, open-ended bereavement groups and closed groups for the spouses of the elderly ill. If one of the purposes of a support group is to develop an enduring self-help group as an outcome, then a closed group is superior to an open-ended group. At the Jewish Family Service of Los Angeles, both open-ended and closed support groups for unemployed professionals were formed. In the leaders' opinion, members received benefits in both structures, but the closed form provided more intensive and "deeper" discussions than the open-ended (Wasserman, 1983–1984).

Location

Where the group will meet is another crucial issue, and the social work literature on support groups demonstrates much sensitivity to it. The question of locale is important not only in terms of the distances that people have to travel (the accessibility issue), but even more so with regard to the problem of stigma and shame. There should be an implicit rule that dictates a meeting place where people *normally* come together to conduct their everyday affairs or a locale that fortifies the members' sense of dignity.

Consider the following examples of meeting places for support group and the rationales for their choice:

1. Social workers chose the conference room of a local bank in which a group of elderly, socially isolated widows met. . . . The bank is central

to the members' neighborhood and was considered convenient for all. Moreover, the setting is not part of a mental health facility, which can be an important consideration when working with the elderly who often see individual and group therapy as appropriate only for "crazy people," whereas a socializing group, meeting in a bank, might be beneficial for anyone (Crosby, 1978, p. 349).

2. In respect to a meeting place for a group of women faced with the common stressor of having moved with their families to a new area, the social workers noted the importance of location. The advantages of conducting the workshop in the library were manifold. A library does not carry a stigma of personal or social problems or failure and thus was suitable to convey that the workshop was dealing with normal problems (Kaplan & Glenn, 1978, p. 434).

3. A group of natural parents whose children were in foster homes met in a community settlement house. The meetings were held there to promote an ambience of relaxation and informality (McFerran, 1958, p. 223).

4. Meetings of Hispanic adolescents in a high school took place in the library workroom "a self-contained room adjacent to the school library. This room represented a neutral environment within the school building. In addition, it offered the needed privacy and a central table arrangement" (Delgado & Siff, 1980, p. 75).

5. Breton (1979) thought about the working place in terms of shelter for a group of abused and abusive mothers. She chose "a place [that] would be easily accessible to the mothers; thus a small flat (one room and attached bathroom) was rented in the neighborhood from which the mothers were recruited" (p. 165).

While social workers may be aware of the importance of the meanings attached to the locale of support group meetings, proper sites may not be available. Wayne (1979) reports, in her work with "isolated mothers" who were high risks for child maltreatment, that the group met at the Crittenton Hastings House, a facility "serving women with unplanned pregnancies." Wayne writes as follows: "Since no other facilities were available, the meetings were going to be held at Crittenton Hastings and the young pregnant women in residence would provide volunteer babysitting service" (p. 11). This arrangement is an example of imaginative thinking. While the worker would have preferred a more neutral setting for the mothers' meetings, she took advantage of what the facility had to offer—child care and an opportunity for young expectant women to have experience in caring for young children.

In regard to prospective members who are known to be resistant to any social work involvement, reaching out in highly assertive ways is sometimes the only means of making and maintaining contact in the period of early group formation. The agency will have to be ready to spend time and money for transportation and, in some cases, to provide a special nonstigmatized locale for the group sessions.

Transportation and Other Physical Needs

How members will get to sessions is the central question. Considerations of who will take care of children when parents are meeting; what kinds of refreshments would be proper and who will prepare them; the physical comfort of the room, including a central table, chairs, lighting, and temperature; and so on are "details" which, singly and together, are of great importance.

In the case of elderly and/or ill and/or physically handicapped people, the question of transportation has to be tackled by the agency and the workers. How will people get to the meetings? Who can come by bus, taxi, or private conveyance? For whom must the agency arrange transportation in one way or another?

Wayne (1979) describes how she picked up the members of a women's group with an agency van. After the women failed to congregate at a designated point, she went from house to house with the van. It became obvious to her that this group of women who were high risks for child maltreatment would not have engaged in an 8-month support group experience without social workers who were willing to seek them out actively.

Child care is a *sine qua non* in forming and maintaining parents' and mothers' groups. There are support group programs in which mothers and children interact at scheduled times during the sessions (Levenson, Hale, Hollier, & Tirado, 1978) and programs in which they are separated physically but in view of each other during the entire period (Holman, 1979). In both kinds of mother-child arrangement, the agency has to have a definitive plan for taking care of the children when they are separated from their mothers.

The serving of food and beverages should be given consideration in planning the group. Perhaps the implicit rule for the serving of food in groups might be that, where the members have suffered early emotional and/or physical deprivation, the serving of food and drinks takes on high significance. Thinking of Freud's assertion that symbolically food is love, if food represents not only a filler of the body but a source of warmth and conviviality, then one can see that the workers' offering of food conveys the messages that members need to "introject" or take in in some symbolic way. If members later take over this function, it may symbolize their increased ability to give and receive similar messages themselves.

Breton (1979) writes with knowledge and sensitivity about the importance of food for her group of abused and abusive mothers:

> Having built into the group programs the means of meeting the need for physical comfort, it was then relatively easy to incorporate the other basic needs, those for food and shelter. Indeed, these last two aspects of nurturing have been time-honored implements for group-work programs since the very beginning of social work with groups.
>
> However, in accordance with the completely giving, nondemanding framework for this particular group, it was decided to seek out a "mothering-type" woman who would look after the preparation of lunch for the mothers. This woman would have to be someone who not only could prepare good meals, but more importantly could give the mothers the feeling that [she] really cared about them. [pp. 164–165]

Here is a thoughtful mind at work, taking into account the members' needs and how these needs might be met through a "mothering-type" woman who cared for them and who served them food.

Confidentiality and Consultation Issues

In respect to confidentiality and communication with other professionals, ethical practice dictates as much openness and discretion in discussing individual group members. We have in mind communications between professionals of the same agency and between those on an inter-agency level. There are two important factors which influence the openness-discretion dilemma. The first factor is the agency regulations and rules covering the issue of communications about clients inside and outside the agency. The second is the nature of the working alliance or contract the group leader has negotiated with members about communications involving them. Ethical issues of this kind abound in social work (Loewenberg and Dolgoff, 1985; Reamer, 1982).

Potential members in individual screening sessions should be informed of the agency's ground rules as well as of any matters that might affect them as individual members or might rebound on the group. If, for instance, a new support group is composed primarily of clients currently in individual treatment in the agency, it must be decided how this fact will be treated. This decision is one that belongs to the agency, after staff discussion and after consultation with those clients who are in both individual and group treatment. If clients are referred from other agencies, rules of communication have to be agreed upon. Here again, the concerned agencies (which is to say, their administrators) should form working agreements as to the nature of the communications, and so on. There is nothing special about support group practice, in the sense that it is a different kind of social work. It is social work and should follow all of the precepts of proper professional practice.

Confidentiality of information in the form of members' disclosures is a matter that should be taken up with prospective group members in intake screening sessions and in the initial group meeting. Group therapy formats generally operate under stricter "rules" than professionally led support groups, which, for instance, do not forbid members' contacts outside the group sessions. If the literature on agency support groups is an indicator of a confidentiality issue, then it is safe to say there is no problem, for it simply is not reported. Yet there must be sensitivity to the question of confidentiality, and it should be discussed with prospective group members.

Unquestionably, a group experience is a public experience. It is unlike the dyadic arrangement of a single social worker and a single client. In a group, several people come together regularly and sometimes the kinds of information is disclosed which ought not to spread beyond the confines of the group. Yet, while social agencies and their staffs ethically must adhere to the principle of confidentiality and urge group members to do so too, no assurance can be made that absolutely safeguards the disclosure.

Content

In the area of content, Kurland (1978) recommends asking the following questions:

> What will go on at the meetings? What supplies and/or equipment are needed? How and by whom will content be planned? (Kurland, 1978, p. 177).

The content of the meetings of professionally led support groups should reflect, in various combinations and permutations, (1) the group leaders' professional knowledge and value positions and (2) the members' priorities, issues, and questions.

Group Leader's Knowledge and Values

The leaders' understanding of a problem—its "causes," development, behavioral manifestations, and outcomes—should be the guide in determining the content of the meetings. Note that this kind of basic knowledge about a psychosocial problem seems to be of a different order than the specific technical skills of leading a group. Yet, in the long term, these two are always related.

There are many possible ways that knowledge plays a role in leading support groups. For example, in an article entitled "Group Treatment for Children in Substitute Care," Mayfield and Neil (1983) discuss their work with children in foster care. They demonstrate their knowledge by pointing out what it means to be removed from one's home:

> Removal and placement interrupt and always distort the process of a child's normal maturation. Children in placement have difficulty in forming close, trusting relationships, and the development of skills necessary for coping with later life is greatly hindered. As children drift through the substitute care system, they learn to survive in increasingly maladaptive ways. [p. 584]

They also demonstrate other important knowledge:

> For many children, behavior problems result in multiple moves through the foster care system, compounding existing emotional problems. When concerted efforts are made to meet the needs of such a child, a referral to a therapist is normally the only resource. It has been observed that individual therapy is often ill-suited to meet the needs of the very young or noncommunicative child; many times it only serves to heighten the sense of isolation felt by a child in substitute care. [p. 579]

It is readily discernible from these citations that these two social workers understand what removal from her own home means to a child, what a searing experience it is; they further understand what happens to many children who are subject to multiple moves, and how individual therapy is not always a proper prescription.

Mayfield and Neil (1983) are also knowledgeable about the four types of survival roles that children develop in foster care—the lost child, the clown, the troublemaker, and the achiever. They know why children may take these roles upon themselves;

> Children in placement suffer common underlying feelings of loneliness, fear, inadequacy, insecurity, and guilt—but most of all, these children feel helpless and victimized. They feel that they are the pawns of adults and that they have no control over their lives. In order to survive and to cope with their pain, they take on one of these four survival roles or some combination of them. [p. 580]

On the basis of their knowledge and experience with children in substitute care, Mayfield and Neil (1983) worked out a "structured eight-week program," the principal goals of which were

> 1. To build self-esteem
> 2. To teach communications and coping skills
> 3. To help children learn to assert themselves and make responsible decisions
> 4. To help children in placement learn to trust
> 5. To assist in alleviating guilt by helping them realize that they are not responsible for the dysfunctions in their natural families [p. 580]

Using a wide variety of the instruments and techniques of child therapy, these two social workers created structured discussions for each of the eight sessions in which the children came together: I) Getting Acquainted; II) Feelings; III) Defenses; IV) Risk Taking; V) Families; VI) Substitute Care; VII) Being Special; and VIII) Saying Goodbye (p. 580). The knowledge of the psychosocial problem, the young age of the children in this particular group, and the power of the group process combine in determining the content of the group.

One more example demonstrates the linkage between knowledge, content, and the group process. In "Nurturing Abused and Abusive Mothers: The Hairdressing Group," Breton (1979) writes at some length about the meanings of nurturing and nonnurturing. Her thinking is summarized in this statement:

> Research findings have indicated that abusive parents do not nurture their children because they do not know how to assume the nurturing role. The findings also indicate that basically this incompetence in the role of nurturer or care giver stems from the fact that these parents have not themselves been properly nurtured, if at all. [p. 163]

Employing Maslow's scheme of a hierarchy of basic human needs, Breton reasons that nonnurturing mothers need physical comfort, but she wonders how this might be supplied in a social work treatment situation. Her thinking develops along the following lines:

> To meet the first basic need of providing physical comfort posed a problem. Indeed, how does one get around to giving physical comfort to adults in our North American culture? Touching is not a readily acceptable feature of our interactional patterns. . . . The problem was dealt with by offering the mothers hairdressing—a socially acceptable way to be touched, as it is considered neither infantile nor sexually questionable. [p. 164]

Here we can detect a social worker's thought process at work, as she forms ideas based on a theory of human needs and a knowledge of how these needs manifest themselves in women who abuse their children and who themselves more likely than not were abused. Her thinking is infused with a refined sensibility. She then moves on to questions of how the group may in the long term meet its members' higher-level needs. How, in brief, might the socialization process be initiated in this group? Let us follow Breton's (1979) thinking once again, quoting at length from her description of how both the content and the form of the group process were determined.

> In terms of authority structure, it was assumed that people who abuse their children have never experienced the security which comes from having had parents who took on the responsibility of guiding, protecting, and controlling them in a beneficent way and therefore have not learned to internalize behavioral controls (which leads to their inability to control themselves and their children appropriately). Consequently, it was decided that the group leaders should enable the mothers to experience this facet of authority.
>
> Thus the leaders took on most of the responsibility for the decision-making in the first phase of the group, demanding very little of the members on this score until they felt the women were ready to participate in this process; the leaders also became models of assertive behavior and encouraged emerging assertive behaviors on the part of the mothers; and finally, the leaders sought to teach the mothers different forms of control than that of punishment, by actively fostering, within the group, norms which stressed positive reinforcement. . . .
>
> Gaining the mothers' trust was therefore seen as a prime focus for the group leaders—*patience was to be the hallmark of their interventions during the beginning phases of the group* [italics added], and "going at the client's pace" was to be a social work practice principle instantly activated. [pp. 165–166]

Later in the article, Breton (1979) comments, "Nurturing, or reparenting, is a slow process: it took nearly a year of sustained giving to the mothers, materially and emotionally, before they themselves could start giving also" (p. 170).

Thus, in the case of abuse, the content of the group meetings will reflect the special stance that a social worker takes toward people who have been hurt and victimized and are now perpetrating the same thing on their progeny. This attitude is combined with nurturing members' growing sense of assertiveness and mastery and developing norms that emphasize giving and receiving clear messages from one another and treating each other with increasing decency.

Members' Priorities, Issues, and Questions

In every support group from which members derive benefits, the content of the group meetings tends to come in greater measure from the group leaders in the early meetings. As the meetings continue and the group progresses, the members' contributions increase while those of the group leaders decrease. What happens in a professionally led support group that meets members' needs is that the group develops what Shulman (1984) calls a "working culture" (p. 295). While Shulman believes that a group's working culture is connected to the group's concerns about authority (members' relationships to the group leaders) and intimacy (members' relationships to each other), the members' thinking, observations, personal experiences, and search for meanings in the form of contributions to the group are a significant aspect of the working culture. It is as much cognitive/intellectual as it is emotional/affective. These two spheres are parts of each other and can only be split off as a heuristic exercise.

How rapidly or slowly the members of a group become the principal contributors to the content of the sessions depends on the interaction of three factors: the duration of the group, the capacity of the members to express their problems verbally, and the willingness of the group leaders to allow a natural progression from a professional leader-led group to a member-led one.

With respect to a short-term group, Empey (1977), in her work with multihandicapped adolescents (including some who were mentally retarded), chose "an unstructured natural group" in which the members decided in favor of a "rap session" (p. 594). In this type of group, the content of the sessions is virtually assigned to the members from the very beginning. The leader saw herself not so much as a presenter of content but as one who would "offer adult role modeling and a parent figure in order to facilitate normal adolescent developmental issues" (p. 595). According to the author's report, this group of multihandicapped adolescents struggled with feelings of exclusion and abandonment, dependency, personal identity, anger, and loss. Empey's writings indicate that members brought these concerns to the rap sessions.

On the other hand, Davis and Shapiro (1979) set up a racially balanced, long-term group for mentally retarded adults aged 22 to 55. During the first 3 months the group leaders took more or less total responsibility for the presentation of the sessions' content. Following that, however, the group reached a somewhat cohesive state and members began to initiate discussions before the arrival of the group leaders.

As one might expect, in short-term groups the members' participation and contribution to content are enhanced by the imposed time structure. There is much work to be done in a relatively short period of time. Conversely, longer-term groups may require more time to involve a larger input from members on content.

Another factor that affects members' contributions is their verbal capacity. This relates to the main vehicle for social work treatment with both individuals and groups, that is, the interchange of words between and among people. It is a truism that people who have suffered great emotional damage are hardly able to talk about themselves and the experiences of their lives in any "normal" kind of way. They are the least able to *be* with others with a comforting sense of mutual warmth. Over and over one reads in the support group literature that the most obvious feature of those suffering from ameliorable and permanent chronic stress is that they are *isolated.* They do not connect with other people; they cannot talk to others without feeling some terrible discomfort. There are populations, including parents who maltreat their children, the mentally retarded, schizophrenic patients, and post-hospitalized ambulatory schizophrenics, who, when formed into support groups, need a social worker who can *take the lead* by structuring both the content and its sequences in the early months of the support group experience. A leader has to work out the topics session by session until the group develops the necessary cohesiveness in which ideas and feelings can be interchanged.

What social workers have to keep in mind for those clients who do not easily express themselves verbally is that talking has either been diverted into relative states of silence and a turning against the self or it has been used for senseless, sometimes violent acting-out against others. Or, it may be used as a way of defending oneself, through excessive shouting, talking too much, or talking without saying anything significant. Regardless, talking and listening to others in a mutual interchange is a new experience that a support group can offer to those who have cut themselves off and/or have been cut off from other people, or for those whose lives have been dominated by acting-out in antisocial ways. Claude Brown, in writing about young people profoundly alienated from other people, states "Most of them possess a hunger for guidance and advice so profound it would be too humiliating to express even if they could." Many of our isolated and stigmatized clients, referred to as experiencing ameliorable and permanent chronic stress, suffer from the same incapacity as Brown's disaffected youth.

While one normally thinks of human support as a helpful, desirable expectation within the human condition, many (but not all) of those populations who might benefit from long-term support groups feel threatened by the support of others. They do not trust it, because they have never developed that basic trust in other human beings that most of us simply take for granted. This is another way of saying that it takes time (several months to a year) for the members of support groups composed of the mistrustful to begin to relate to each other differently so that cohesiveness and the development of a work culture can take place. It takes a great deal of time for the disaffected to sense that group leaders and other members are not there to hurt or betray them. In other words, some groups do not become true support groups until they have been in existence for several months.

All things being equal, the members of short-term support groups composed of people who are going through some crisis (e.g., divorce) or who need some temporary guidance and sustenance in a new role (e.g., foster parents) are capable of talking about their common situation with relative ease. That is not to say that some people are not more talkative or active generally than others, but the interchange almost from the first session is of a different quality. There is a willingness mixed with inhibition about speaking about oneself, but usually the lack of basic trust is not the issue. What is at issue in the short-term group is the normal resistance to self-disclosure and thus exposure to others. In sum, the most difficult task for group leaders is to help people to learn how to listen and talk to others when their whole lives have been directed in ways that have abjured these most human capacities.

Transfer of Authority and Control

In looking at group leadership and membership growth, the question arises, "What might be an appropriate, healthy, life-sustaining role for professional leaders of support groups?" The most important principle in the philosophy of social work leadership of support groups is the inherent belief in the problem-solving and "growth" capacities of group members. In some groups, depending on the psychosocial circumstances of their members, these inherent capacities are quite apparent, such as in groups of foster parents in training. They are much less apparent in a group of chronic ambulatory schizophrenics. In the latter situation, the duration of the group, the patience and understanding of the leaders, and the quantity and quality of all of the components of the treatment philosophy and "package" all play some determining influence in the members' capacity to deal with their problems and take some initiatives in making some important decisions with respect to their life circumstances.

In accord with this principle, the leaders' goal in support group work is to transfer group leadership from themselves to the members. This principle values the democratic dispersion and use of authority and power. The more people can do for themselves—with minimal influence of experts, such as professional group leaders—the better. Substantial evidence on the proliferation of nonprofessionally led self-help groups indicates that people can come together and help each other, even without professional intervention, or with minimal help. In effect, when members of a professionally led support group decide to become a self-help group—with or without professional consultation, but with the latter always being available—this is a transformation in the right direction. Rather than viewing self-help groups as a threat, social work ought to view this development as a beneficial advice for thousands of people. Although it is clearly true that some people have been hurt in these groups and that these self-help casualties are not to be ignored, greater autonomy is in general a hopeful direction.

It should be noted that, despite the belief in members' ability to grow and learn to help themselves, there is a reality principle: It may well be that some support groups cannot allow for the transfer of leadership authority to the members. For instance, wife batterers and other persons who have long histories of violence against others may not be able to create a consistent, dependable subculture of nonviolence as a group norm. Without this development, it is highly probable that group members will continue to behave in their habitual ways. Thus, the principles set forth are not absolute and need to be tempered according to the reality principle. Nevertheless, this caveat should not be used as a rationalization for impeding appropriate transfers of leadership.

Social work cannot merely assume people's inherent strengths for self-leadership, problem solving, and growth. If, as it seems likely, the great majority of group leaders continue to come from the ranks of psychodynamically oriented clinical social work, there may be a tension or, better, a contradiction in basic assumptions. On the one hand the profession of social work adheres to a belief in people's capacities for democratic leadership and decision making; on the other hand, training in psychodynamic theory revolves so much around unconscious processes that social workers can find this orientation overshadowing beliefs in self-determination and individual choice. When this occurs, knowledge becomes the privilege of the expert and the client's well-being is seen as more dependent upon a social worker's skill in transfering that knowledge to the client. In social work with groups the assumption presupposes less social and intellectual distance between group leaders and members, whereas the psychodynamic perspective rests on a larger social distance and knowledge gap between social work therapist and client.

In brief, support group leaders who have been trained in and have practiced according to psychodynamic theory may have to undergo a radical shift in perspective. In order to function as effective, successful support group leaders, they will have to experience a paradigm shift, away from a fairly distant, expert position vis-à-vis the client and toward a social status and role within the group that tends toward greater equality between leader and members as they both contribute to content.

Pregroup Contact

Kurland (1978) suggests the following questions be asked with regard to pregroup contact.

> How and by whom will intake, screening, recruitment, and orientation to the group be carried out? What will be the content of intake, screening, recruitment, and orientation processes prior to the first group meeting? [p. 177]

In general, it is good social work practice for group leaders to do the intake, screening, and orientation work. Assigning these initiatory responsibilities to the leaders is one means by which the potential members of the group can sense a genuine interest in their situations. This arrangement avoids the bureaucratic misfortune of clients having to disclose their "stories" to many different people, with whom they have fleeting contacts.

What might be the nature of these initial contacts between social workers and potential members? The following excerpt from Shulman-Miller and Rubin (1982) represents an example of good social work practice. In this case, the authors are describing a short-term support group of parents who intend to separate or have recently separated from or divorced their spouses.

> The first step in the intake process is a prescreening telephone contact initiated by the prospective client. During this phone call the worker begins to set the ground rules for participation by stating that all prospective Parents-in-Transition members come in for an appointment to help determine if the group will best meet their need. The worker stresses that the meeting in no way obligates participation; rather, by talking together, gaining an understanding of the situation, and clarifying needs, the worker and client will mutually be able to decide if the group is appropriate. . . .

> The intake lasts from 35–60 minutes, and is divided into 3 major components. In the first part of the intake the worker shares information about the group—what it looks like, what happens during a group meeting, issues discussed, guidelines for participation. In the second component of the in-

> take, the worker engages the client in discussion about what she is looking for. Why does she want a group experience? What issues does she want the group to address?
>
> The third component, and the major portion of the interview, is the taking of a family history. This background information enables the worker to have a better understanding of the individual and her family system. Questions include who initiated the divorce, family reactions and alliances, role changes, financial and legal questions, support system availability, as well as present coping mechanisms.
>
> The worker's role, in addition to asking questions and setting a tone of acceptance, is to highlight common themes that other recently divorced people are also experiencing. In this way the worker begins to make linkages between people who are feeling isolated. By the end of the intake the worker should have a better sense of the prospective group members. Together they should be able to assess if a group experience is desired and appropriate. [pp. 4–6]

This article is quoted liberally because it offers one of the fullest descriptions of the intake, screening, and orientation process in respect to support group formation. The process serves both as an assessment of the prospective member and as a connecting medium to the group.

Are there any foolproof methods of excluding people who cannot benefit from a support group experience and/or whose presence in a group would not be helpful to others? The answer is no. Leaders can, of course, screen out the more grossly disturbed persons who would be disruptive of the group process. What is a more difficult and elusive diagnostic task is to exclude those who, in a dyadic situation, appear to be capable of a beneficial group experience, but who, once in the group, prove to be disruptive members. In brief, a dyadic encounter is not always a predictor of a person's behavior in a group. There is no foolproof prescription for inclusion and exclusion in groups. The best judgment relies on a mixture of professional assessment skills, intuitive hunches, and common sense.

In Schulman-Miller and Rubin's (1982) parents-in-transition groups, the same members begin and end the group experience. The agency and its social workers have a professional obligation to do screening interviews, to enhance all prospective members' well-being. However, in an open group format where people "show up" for the group, screening efforts are usually impossible, except in some institutional settings. In hospitals, for either medical or psychiatric reasons, patients can be prohibited by medical authority to attend group sessions, but even here it is quite rare. In agencies and clinics where people come in off the street, people join the group by virtue of their presence. The literature indicates that this "uncontrolled" arrangement works very well. Apparently people join helping groups with serious intent and adapt themselves to the group structure and process over a period of time.

Another facet of pregroup contact involves recruitment of members, which can take various forms. The most common method, perhaps, is the acceptance of in-house referrals in an agency. Frequently, in this case, the clients are already involved with the agency and may be receiving individual casework treatment. In her work with adult victims of childhood incest, Gordy (1983) obtained referrals in this manner. If this method is used, it is important for group workers to coordinate services with other clinic staff.

Recruitment can also be done by mail, with agency follow-up by phone. If this is done, it helps to use already existing resources or institutions to obtain mailing lists. For example, in a support group for surviving parents of homicide victims, contact was made with the individual who provided victim identification for the coroner's office.

Other recruitment possibilities include flyers, interagency referrals, advertisements, public service announcements, and face-to-face outreach work. Most referrals for support groups are of a voluntary nature, but in the future more use of court-ordered referrals (drug users, battering men, abusive and neglectful parents) may be a possibility.

To close this section, a caveat: No matter what the method of recruitment, it is recommended for any closed-membership group to screen the members prior to group formation. Screening will help insure that the group members' expectations are compatible with the group purpose, and that the individual and the group are appropriate for each other. This process helps to avoid unnecessary group casualties.

SUMMARY

This chapter has offered a fairly extensive discussion of the process of creating a support group. A step by step summary is listed in the appendix, but the following are the general highlights to keep in mind during the planning stage:

1. *Clarify the agency or organization's commitment* to sponsoring the support group. Commitment may include many areas, such as monetary backing, staffing availability, philosophical and theoretical goals, as well as access to material resources.
2. *Establish the need* for the support group. Basically, any group of people with a common problem, experience, or situation may contain candidates for support group information.

3. *Be clear about the purpose* of the group. Be aware of the type of stress facing the group membership; acute, ameliorable chronic, or permanent chronic. Usually the group purpose will involve the relief or reduction of the psychosocial correlates of the stressor, such as isolation and stigma. *Limit the purpose to the actual needs and realistic possibilities* of the group.
4. *Focus group composition on the commonality of experience.* Support groups revolve around homogeneity of the stressor, not necessarily other membership characteristics. It is often helpful to separate identified patients or victims from families and friends.
5. *Carefully plan the group structure,* attending to the following:
   a. Longer-term stressors generally need longer-term groups.
   b. Meetings are typically once a week for 1- or 2-hour sessions.
   c. When possible, short-term groups do best with closed membership. However, remember that open membership groups *can* be supportive.
   d. Arrange meeting places in the most convenient, least stigmatized settings.
   e. Be sensitive to members' specific needs with regard to transportation, child care, medical needs, and so forth.
   f. Refreshments and snacks often help bonding.
   g. Plan for issues of confidentiality and communication of information.
6. *Expect group leaders to have the most influence on content early in the life of the group. Be knowledgeable about the stressor and related values.* Members will eventually determine increasing amounts of content, depending on the duration of the group and their verbal capacities. Aim to decrease any sense of distance between the leaders and members.
7. *Arrange for pregroup contact* if possible, to determine appropriateness of membership, review group purpose, and begin the rapport-building process.

REFERENCES

Atwood, N., & Williams, M.E. (1978). Group support for the families of the mentally ill. *Schizophrenia Bulletin, 4*(4), 415–425.

Avery, N., & Wayne, J. (1978). Group development and grief therapy for non-nurturing mothers. *Social Work with Groups, 1*(3), 287–298.

Barth, R.P., Blythe, B.J., Schinke, S.P., & Schilling, R.F. II (1983). Self-control with maltreating parents. *Child Welfare, 62*(4), 313–324.

Beaulieu, E.M., & Karpinski, J. (1981). Group treatment of elderly with ill spouses. *Social Casework, 62*(9), 551–556.

Beck, L., Lattimer, J., & Braun, E. (1979). Group psychotherapy on a children's urology service. *Social Work in Health Care, 4*(3), 275–285.

Blythe, B.J., Gilchrist, L.D., & Schinke, S.P. (1981). Pregnancy-prevention groups for adolescents. *Social Work, 26*(6), 503-504.

Bonkowski, S.E., & Wanner-Westly, B. (1979). The divorce group: A new treatment modality. *Social Casework, 60*(9), 552-557.

Breton, M. (1979). Nurturing abused and abusive mothers. *Social Work with Groups, 2*(2), 161–174.

Brown, D.H., Glazer, H., & Higgins, M. (1983). Group intervention: A psychosocial and educational approach to open heart surgery patients and their families. *Social Work in Health Care, 9*(2), 47–59.

Brown, K.A., & Sunshine, J. (1982). Group treatment of children from alcoholic families. *Social Work with Groups, 5*(1), 65–72.

Cahners, S.S. (1978). Group meetings for families of burned children. *Health and Social Work, 3*(3), 165–172.

Carbino, R. (1982). Group work with natural parents in permanency planning. *Social Work with Groups, 5*(4), 7-30.

Chinitz, S.P. (1981). A sibling group for brothers and sisters of handicapped children. *Children Today, 10*(6), 21–23.

Citron, P. (1978). Group work with alcoholic polydrug-involved adolescents with deviant behavior syndrome. *Social Work with Groups, 1*(1), 39–52.

Crosby, C. (1978). A group experience for elderly isolated widows. *Social Work with Groups, 1*(4), 345–354.

Daniel, S.W., & Barrett, C.J. (1981). The needs of prisoners' wives: A challenge for the mental health professions. *Community Mental Health Journal, 17*(4), 310–322.

Davidson, B., & Dosser D.A. Jr. (1982). A support system for families with developmentally disabled infants. *Family Relations, 31*(2), 295–299.

Davis, K.R., & Shapiro, L.J. (1979). Exploring group process as a means of reaching the mentally retarded. *Social Casework, 60*(6), 330–337.

Delgado, M., & Siff, S.A. (1980). Hispanic adolescent group in a public school setting: An interagency approach. *Social Work with Groups, 3*(3), 73–85.

Dincin, J., Selleck, V., & Streicker, S. (1978). Restructuring parental attitudes: Working with parents of the adult mentally ill. *Schizophrenia Bulletin, 4*(4), 597–608.

Empey, J.L. (1977). Clinical group work with multihandicapped adolescents. *Social Casework, 58*(10), 593–599.

Erf, L.A. (1981). A moratorium for growth: Group work with adolescent mothers. *Clinical Social Work, 9*(1), 44–56.

Feldman, W.S., Manella, K.J., & Varni, J.W. (1983). A behavioral parent training program for single mothers of physically handicapped children. *Child Care, Health and Development, 9,* 157–168.

Friedlob, S.A. (1984). *The development and use of the facilitator training scale: Project return.* Unpublished master's thesis, UCLA School of Social Welfare.

Getzel, G.S., & Masters, R. (1983). Group work with parents of homicide victims. *Social Work with Groups, 6*(2), 81–92.

Giarretto, H. (1982). *Integrated treatment of child sexual abuse: A treatment and training manual*. Palo Alto, CA: Science and Behavior Books.

Gitterman, A. (1982). The use of groups in health settings. In A. Lurie, G. Rosenberg, & S. Pinsky (Eds.), *Social work with groups in health settings* (pp. 6–24). New York: Prodist.

Gitterman, N.P. (1979). Group services for learning for disabled children and their parents. *Social Casework, 60*(4), 217–226.

Gordy, P.L. (1983). Group work that supports adult victims of childhood incest. *Social Casework, 64*(5), 300–307.

Guerney, L., & Jordon, L. (1979). Children of divorce: A community support group. *Journal of Divorce, 2*(3), 283–294.

Harris, P.B. (1979). Being old: A confrontation group with nursing home residents. *Health and Social Work, 4*(1), 152–166.

Hartford, M.E., & Parsons,R. (1982). Groups with relatives of dependent older adults. *The Gerontologist, 22*(3), 394–398.

Hess, P., & Williams, L.B. (1982). Group orientation for parents of children in foster family care. *Child Welfare, 61*(7), 456–466.

Hill, B.M., Raley, J.R., & Snyder, D.K. (1982). Group intervention with parents of psychiatrically hospitalized children. *Family Relations, 31*(3), 317–322.

Holman, S.L. (1979). An early intervention program for developmentally at-risk toddlers and their mothers. *Clinical Social Work Journal, 7*(3), 167–181.

Hughes, M.C. (1982). Chronically ill children in groups: Recurrent issues and adaptations. *American Journal of Orthopsychiatry, 52*(4), 704–711.

Jacobs, M. (1980). Foster parents' training: An opportunity for skills enrichment and empowerment. *Child Welfare, 59*(10), 615–624.

Kaplan, M.L., & Glenn, A. (1979). Women and the stress of moving: A self-help approach. *Social Casework, 59*(7), 434–436.

Kessler, S. (1976). Divorce adjustment groups. *Personnel and Guidance Journal, 56,* 251–255.

Kessler, S. (1982). Building skills in divorce adjustment groups. *Journal of Divorce, 2,* 209–216.

Kornfeld, M.S., & Siegel, I.M. (1980). Parental group therapy in the management of two fatal childhood diseases: A comparison. *Health and Social Work, 5*(4), 28–34.

Kruger, L., Moore, D., Schmidt P., & Wiens, R. (1979). Group work with abusive parents. *Social Work, 24*(4), 337–338.

Kurland, R. (1978). Planning: The neglected component of group development. *Social Work with Groups, 1*(2), 173–178.

Lee, J.A. (1979). The foster parents workshop: A social work approach to learning for new foster parents. *Social Work with Groups, 2*(2), 129–143.

Leon, A.M., Mazur, R., Montalvo, E., & Rodriguez, M. (1984). Self-help support groups for Hispanic mothers. *Child Welfare, 63*(3), 261–268.

Levenson, P., Hale, J., Hollier, M., & Tirado, C. (1978). Serving teenage mothers and their high-risk infants. *Children Today, 7*(4), 11–15, 36.

Loewenberg, F., & Dolgoff, R. (1985). *Ethical decisions for social work practice* (2nd ed.). Itasca, IL: F.L. Peacock.

Lonergan, E.C. (1982). *Group intervention.* New York: Jason Aronson.

Massenzio, S.E. (1977). A supportive group experience for mothers of severely retarded children. *Dissertation Abstracts International, 37*(11-A), 6975-A.

Mayfield, J., & Neil, J.B. (1983). Group treatment for children in substitute care. *Social Casework, 64*(1), 579-584.

McFerran, J. (1958). Parents' groups in protective services. *Children, 5*(6), 223-228.

Moore, J.B. (1982). Project thrive: A supportive treatment approach to the parents of children with nonorganic failure to thrive. *Child Welfare, 61*(6), 389-399.

Oppenheimer, A. (1978). Triumph over trauma in the treatment of child abuse. *Social Casework, 59*(6), 352-358.

Park, D.N. (1979). A workshop for foster mothers of special children. *Social Casework, 60*(3), 171-175.

Park, S., Song, K., Fujita, Y., Forrest, V., Montgomery, P., & Bennett, K. (1982). *Pan asian child rearing practices.* San Diego, CA: Pan Asian Parent Education Project.

Phillips, N., Gorman, K.H., & Bodenheimer, M. (1981). High-risk infants and mothers in groups. *Social Work, 26*(2), 157-161.

Polansky, N.A., Chalmers, M.A., Buttenwieser, E., & Williams, D.P. (1981). *Damaged parents: An anatomy of child neglect.* Chicago: University of Chicago Press.

Reamer, F.G. (1982). *Ethical dilemmas in social service.* New York: Columbia University Press.

Rodkin, L.I., Hunt, J.E., Cowan, S.D., & Dunstan, S. (1982). A men's support group for significant others of rape victims. *Journal of Marital and Family Therapy, 8*(1), 91-97.

Roy, P.E., & Simpter, H. (1983). Group support for the recently bereaved. *Health and Social Work, 8*(3), 230-232.

Samit, C., Nash, K., & Meyers, J. (1980). The parents' group: A therapeutic tool. *Social Casework, 61*(4), 215-222.

Schopler, J.H., & Galinsky, M.J. (1984). Meeting practice needs: Conceptualizing the open-ended group. *Social Work with Groups, 7*(2), 3-21.

Schulman-Miller, J., & Rubin, J. (1982). *Parents in transition groups.* Unpublished manuscript.

Shulman, L. (1984). *The skills of helping individuals and groups* (2nd ed.). Itasca, IL: F.E. Peacock.

Stephenson, S.J., & Boler,M.F. (1981). Group treatment for divorcing persons. *Social Work with Groups, 4*(3/4), 67-77.

Thompson, E.H. Jr., & Doll, W. (1982). The burden of families coping with the mentally ill: An invisible crisis. *Family Relations, 31*(3), 379-388.

Walker, K.N., MacBride, A., & Vachon, M.L. (1977). Social support networks and the crisis of bereavement. *Social Science and Medicine, 11*(1), 35-41.

Wandersman, L.P. (1982). An analysis of the effectiveness of parent-infant support groups. *Journal of Primary Prevention, 3*(2), 99–115.

Wasserman, D. (1983–1984). Personal interview with co-leader of groups of unemployed professionals, Jewish Family Service, Los Angeles.

Watkins, H.D., & Bradbard, M.R. (1982). Child maltreatment: An overview with suggestions for intervention and research. *Family Relations, 31*(3), 323–333.

Wayne, J.C. (1979). A group work model to reach isolated mothers: Preventing child abuse. *Social Work with Groups, 2*(1), 7–18.

Wood, P., Milligan, M., Christ, D., & Liff, D. (1978). Group counseling for cancer patients in a community hospital. *Psychosomatics, 19*(9), 555–561.

Yalom, I.D. (1975). *The theory and practice of group psychotherapy* (2nd ed.). New York: Basic Books.

6 Leading a Support Group

Volumes have been written concerning group leadership from numerous theoretical perspectives, ranging from psychotherapeutic to encounter to Tavistock groups. Regardless of the orientation, leaders operate with a knowledge of small-group behavior, understanding concepts such as power, roles, norms, and boundaries. Support group leaders will likewise be more effective with a foundation in small-group theory and dynamics; however, it is not the intent of this chapter to reiterate previous, well-substantiated group-work theory, but rather to highlight those aspects of leadership and process that characterize support group work.

The fundamental task of a support group is to develop a mutual-aid system, facilitated by the leader's intervention. Building mutual aid requires a commitment to the belief that people can help one another, a sensitivity to the group's phases and processes, and skill in utilizing support-building techniques. Clearly, at times, mutual-aid systems do develop without professional intervention, but, as Lee and Swenson (1986) point out, "Helping is not effortless" (p. 373). The social worker assists with this effort by engaging the members, by modeling, by supporting the group's growth through augmenting interdependence, and by confronting barriers to the helping process. What follows is a discussion of the leader's role in eliciting and sustaining mutual aid, while emphasizing that "the worker's faith in the helping and healing potential of the group itself, through the process of mutual aid, is the most essential ingredient" (Lee & Swenson, 1986, p. 373).

BUILDING MUTUAL AID

Papell and Rothman (1980) declare that "the conception of the group as a mutual aid system has become a universal one in all group work practice" (p. 8). By establishing mutual aid as a goal for social work groups, these theorists, along with Schwartz (1961) and Shulman (1979), recognize the human desire and need for people to cooperate and extend help to each other. Shulman makes the important point that "the *potential* for mutual aid exists in the group; simply bringing people together does not guarantee that it will emerge" (p. 110). Forces may operate within groups which militate against the development of mutual aid. Group leaders, for example, may not embrace mutual help as a high value and will not work toward creating the conditions for its emergence. Negative group experiences of some participants may also hinder its development, where those members are unable to overcome their disenchantment. In some support groups with members who live with permanent chronic stress, such as the mentally ill, the inherent tendency is toward self-absorption and a profound difficulty in forming and maintaining interpersonal relationships. As Shulman points out, perhaps the most important dynamic in forming mutual aid is the group leader's faith in the hidden strength of the group and its potential to create a system of support.

Schwartz (1961) defined the helping group as follows:

> The group is an enterprise in mutual aid, an alliance of individuals who need each other, in varying degrees, to work on certain common problems. The important fact is that this is a helping system in which the clients need each other as well as the worker. This need to use each other to create not one but many helping relationships, is a vital ingredient of the group process and constitutes a common need over and above the specific tasks for which the group was formed. [p. 18]

This statement about mutual aid in helping groups represents a philosophical position, not simply an observational conclusion. Schwartz's conception of social work hinges on the notion that one of the profession's principal goals is to bring people together to help one another and cooperate on common tasks. Essentially this is an expression of social idealism where human attachment and cooperation are valued.

Thus, in running a support group, it becomes essential to promote the development of mutual aid. Shulman (1979) identifies eight processes that strengthen mutual aid: sharing data, the dialectical process, discussing a taboo area, the "all-in-the-same-boat" phenomenon, mutual support, mutual demand, individual problem solving, and rehearsal. Increased awareness of these processes enables group leaders to encourage mutual aid.

Sharing Data

The term *sharing data* is synonymous with a term previously in vogue, namely, *imparting information.* In group life, the members disclose various information, some correct, some erroneous. Sometimes the leaders or other members can make corrections on the spot; sometimes that is not possible. But there are types of information that are not only factual in nature but can help some group members do things differently. For instance, in a group of unemployed people, some member may clue in others about a particularly effective employment agency or some particular job counselor. In a group of people going through divorce, members give each other advice about social clubs, lawyers, new ways of dealing with divorce (mediation court), and where and how to conduct a job search, sometimes a particularly useful piece of information for people who have been out of the labor market. This data sharing is a form of mutual aid. It is a way of building mutual trust, a demonstration of people caring for each other.

The Dialectical Process

Group members have different ideas and different ways of doing things in regard to almost every aspect of living. It is important—in fact, it is critical—that these differences be revealed in the group, where people can think about them and discuss the pros and cons, and where their own affirmations and doubts about a topic can be challenged. The argument or debate that ensues usually involves centrally two or three people, but others are free to enter into the fray. Those who choose not to can still benefit from the discussions.

What might be some examples of people holding wide differences of opinion or polar expressions of behavior in a specific area? In a group of stepparents, two stepmothers may differ radically on how they see themselves relating to their stepchildren. One may insist that she be viewed as "mother," while the others may hold the view that she cannot be "mother" to her stepchildren, or doesn't want to. In a support group of first-time parents, one new father may recount how he shares taking care of the baby at night with his wife; another new father says he will only do so when his wife for some reason cannot physically do it.

There are two important consequences of the dialectical process in behalf of mutual aid. First, it is important for the group members to see, to live through, an "argument" where no one has come up with the right answer, and where no one loses self-respect as an outcome of expressing differences. In a group where members have histories of family violence, it is critical to their healing to experience the airing of differences where people are not physically harmed. Second, differences do not necessarily signify rejection. Differences emphasize the members' individuality, and the fact of individuality is no threat to the workings of a group. It is possible for members to attain high degrees of individuality and still maintain group solidarity. The cohesion of groups does not depend on the suppression of individual differences. Both individuals and the group, in other words, stand to gain from each other in a dialectical relationship.

Discussing a Taboo Area

One usually thinks of incest as being the greatest taboo. There is a proscription not only against the act itself, but against talking about incestuous happenings. What does it mean for women to meet in a support group where the lifelong prohibition of talking about what happened is finally dissolved in a public (albeit restricted) forum? At last there can be catharsis, examination of feelings of guilt and shame, expressions of hate and hostility, and grieving over the absence or the gross distortions of a needed parental-child relationship. All of these issues may be aired within a group of people who do understand and, beyond that, can help one another regain self-respect and self-esteem. The shared secret is the basis for the formation of the support group, and the small community (the support group) of mutual helpers is the source of strength for surmounting an internalized "scarlet letter."

There are lesser taboos, but taboos nevertheless. These include taboos around women taking initiatives and being assertive; taboos around "washing one's dirty linen in public" (talking about personal and family affairs to strangers); and taboos about men weeping in public. The breaking of a taboo in a support group is not as difficult as it is in other helping groups, since the group is formed around a common problem or situation, a shared affliction, or a mutual degraded status. In the support group there exists at the outset a powerful potential to confront a taboo area. There is no social arrangement that carries the same possibility.

The "All-in-the-Same Boat" Phenomenon

People who are confronted with a common situation of an aversive or enfeebling nature possess a special bond that not only *includes* but *excludes*. Members know what it means to be struggling with this set of special circumstances, which one really cannot know unless one is in the "same boat" with others. There may be differences among those who face a common situation, but, above all, they share this unity of situation, which is the source of common pain. Members gain strength as individuals and as a group by coming together and struggling against a common plight and a new way of looking at themselves and how they regard those outside "our group."

What is clear is that this all-in-the-same-boat situation contains a hopeful possibility for mutual help. There is, of course, no inevitability of this outcome. Much depends on the evolving process of the group and the conditions of the larger environment.

Mutual Support

The support group is a potential source of emotional support for every member of a group. Once again, the commonality of situation practically guarantees empathic feelings flowing among people. This is made poignantly clear in Getzel and Master's (1983) explanation of the special excruciating circumstances the parents of homicide victims have to face:

> Death by the direct hand of another human being creates a special type of survivorship. Through their close contact with murder, survivors are forced to re-examine the conventionally held assumptions about the fairness and stability of their society. Their reaction to the shattering of their illusions is nihilism and despair. [p. 85]

It is evident that the members of such a group see themselves as possessing a bond created by their personal and collective pain. Their empathy for each other is based on the kinship of suffering. Thus they must care for each other in order to experience release from the horror of the event and the crushing blow of their loss. Yet we must register again this caveat: There is no guarantee that people can invariably care for each other and give each other mutual support, even in such a circumstance. If there are more than one or two people in the group who are so exclusively centered in their own pain that they cannot reach out to others in empathic ways, then of course the group may fail, not only as a medium of mutual aid, but as a group. In such situations, the leader's expertise is of critical importance.

Mutual Demand

Shulman (1979) writes that, "as the group 'culture' develops, it can include the mutual expectations that members must risk their real thoughts and ideas, listen to each other, put their own concerns aside at times to help another, and so on. These expectations help to develop a productive 'culture for work'" (p. 167). The members of a professionally led support group are expected to work, and it is the role of the group leaders to encourage this. More important, as the members of a group develop closer ties and begin to care for each other, they also begin to make demands on each other to disclose their own thinking, feeling, reactions, quandaries, perplexities, and so on. It is a demand for "interpersonal learning output" as well as "interpersonal learning input." Yalom (1975) defines the former as "learning how I come across to others" (p. 79) and "other members honestly telling me what they think of me" (p. 79). The latter Yalom defines as "feeling more trustful of groups and of other people," and "learning about the way I related to the other group members" (p. 79). Taken together, mutual support and mutual demand are powerful forces in helping the members of the group, for they combine, in a dialectical fashion, both giving and caring, on the one hand, and expecting oneself and others to work, on the other.

Individual Problem Solving

While the members of a group share a common problem, they still have their own individual, unique troubles to contend with. For example, in a group of foster parents, one particular foster parent may have a specific problem with a difficult foster child. In another setting, a mentally retarded mother may be very upset because her baby cries a great deal. In a group of parents of mentally ill young adults, a father may be alarmed at his daughter's staying out late every night. In such situations, the members of a group and its leader(s) become consultants, assuming the roles of supporters (showing empathy), clarifiers (helping a member think through a problem), challengers (helping a member to think and do things in new ways), and listeners (showing that they care). The group, at its best, can serve as a healing agent in its function as caring consultant.

Rehearsal

The group can be used as an arena in which people can engage in behavior rehearsals, which frequently take the form of role playing. A recently divorced man may want to practice talking to one of his children; a 50-year-old woman may have some difficult things to say to her 75-year-old father; an abusive mother may want to talk to the principal of her son's school. What all of these people face, in their own eyes, are terribly difficult, frightening social situations. Perhaps these are first-time attempts at problem resolution, or they may be fraught with anxiety because of confronting an authority figure. The support group is a safe place to risk some "run-throughs" of anxiety-provoking social situations. The group can support, guide, and offer criticism of the individual's rehearsals. Members can try out, via rehearsals in support groups, behaviors which if not new are not customary or habitual. If the try-outs work in a safe place, then they might be attempted or risked in a less secure one. In any case, whether the results are success or failure or a mixture of both, the group is there to rely on, to help sort out feelings and thoughts, and to encourage the risk of taking initiative.

The Leader's Supportive Role

Shulman's (1979) eight processes by which mutual aid may be strengthened offer a helpful description of support group interactions, but these processes do not always occur spontaneously. Thus, the leader's activity should promote and reinforce these eight patterns by

1. Encouraging and modeling information sharing, while relating this process to goals of building trust and caring
2. Eliciting, and if necessary, mediating differing opinions, while pointing out the group's ability to build individuality within group solidarity
3. Giving permission to discuss taboo areas, while strengthening the group's commitment to confidentiality and safety
4. Calling attention to the members' shared situation, thus emphasizing the common bond
5. Reinforcing and demonstrating empathic responses, with the intention of building mutual support
6. Supporting mutual demands, while validating the expectation for all members to work

7. Allowing individual problem solving to take place, while helping group members assume consultant roles
8. Engaging members in rehearsal of behaviors, giving the message that risk-taking is safe.

Mutual Aid and Belonging

Quotations from participants offered in the support group literature illustrate the theme of belonging and mutual aid time and again. Here are a few examples, this first one from a nursing home resident:

> It is the responsibility of everyone living here at the home to help each other. It makes a difference when we old people try to help each other, in any way and as much as we are capable of. [Harris, 1979, p. 161]

A recently relocated woman said of her support group experience,

> At a time when one feels no roots, when one doesn't fit in, or belong to anything. I feel a sense of belonging here. [Kaplan & Glenn, 1978, p. 436]

A member of a woman's vision-impaired diabetes support group said,

> I think I would have gone crazy without this group. Now I know I'm not the only one in this situation. I'm not afraid to talk about it, and I know there are places I can go for help. [Denney, 1983, p. 215]

A worker paraphrased as follows a member's statement during a terminating session of a group for depressed foster adolescents:

> Cherise spoke of nursery school and of moving south with her foster family. Then she added quietly, "I wish I could stay here with the group. I've changed in the group. I've grown from the hate into kindness . . ." [Lee & Park, 1978, p. 525]

A member of a group for natural parents with children in foster placements said,

> We belong to a group where for once we can share our feelings. We can let our hair down. We were in it all alone . . . It's a blessing that I found the group . . . You have to remember how very tired you were after all the struggle. There are other people, I'm sure, who are going through it who are, at this point, very, very tired, exhausted. We all know what [the others are] feeling and we have this bond . . . [Carbino, 1982, pp. 17–18]

Potential Obstacles

This section ends where it began—with Shulman's (1979) dictum that "the *potential* for mutual aid exists in the group" (p. 110). There are four obstacles to the development of mutual aid in groups, including support groups. One obstacle has already been mentioned, namely, the difficulty, perhaps the inability of some group members to identify with the pain and suffering of others. This failure of empathy signifies an early developmental lacuna in the area of trust and attachment, and hence a weakness in the capacity to form caring relationships. In the language of object relations, the self as the core of the person lacks integrity and the person feels buffeted and bruised as a result of feeling unsafe and insecure in a world of other people.

A second obstacle is a more general failure in group development. As Shulman (1979) points out, all groups have to develop rules and procedures, and group members play out certain roles within the group. In developmentally "deviant" groups, both rules and roles operate in ways that militate against any sustained cooperative efforts. Unstated rules, such as who may or may not address certain topics or what may or may not be talked about in the group, obviously are in opposition to the "rule" or value of openness among members. Roles, too, are assigned and assumed unconsciously by members of a group, and this can counteract people caring for themselves and each other and helping each other with the task of problem solving.

The third obstacle is a group's difficulty in establishing the norm of honest communication, that is, establishing a working culture. Maltreating parents and violent men such as child beaters, wife batterers, and incest perpetrators frequently cannot "own up" to what they have done, to the pain and harm for which they are responsible. Thus the failure of honest communication in groups composed of violent people is synonymous with an evasion of responsibility. Mutual aid in a group cannot eventuate under this condition.

The fourth obstacle, already suggested, is a group leader's lack of awareness or interest in mutual aid as a high human value. The reasons may range from indifference to arrogance. There is no reason to believe that all or even a majority of social workers in the current epoch conceptualize the profession as fostering mutual aid among clients.

As the leader sets out to build mutual aid, she should be cognizant of these four possible obstacles. In particular, when facing the second and third, the leader should have a grasp on group phases and group processes. Because of their impact on successful group development, support group phases will be discussed in more detail.

GROUP PHASES

In discussing small-group theory, the concept of progressive phases generally arises when exploring the pattern of group development. Perhaps the most generic theories are those that describe beginning, middle, and ending stages, such as those delineated by Tropp (1976). In such conceptualizations, the beginning and ending stages are just that—the starting and parting of groups—with most of the group work falling within the middle stage. Other thinkers have expanded upon this basic model, often while addressing specific types of groups. For instance, with regard to social work with groups, Schwartz (1976) proposes four phases of work: tuning in, beginnings, tasks, and transitions and endings. This is quite similar to the three-phase model, with the addition of the first stage, that of tuning in to the "life processes" of the group and its potential members (p. 187).

Another example is the work of Anderson (1984), who describes five counseling-group phases: trust, autonomy, closeness, interdependence, and termination. These five comprise what he calls TACIT, an acronym of the five stages. Anderson presents the model in a novel way, describing the tasks facing the individual, the group, the interpersonal relationships, and the leader in each phase. Thus, in the first stage, that of trust, Anderson not only describes the interpersonal challenge of establishing trust, but also the individual question of involvement (Should I join?), a group issue of security (Let's protect each other), and the leader's parallel task of building an atmosphere that promotes trust. Anderson's book is most helpful in objectifying many tasks and necessary sequences in the group counseling process.

With regard to phase theories in support groups, however, there exists a paucity of information in the literature. Without good empirical research findings, it is questionable which of these concepts in previous group-work theory might represent the process in support groups. A few authors, in describing groups with a rather supportive focus, have offered their impressions of the stages of group development. For instance, Beaulieu and Karpinski (1981) delineate their 12-session support group according to the following paradigm: "Sessions one to three formed the introduction and the beginning of sharing and trust; sessions four to six revolved around power, control, and decision-making issues; sessions seven to nine focused dramatically on intensity of feelings of intimacy; and sessions ten to twelve allowed for closure and winding down" (p. 554).

Beaulieu and Karpinski's (1981) analysis is close to that of Garland,

Jones, and Kolodny (1965), with some modifications. It might be noted that Garland et al.'s five-stage model of group development was derived from an analysis of the group process at a children's agency over a three-year period. The groups were composed of boys and girls from the ages of 9 to 16 and were designed to improve their intrapersonal and interpersonal development. The five stages were (1) pre-affiliation, (2) power and control, (3) intimacy, (4) differentiation, and (5) separation. The first stage is characterized primarily by ambivalence toward involvement; the second, by members testing each other and the worker; the third, by greater disclosure of personal problems and feelings and by the members growing closer to each other and at the same time being rivalrous and competitive; the fourth, by a simultaneous recognition of members' individuality and a greater sense of belonging (cohesion); and the fifth, by the members preparing to leave each other while protesting their need to stay together.

Such descriptions have clear similarities with models like Anderson's TACIT. Two concerns arise, however, in applying this theory to support group work: (1) the group phases described by the numerous other theorists tend to be more treatment focused than a support group and (2) in synthesizing a gestalt with regard to support group phases as presented in the literature and from clinical experiences, an impression remains that these paradigms do not quite capture the essence of support group development.

The differences surface in the more conflict-laden stages, such as those involving power and control. The counseling or treatment group inherently implies a reworking of a conflictual area, necessitating emotional struggle and often interpersonal tension. That struggle is often imperative for reenactment and problem resolution to occur. Typically, such reparation is not the primary goal in support group work, even if it happens as a natural course for some individuals. In support group work, the essential foci involve mutual aid, support, and coping with stress. This is not to suggest that support groups are without conflict, yet intragroup or leader-member conflicts do not seem to be sufficiently marked to comprise a specific phase of group development.

For this reason, a framework similar to Budman's (1975) delineation of four psychoeducational group stages appears more appropriate to the support modality. His stages will be reviewed here, and we will note their applicability to support groups and expand on them as needed. Budman writes descriptively of the stages, so we will give them numbers but not labels.

Budman's Phase 1

Budman (1975) sees the beginnings of group formation as follows:

> In this first phase, since the group members are aware of their common issue, there is a general coming together around this issue with comparisons and an examination of similarities and differences. [pp. 395-396]

The group members "share" a common issue (similar life circumstance, same illness, and so forth), which creates the sinews of cohesiveness.

Budman's (1975) observations about "comparisons and an examination of similarities and differences" speak to dynamic psychological activities inherent in the beginning phases of group life. Lakin (1985) comments on these as follows:

> The group experience tends to be characterized by social comparison. The participant is impelled to compare himself with other group members and to attend to their reactions to him. . . . Thus, the group inevitably generates a greater awareness of how other manage—or fail to manage—their lives. We may describe the sensitivity that is elicited by the group as an interpersonal one, a concern with how one perceives others and how one is perceived by them. [pp. 48-49]

For example, in a support group of parents of severely asthmatic children, Bernstein et al. (1963) noted that parents often compared their behaviors during a child's asthmatic attack. In some cases both parents would try to help the child during an attack; in other cases, only one parent would be present because the other might be a hindrance. The comparisons were made around parental cohesiveness or separation in the face of a specific crisis. It seems that such social comparisons are an integral part of the beginning phase. Inevitably this process takes place and is particularly powerful in its impact upon people who have felt the social pangs of stigmatization.

In the first phase, ideally everyone has a chance to tell her story: This is who I am; this is what happened to me, my family, my marriage, and so on; this is what I have tried or not tried to do about it. Often, but not always, these stories are told at first in a matter-of-fact kind of way, as if there were little or no deep feeling behind them. They are "introductions of myself" to the group. Group members are often reserved in their early verbal contributions, not wanting to reveal too much about themselves, but just enough to make their presence known: I'm here, and I have a story; there is more to come later. At the outset of group meetings, what is at stake for participants is a profound wish for a more solid self-esteem and the approval of others. The making of a good impression, through being careful and circumspect in the beginning stages of the group, is an appropriate social behavior. It is no different in other phases of life when first meetings are held between and among people.

In the early meeting(s) of the support group, the members do not know what they will gain from the group. Here they find themselves with a group of strangers, all of whom are in the same boat, but the underlying question for everyone is, What am I going to get out of this? There is then much uncertainty and ambiguity in the beginning phase, when members neither know each other nor have much sense of who the leader(s) are and what they have to offer, except for what they were told about the group in their individual screening sessions.

In "Groups for Foster Children," Ludlow and Epstein (1972) describe how the children in the group moved into the discussions with what was apparently a great pent-up need to talk about the questions and issues they all shared in common. These all revolved around their biological parents and their foster home status. Apparently there was little of the circumspection and hesitation that accompanies the usual beginning meetings of a group just described. The workers soon abandoned their agenda because

> the children soon made it clear that they knew what they wanted to discuss. The agenda grew out of their questions, which included the following: Why am I in foster care? Who is responsible for me when my real parents visit me in my foster home? Where are my brothers and sisters? Why do people become foster parents? What do social workers do? Why are our workers changed? Why are the rules different in my foster home and at home with my real parents? Where will I live when I grow up? [p. 97]

So it can be seen that some groups will approach the first phase with less caution. This may depend on the issue at hand or the age of the members.

Included in Budman's (1975) first stage is the group's first meeting, a pivotal point in the life of the group. The primary focus of a support group's first meeting is the clarifying of the worker-member discussion during the individual screening interviews. This involves a group exploration of the following:

1. Stated purpose. A support group is the members' group, and it is essential that they agree with the purpose of the group. Leaders should maintain as much flexibility as possible in molding to the group's needs.

2. Agreement on format. Certain groups will request greater structure than proposed and vice versa. The format should be adjusted to maximize group comfort, not the leader's plan. This should include a discussion of what modalities (lecture, film, discussion, group interaction) will be used in the group, what is meant by support, what expectations are realistic, and what limitations can be expected.
3. Maintenance issues. These include meeting time, meeting place, transportation alternatives, child care alternatives (in mothers' support groups, the agency usually has to make arrangements for the children), fees charged, and so forth. Whatever *support* the agency can offer to enable member attendance is an asset for group continuity and success.

In general, the beginning meetings (the first two or so) are characterized by a "getting acquainted" process in which the common issue is identified, mutual comparisons are made, personal stories are exchanged, and strong feelings are controlled by an unsureness of the nature of the interaction. There are exceptions to this generalization: Some groups, such as the one in the Ludlow and Epstein (1972) example, delve quickly into the issues at hand. Other groups, particularly those composed of more-or-less involuntary participants who feel stigmatized and isolated, may begin more slowly as a result of resistance to group involvement.

Budman's Phase 2

Budman (1975) describes the second phase as follows:

> In the next major phase, the group usually turns toward the leader(s) for specific information regarding the stress around which the group organized. Traditionally oriented leaders who are not experienced in leading psychoeducational groups may be tempted to frustrate the members' desire for information and throw all of their questions back to them. Experience indicates that this is not a wise strategy and may lead to a rapid dwindling of group membership. Rather, the leader should steer a course somewhere between the "all-knowing" expert . . . and the "blank-screen" therapist. Often, it is useful, if possible, to colead such a group with someone who is quite knowledgeable regarding the area in question. [p. 396]

Thus the second phase involves turning to the leader and other members, seeking information on a common issue or stress. What should be kept in mind in regard to the second phase is that the group process and the main work of this phase are to some considerable extent shaped, if not determined, by the agreed-upon format. For example, one of the prominent short-term support group formats consists of sessions divided into two parts: educational/didactic and experiential/interactive. This format appears to be increasingly popular. The typical 1- or 1½-hour session begins with a lecture or a film (the didactic material) and is followed by group discussion and interaction (the experiential material).

Related to this, in social work circles there has evolved a growing appreciation for the cognitive aspects of problem solving and, even more important, the understanding of the components and requirements of the situation(s) in which people find themselves. For instance, biological parents, foster parents, and foster children need a better understanding of the legal aspects of their situations and of their relationships to child welfare agencies and with the social workers with whom they are engaged (Carbino, 1982). This kind of "knowledge" can help people better understand what they can and cannot do, how they might conduct themselves in the present, and the choices and decisions they may have to face in the future.

In the case, for instance, of people going through divorce, the same kind of format can be followed, albeit with some changes in the allotted time for the segments. Schulman-Miller and Rubin (1982), in their parents-in-transition groups, have worked out topics for each session. Their modified format relies more heavily on experiential material, but the group leader "teaches" by delineating and explaining the "normality" of the responses the people are feeling about their separation from spouses. Their format, which is an analysis of the divorce process, is broken down into the following session topics.

Session 1: Introductions—Who we are/sharing our experiences
Session 2: Ourselves—Looking at ourselves, our feelings, and our experiences
Session 3: Our Children—Explaining our new lifestyles to our children
Session 4: Our Children—Our feelings, their reactions
Session 5: Changes—How my separation has changed me and my life
Session 6: New Roles—Reentering the world as a single parent
Session 7: Conclusions—Where do I go from here?

The topics of the sessions are a reflection of the most important issues and problems with which the divorced person has to contend. The sequence of the topics may or may not represent a hierarchy of priorities. People going through divorce or who are contemplating divorce think about every aspect of their and their children's lives, at times simultaneously. It is partially for that reason that no mutual concern or common problem that surfaces in group interchange is ever permanently shelved or solved for good. The group leader needs to be prepared for this resurfacing of issues, despite the scheduled format.

In general, members seek information in the second phase, and the process of imparting such knowledge will be affected by the established format, whether tightly or loosely structured. Members should be encouraged to do much of the information gathering themselves. This provides a continuity with the first phase, a time of finding their mutuality yet observing their differences; and it helps the transition to phase 3, in which members tend to look at themselves and identify their own style of coping.

Budman's Phase 3

In the third phase, according to Budman (1975),

> members begin to examine their own characteristics in dealing with a particular life stress . . . A new father may be able to see that as he becomes anxious when his infant cries, he deals with this anxiety by becoming exceedingly critical of his wife's handling of the child. . . . There are strong similarities between the issues examined during this phase and issues usually examined in group psychotherapy. [p. 397]

Despite the similarities here with a psychotherapeutic process, distinct differences exist. In the support group, the self-examination typically involves an identification of one's problem-solving techniques and coping styles and the naming of specific anxieties. This stage often represents a more frank communication of the stories recounted in stage 1. More details, more vulnerability, and more personal accounts may be shared. Members may examine their own behavior patterns and their own way of thinking and feeling and how these influenced their responses and choices, but this process does not occur with the intensity of interpersonal and intrapsychic analysis characteristic of psychotherapeutic groups. At times, particularly in longer-term support groups, more of an intrapsychic-type healing can take place in deeply moving ways. This is especially true for support groups composed of people who have suffered deep psychic wounds as a result of physical and/or psychological trauma. The intensity and duration of this self-examination phase will greatly depend on group length and composition. Success in this phase facilitates the progression toward cohesiveness; that is, more open and honest communication and sharing propel the process on toward the fourth phase.

Budman's Phase 4

Budman (1975) characterizes the fourth phase as one in which

> a strong cohesiveness and mutual support develops. Often members become friends outside of the group. Thereby, they develop a mutual support network that can operate without leaders. The group leaders become less and less prominent. [p. 397]

From this final phase emerges the essence of the support group — a working mutual-aid system. Organized by a leader, members have come together around a common issue, shared their stories, sought information, risked self-examination, and emerged with a supportive, mutual-aid system. While a supportive atmosphere is nurtured throughout the group's life, the mutual-aid system only reaches maturity in this phase. The focus becomes one of helping each other. Unity grows when strangers join together, experiencing the universality of their feelings and vulnerabilities amidst a supportive community of peers. At this period, members tap into the healing aspects of decreasing self-focus and greater helping of one another. It is this process that decreases the leaders' prominence in the group: instead of dependence upon the expert, the members function in mutually helpful interrelationships.

An Additional Phase

Although Budman (1975) does not address this as a separate stage in psychoeducational groups, in support groups there exists a prominent period of helping members move on from the group proper. Similar to traditional termination periods, the focus of the fifth step is to assure support and coping beyond the group's ending. This process can take many forms, such as:

1. Evolving the support group into a self-help group, or members joining an established self-help group
2. Forming dyadic supportive relationships or buddy-type systems
3. Linking members with preexisting community supports and services
4. Arranging reunion or check-in meetings of the group

5. Exchanging phone lists
6. Reviewing available crisis services or agreements around contact with group leaders.

This recognition of the need for continuity in the support work is fundamental to support theory and epitomizes the mutual-aid process. This final phase is viewed more as a period of transition rather than termination.

Conclusions

Borrowing heavily from Budman (1975), the support group can be conceptualized as a five-stage process. For the sake of brevity and clarity, these phases can be labeled as follows:

1. Common ground
2. Information seeking
3. Self-examination
4. Mutual aid
5. Transitions

This discussion of group phases is offered as one possible model and not as a conclusive finding in regard to stage development. In fact, the stages can be expected to merge into each other and are not discrete in the sense that the principal activity during one phase does not appear, even prominently, in another phase. For instance, there may already be elements of ''strong cohesiveness and mutual support'' in the second phase. In the third phase, the participants may demonstrate a very strong sense of belonging to the group, a sense of ''we-ness'' and mutual support.

There is much observation and research yet to be done on the pattern of phases or stages in support groups. In all likelihood there is no one pattern, given the different kinds of focal problems, populations, and formats that constitute these groups. Yet other paradigms will surely have certain processes in common with one another. Lakin (1985), who is a seasoned observer of groups, believes that ''helping group processes rarely involve sequentially ordered progressions, say, from issue to issue — unless they are heavily structured'' (p. 145). Researchers in this field will have to incorporate a series of important variables into their investigations — types of problems, ethnicity, social class, location of meetings, a single leader or two or more coleaders, voluntary/involuntary membership and so on. There is much work to be done.

GROUP PROCESS IN SHORT-TERM SUPPORT GROUPS

What do we mean by group process? Mackey (1980) refers to it as "the change taking place in interactions among individuals over time" (p. 26). Yalom (1975) writes, "in interactional psychotherapy, 'process' refers to the relationship implications of interpersonal transactions" (p. 122). These two definitions are in accord in that they both emphasize the dynamics and meanings of the interaction among the participants of a group. Here it must be kept in mind that support group process is somewhat different from that in therapy and growth groups, in that support groups place a heavier emphasis on diminishing the members' sense of isolation and concomitantly increasing their sense of solidarity, whereas therapy and growth groups stress undergoing some beneficial inner (intrapsychic) change(s) through interpersonal interaction.

The group process in short-term support groups is influenced essentially by the format and the goals through which the work of the group is accomplished. Many short-term support groups contain both didactic/educative and experiential/interactive approaches. In this type of group, the lecture, tape, or film comes first (after a brief warm-up or introduction); and then a discussion ensues on the topic. In other short-term support groups the emphasis is almost wholly on the interactive, except for occasional information items which might be introduced by either leaders or members. Thus it is not surprising that a somewhat different group process takes place, although there are undoubtedly similarities between the two.

In discussing group process, it helps to examine the workings of a particular group. Our example here is Mayfield and Neil's (1983) 8-week, 8-session structured program for children in foster placement, selected because it demonstrates how structure in a time-limited group can affect process and phase development. In addition, it provides an opportunity to point out some differences in process in support groups for children as compared to adults. Although Mayfield and Neil refer to this program as a treatment and support group, much of its focus is supportive, uniting children around an emotionally powerful situation they all share.

In Chapter 3 we reviewed Yalom's (1975) curative factors, that is, those processes that facilitate healing in groups. As was also noted, many of these factors are applicable to the support group process, and these will be highlighted throughout this section in relation to our example group.

How do format and group goals affect process? In Mayfield and Neil's (1983) group, sessions last 1½ hours, consisting of an introduction, a short topic or specific lecture, a creative project, a refreshment break, sharing time, and a closing statement. The primary goals are

> (1) to build self-esteem by aiding the children in becoming aware of their own specialness and individual strengths; (2) to teach communication and coping skills; (3) to help the children learn to assert themselves and make responsible decisions; (4) to help children in placement learn to trust; (5) to assist in alleviating guilt by helping them realize that they are not responsible for the dysfunctions in their natural families. [p. 580]

The two social workers, who refer to themselves as "facilitators," see their roles as not imposing their will upon the children in respect to the format, but guiding them "gently." They write, "The children are governed by group rules that they themselves compose. Developing their own methods of guidance, with rewards and consequences, familiarizes the group members with the concept of self-responsibility and gives them a measure of control" (p. 580).

What is the nature of the group process in this short-term group? What goes on between leaders and members and among the members themselves?

Session 1

In the first session ("Becoming Friends"), the children become acquainted with each other. The leaders of the group explain its structure, and the children make up their own group rules. Noncompetitive games are played, encouraging members to relate to each other in positive ways. Here it is noted how the workers, without explicitly stating it, attempt to introduce the children to the concepts of human connection and solidarity, through playing noncompetitive games. One sees how workers' values influence not only format and goals but process—the interchange among the children. The emphasis is on cooperation, not competition.

Session 2

In the second session, primarily through creative dramatics, the children are helped to express their feelings. The leaders aim to "help the children accept their feelings—even those they consider negative—and to remove their sense of isolation" (Mayfield & Neil, 1983, p. 581). For the children, the expression of a wide range of feelings (sadness, guilt, loneliness, and anger) begins the experience of participating in and witnessing the *universality* of these feelings, and learning that "feeling bad doesn't make one a bad person" (p. 581). The interactive process, in other words, is designed to fortify the children's sense of their belonging to a common humanity.

Taken together, the process of the first two sessions—the activities and interactions of the members and leaders of the group—builds toward a sense of belonging or *cohesiveness* in the group. Development of cohesiveness is central to the first phase in all support groups—the time of coming together and finding a common ground. Yalom (1975) sees group cohesiveness as the analogue of the dyadic relationship in individual treatment and "the resultant of all forces acting on all the members to remain in the group" (pp. 45–46). According to Lakin, (1985), the centrality of cohesiveness in group process lies in the following factors:

1. It emotionally binds members to shared tasks as well as to one another.
2. It assures greater stability of the group in the face of frustrating circumstances.
3. It develops a shared frame of reference, and consequent tolerance for divergent aims of group members. [p. 84]

Thinking for a moment about the life experience of foster children, who have been removed from their own homes and forced to adapt to new and strange people and environments, one can begin to understand the potential curative effects of the group process.

Session 3

The third session is devoted to defenses and how everyone possesses and uses them. As they guide the group into the second or information-giving phase, the facilitators in their didactic role inform the children about defenses, and "let them know that there are times when they can lower defenses to have needs met" (Mayfield & Neil, 1983, p. 581). They further define defenses as "masks that people wear or walls that they build around themselves as protection" (p. 581). Then the children do a sentence-completion exercise to see how people use defenses as protective devices. The authors observed that understanding defenses taught the children about self-responsibility and increased their sense of control.

The social workers in this third session assumed the role of sensitive educators. Although the children are young, it is thought that they can understand the use and meanings of defense, that this understanding can be achieved through the facilitators' careful use of language, through playing a game, and by encouraging the children to express artistically their knowledge about defenses. The main points are that (1) the *imparting of information* in sensitive ways is a curative factor and (2) the *interpersonal learning* and the *catharsis* that take place in this and other sessions carry therapeutic powers.

Session 4

In the fourth session where risk taking and decision making are the principal topics, the children "are encouraged to take feeling risks—to reach out to others and make needs known" (Mayfield & Neil, 1983, p. 581). This structure gives a gentle push into the third phase, self-examination. The children are encouraged to think for themselves while taking into consideration in their lectures how children are influenced by "peer pressure and media advertisement" (pp. 581-582). The children play a game called "Take a Risk," in which they earn rewards by sharing feelings and lose spaces by withholding feelings. The facilitators also teach that risk taking does not always have a positive outcome. One facilitator disclosed how some risk taking on her part had proven to be a painful experience. Even so, the teaching is that, on the whole, it is better to share how one feels rather than hold it tightly within or hurt others when feeling badly inside.

This is an important session in terms of the curative factors that are at play in the group process. First, as in previous sessions, the facilitators encourage the children to engage in *imitative behavior*, which is thought of as positive reinforcement of healthy behaviors such as lowering defenses, taking risks, and so on. Second, the social workers' self-disclosure on how they, as people like the children in the group, meet up with frustrations and disappointments, carries with it a higher meaning to the children. The workers' self-disclosure is a gift to the children, a form of *altruism*, in which adults convey to children that they are people too, with difficulties, troubles, and defects. The third curative factor in the risk-taking and decision-making sessions lies in the message that, even though sharing feelings and lowering defenses are, on the whole, healthier for intimate interactions, there is no guarantee that there will always be a positive outcome. This moral lesson is what Yalom (1975) refers to as an "existential factor." Also, the workers confront the children's feelings of guilt that they were the cause of their families' problems. Workers do so by asserting that all families have problems and that children are not responsible for them.

Running through this session are the aforementioned curative factors as well as another dynamic that undergirds group cohesiveness and the sheer rightness of being part of the group. In everyday life these foster children experience themselves as a minority in a majority world, but in the group they are the majority; that is, they all live in substitute homes. In essence, being the member of a majority in a group helps them to feel normal rather than abnormal or deviant. Levine and Schild (1969) observed that, in the group treatment of depression, the most important therapeutic factor for the members of the group was perceiving themselves as a majority rather than as a minority in the larger environment. This gave them a sense of the legitimacy of their feelings and situations. For the foster children as well, legitimizing their status can be a boost to their self-esteem.

Session 5

This theme of normalizing the children's self-view continues in the fifth session, where the theme of children not bearing responsibility for family difficulties is pursued. The universal reality of family problems strengthens the members' cohesiveness, while allowing the children to continue looking at themselves in the context of their family and a community of peers.

Session 6

The sixth session revolves around the theme of substitute care. This is a fact of their lives: All of the children live outside their own homes with foster parents or in a congregate home or facility. This fact is the basis of their cohesivenesss. This existential fact brings them together and provides them with a sense of solidarity and legitimacy. The session is a mixture of educative and interactional modes of personal and interpersonal learning. The workers use puppets to play out the dramas of troubled families and children who leave their own homes. To greater or lesser degrees all of the curative factors mentioned thus far are involved in the session, which touches most directly upon members' stigma and pain.

Session 7

The seventh session (''Specialness'') accentuates every child's uniqueness. The authors write, ''This session is designed to help the children feel pride in themselves, to gain awareness of their self-worth, and to recognize their own special gifts or that there is less need to hide behind a facade'' (Mayfield & Neil, 1983, p. 583).

The workers employ handmade autograph books and ''warm-fuzzy bags,'' which the children use to make positive comments about each other. As the authors point out, many of these children have never enjoyed the experience of friendship. The group has been the social context, the source of this new set of positive feelings about other people. The whole group process, one might reasonably say, has helped to develop the children's socializing techniques, which is another curative interactional factor. Here, as the children support one another's specialness, one sees the blooming of the mutual-aid phase.

Session 8

The eighth and last session, which is called ''Celebration,'' is the time for the children to say goodbye to each other. The children's caretakers and caseworkers attend this last session. The children play a series of games that ''promote communication and understanding between the children and significant others in their lives'' (Mayfield & Neil, 1983, p. 583). The most helpful dynamic happens when the children present themselves to the outside world (caretakers, caseworkers) as a group of people who have felt good being together. Assuming that the group has been a positive experience, it validates children's feelings when they see outsiders view it in the same light. This is confirmation by important people in their lives.

In discussing the children's experience of group process, many elements that Yalom (1975) has listed as the curative factors in group therapy have been mentioned. This short-term support group demonstrates the impact group structure will have on the development and processes of the group. In a program as structured as Mayfield and Neil's (1983), the processes and phases appear more distinctly than in a looser format. It can also be seen with this group, in comparison to some of the adult groups discussed earlier, that the mutual-aid system for children may not reach the stage of being a sophisticated, mature network of people helping one another. Research needs to be conducted in this area, but it would be anticipated that the mutual-aid potential for young children will look somewhat different than that for adults, reflective of their cognitive and moral developmental levels.

For most short-term groups, it takes 8 to 12 weeks to establish a viable interactional mutual-aid system. In some sense, then, the short-term experience becomes a lesson in the human potential for mutual aid. For children who are likely to be in more ongoing substitute care, a long-term group may prove to be more helpful, allowing the child not only to reach a mutual-aid phase but to reap the benefits over a greater time period. However, the exigencies of agency life (the combination of facilitating and constraining circumstances) and of social workers' caseloads, energies, time, and so on do not always allow the optimal and the ideal to be practiced. In the short run the support group experience was helpful for these children, in the sense that they began to view themselves and others in the same situation in healthier ways. We cannot know about any long-term consequences of the group. It may be that for one child or for many of them the experience may have been a significant turning point in their lives.

GROUP PROCESS IN LONG-TERM SUPPORT GROUPS

Long-term support groups have been defined as those that meet more than 12 weeks and often endure for 2 to 3 years. For the purposes of this section, *long-term* shall be defined as lasting from 6 to 9 months to 3 years.

Long-term professionally led support groups should be composed of people who are at risk and are suffering from one or more of these different conditions: (1) a weak existing social network, (2) a stressor with high social unacceptability, (3) a negative or self-punitive definition of the stressor, (4) failing coping skills, (5) a stressor outside the average expected norm, and/or (6) barriers to the fulfillment of basic human needs. Specific examples of people who can benefit from long-term support groups are parents of homicide victims, maltreating and non-nurturing (abusive and/or neglectful) parents, biological parents whose children are in foster homes, unwed mothers, mentally retarded adolescents and adults, the children of alcoholic parents, and depressed adolescent girls in foster homes.

In reviewing Table 4–1, which lists the psychosocial correlates of ameliorable and permanent chronic stress, one will notice that these factors describe the burdens of social work clients who have often been characterized as "unmotivated for help" and suffering from "weak ego development," "super-ego lacunae," "early affect deprivation and loss," and so on. These are not exact diagnostic formulations. A problem arises out of these psychological descriptions, which are intended to serve as explanations, because they connote a sense of therapeutic pessimism. One might conclude that there is little or nothing to be done. Yet, from their historical experience, social workers and other mental health professionals know that those people who are in the most need of help are the least able to ask for it.

The fact is that even the most recalcitrant of clients in dyadic (worker-client) situations are sometimes able, often in conjunction with their individual therapy, to benefit from a support group experience. Reading some social workers' experiences leads one to the conclusion that many short-term support groups are formed of the most vulnerable, at-risk people when, in reality, these people would profit more from a long-term experience. There is a widely held belief in professional circles (and there is undoubtedly some truth to it) that the most needy cannot tolerate the frustration of "just talking"; that they are primarily impulse-ridden and do not have the psychic integrity to invest in a long-term support group. Yet, there *are* some severely damaged clients who seemingly can benefit from a long-term support group experience led by professional social workers (Avery & Wayne, 1978; Breton, 1979; Holman, 1979; Lee & Park, 1978; McFerran, 1958; Phillips, Gordon, & Bodenheimer, 1981; Rosenberg & McTate, 1982; Wayne, 1979).

Beyond the obvious advantages that long-term support groups hold for the members, an added benefit should be noted. As suggested, many individuals appropriate for long-term groups are also in individual therapy. Clients with fragile ego structure and a propensity for fragmentation or acting out can be quite draining over a long period of time, often depleting the resources of individual therapists. A well-run support group can bolster not only the member, but can indirectly help relieve the burden experienced by primary clinicians.

In forming a group of at-risk clients, the leaders ought to consider a long-term group, but, in actuality, they should leave that issue open. Indicating to a group of prospective members, either in the individual screening interview or at the beginning of the group meeting, that the group expects to last, say, a year and a half would only frighten people into "no-shows" or early terminations. It is best to leave termination open and simply tell the group that it will last as long as people think they are deriving some benefit out of it.

In explaining or justifying the need for a group to its prospective members, it is often advisable not to be pointedly specific about the reason for its formation. To a group of abusive and/or neglectful mothers, one might simply say, "Parents are having a difficult time raising kids today, and this will give us a chance to get together to talk about these things." To a group of depressed girls living in foster homes, one might initially offer to talk about their being in foster homes and not mention the depressive part. On the other hand, with men who batter or with women who are battered, there is little sense in not being direct in stating the purpose of coming together.

What is the nature of the process in long-term support groups? Carbino (1982) sheds much light on this subject in her work with abusive and neglectful parents. In her review of the literature in this area, she notes the following about group work with abusing parents:

> Abusive parent group members were in seriously disadvantaged circumstances economically, socially and personally. They were isolated, lacking familial and community supports. *They were in need of multiple simultaneous services for a host of problems, of which child caring was just one [italics added].* They were in obvious need of nurture and attention for themselves as well as on behalf of their children. [p. 15]

The group's purpose was to enhance personal support and growth while improving understanding and parenting abilities. Social workers ran small groups that met one to two times per month over periods of 12 to 22 months. Despite members' willingness to participate and discuss early on in the group, she notes that "it was clear that groups remained in the pre-group and early group formative stages for a long time" (p. 15). The workers needed to assume a great deal of responsibility for group development and member support.

Carbino's (1982) main points appear accurate. First, it takes from 6 to 12 months for a group of abusive and/or neglectful mothers to become a cohesive community. While it is true that members are "active and vocal from early on" (more true of abusive parents than neglectful ones), much of the talk is in the form of external blaming—accusations against social workers, the agencies, housing authorities, and so on. Some of these are gross distortions, while others are on the mark. The externalization of their problems allows the parents to ventilate their anger and frustration against what they view as the hardness and cruelty of an unyielding institutional system. The experienced professional social worker leading a support group will understand the need to vent rage and fury. The members are unloved people who do not know how to love except in ways that are painful to themselves and/or others. Close relationships, or better, the shadows of close relationships, have meant hurt and suffering, which in turn have led to their striking out against their own putative love objects, their children.

Forming a cohesive group requires that the participants have the capacity (in some minimum way) to trust the group leaders and their fellow members. This is precisely what many at-risk, highly vulnerable people cannot do. Even if the lack of basic trust is not precisely true for every participant, it would be, it seems, realistic and practical for group leaders to make the assumption that maltreating parents have a basic problem in the area of trust.

Thus the early months of the group experience must necessarily be a time during which the workers are in the position of givers or nurturers. The leaders give and nurture by (1) taking responsibility for the content of each session, allowing for spontaneous developments within the group; (2) by not challenging the members' habitual defenses of denial and projection; (3) by doing such concrete things as providing or actually doing the transportation; (4) by preparing and serving food; (5) by arranging for child care during the sessions; and so on. Beginning where the clients are in this type of support group necessitates a profound, empathic understanding of these participants as psychologically damaged people. This must be combined with a great deal of patience and faith in the plasticity of the human organism, that is, its capacity to change in a positive direction.

Thus, in the first 6 to 12 months, the main interactions that characterize the group process are those that occur between group leaders and participants. The minor arena of interactions lies among the members themselves. They begin at a point of solipsism or self-absorption and proceed slowly, hesitatingly, in faltering steps, toward connecting with others. They begin to recognize slowly that their deprivation, hurt, and pain have something to do with how they have conducted their own lives; and at the same time they become aware that their co-participants' lives and theirs revolve around similar events, themes, and patterns.

It is a circular process, a time filled with expressions of rage against the workers, who are perceived as the representatives of an uncomprehending and unyielding society. In the negative transference, the members may project a distortion, viewing the leaders as threatening, punitive parents. Sibling rivalry and the difficulties of becoming a socialized human being can give way slowly to the normal give-and-take of a civilized society. Slowly the members become attached to each other, when both intrapsychic and interpersonal workings and experiences are transformed into different meanings and changed perspectives.

Thus, a phase of intimacy and common ground develops among the participants in which the group process is characterized by sufficiently cooperative behavior to allow members to engage in collective planning, the execution of projects, and interactions that indicate that the group is highly valued as a source of well-being. At the same time, the participants manifest "greater personal involvement and openness" (Wayne, 1979, p. 14). The participants interact more with each other and less with the group leaders. The latter initiate less activities, and they do not dominate the decision-making process of the group, as in the early stages.

It was during this period of intimacy and the next phase of differentiation (Garland, Jones, & Kolodny (1965) that Breton (1979), for instance, embarked on teaching problem-solving skills to the participants of the group. Breton points out that, in her group of abusive mothers, she focused on nonthreatening areas first and stayed with these so that they could better manage their lives in general. This enabled the members to move on to the informational phase. As the participants in Breton's group became increasingly attached to each other, they began to give to each other, bringing in food for the group and clothing for each other or one another's children. In their giving to each other, they had become a mutual-aid group, where as Breton (1979) writes;

> the major source of help comes from the members themselves as they interact. . . . As the group becomes a system of mutual aid, the members will have to develop the skills necessary to relate to others in a peer power structure. This will entail learning . . . behaviors that are assertive without being controlling, firm without being rigid, just without being punitive, and discipline, without being abusive.
>
> Participating actively in a mutual aid group also entails sustaining frustrations and controlling oneself. Parents of abused children have grave difficulties in both these areas; the experience of giving as well as receiving help in a group, of taking responsibilities willingly and assuming unattractive tasks, will go a long way in helping the mothers learn appropriate parenting skills. [p. 172]

What can we conclude about long-term support work with at-risk clients? Lang (quoted in Breton, 1979, p. 173) makes a distinction among "allonymous," "transitional" and "autonomous" group systems. The allonymous are "worker-governed," the transitional are "worker and group-governed," and the autonomous systems are "group-governed." In examining the governing aspect of the group process, which includes rule-devising and decision-making, the desired direction for all groups, including those comprised of at-risk clients, flows from the allonymous through the transitional to the autonomous. In effect, this happens when a professionally led support group becomes a member-governed self-help group with minimal or no consultation with a professional source.

It may well be that not all at-risk groups can reasonably be expected to become autonomous. For example, in open groups of battering men and in the mixed worker-member leadership groups of Parents United, the history of violent acts and the legal implications and exigencies revolving around strict social and legal control may not allow the desired sequence of governing leadership. It does seem apparent that some long-term groups do, however, have the potential to achieve an autonomous life.

Periods of greater conflict may be more common in these longer-term support groups. This may result from a more troubled group membership as well as from the prolonged period of interaction. The advantage of the longer-term group, despite the more painstaking efforts required to reach the mutual-aid phase, is that, once achieved, there remains time to experience healing through helping. It is also reasonable to expect that the course toward the final stages of mutual aid and transition will be more fluid and less discrete than in a short-term group.

In general, the group process of long-term support groups has yet to be determined through research. Perhaps films or tapes of long-term groups, analyzed according to agreed-upon conceptual categories and ways of observation, recording, and so on, will bring a better understanding of the group process. It might be noted here that the curative factors referred to in the short-term support group process are the same in the long-term arrangement.

Anthropologist Victor Turner (1974) believes that people who suffer from various forms of stigma, impairment, and displacement (foster children, maltreating parents, the mentally retarded) need to undergo a process of "reritualization." Reritualization refers to all of the culturally patterned ways a society provides for people to become members of a community. The helping group can be a source of this reritualization, by restoring the individual's sense of community through sanctioned group membership.

The support group can provide a safe and secure context in which people can "confess their sins." In a group of their peers they can confess (ventilate, express feelings of guilt and shame, and self-criticize) in a community of other "sinners." The participants thereby gain relief and also "overcome their estrangement and achieve reconnection" (Lakin, 1985, p. 181). It may take a relatively long time for the highly at-risk individual to find reconnection.

Not all abusive and neglecting mothers will engage in heart-rending *mea culpas*, but they may do it indirectly, once they feel safe in the group, by asking the group leaders or visiting nurses, for instance, for advice about various aspects of child rearing. This constitutes an awareness and a public acknowledgment of the desire to stop doing the "wrong thing" and start doing "the right thing." Confessions take many forms, and in social work with groups, there exists no ideological imprimatur for the correct way of expression.

In finishing this section on long-term support groups, we turn to an important point articulated by Carbino (1982):

> For parents in disadvantaged circumstances, group work can be an excellent means of countering the problems of isolation, of lack of familial and community support, and of lack of information about the foster care system and their legal rights. *At the same time, such parents can be expected to need a number of intensive and simultaneous services, thus, group service cannot be conceived of as the sole service to be rendered* [italics added]. [pp. 16–17]

Again, with disadvantaged clients experiencing ameliorable and permanent chronic stress, the most advantageous approach is the ecological one. This perspective broadens one's vision to include all of the ''environments'' of client interaction which may be sources of difficulty. It informs one, specifically in regard to disadvantaged clients, of the guaranteed failure of relying upon a ''sole service'' in trying to help people with multiple problems. The long-term support group represents but one piece in a holistic, ecological view of needed services.

THE SOCIAL WORKER'S ROLE

In his examination of the current trends in social group work, Garvin (1984) suggests there exists a need for increased use of group modalities, particularly those that function on mutual-aid principles. Yet he recognizes that not all groups with such an emphasis can be run strictly by traditional group psychotherapy techniques. He suggests a need for a broader understanding of the group-work process and comments on the necessity for more extensive training geared toward this expanded utilization of groups.

Rethinking the social worker as a mediator in the mutual-aid group process (Lee & Swenson, 1986) further accentuates the need to understand leadership tasks. Although in some ways it is a very old concept to view the leader as one who ''helps them help each other'' (Klein, 1972, p. 32), examining this role within the support modality remains a relatively unexplored area. Leadership of other group types has been well discussed, as in Yalom's (1975) work on psychotherapy groups or Anderson's (1984) description and analysis of counseling groups. Anderson, in fact, refers to Lieberman, Yalom and Miles's (1973) important encounter group analysis. In this research, it was found that the most effective leaders provided high amounts of caring and willingness to attribute meaning to processes, but only moderate emphasis on eliciting ventilation and maintaining an executive role.

A prodigious work, completed in the 1970s in the San Francisco area, Lieberman et al.'s (1973) study results have implications for effective intervention styles and formats. Because the work addresses encounter groups—usually an intense, growth-oriented process—generalization of its findings cannot be made for support groups. However, Lieberman et al.'s and Anderson's (1984) work are referred to as examples of the type of research that is needed to identify the helpful and the not-so-helpful leadership styles in support groups. We are in full agreement with Garvin's (1984) contentions for improved understanding of social work with groups; in addition, we recognize the need to make some attempt to operationalize the actions of the support group leader. Despite support group theory's infantile stage of development, in this section we will identify some aspects of what a support group leader does. We will include in this synthesis many elements of the group leader's role that have been discussed earlier, encapsulating the intended qualities characteristic of a support group and making suggestions for workers on how to achieve the desired atmosphere and life of the group.

In identifying the desired characteristics of a support group, six particularly jump to the forefront: cohesion, safety, support, reinforcement, stress reduction, and information giving. Each of these can be promoted by particular approaches and interventions.

Cohesion

In discussing support groups, the concepts of universality and commonality repeatedly appear. It is precisely these elements of the support group which build its cohesion. Several techniques are available to the worker for use in fostering the connectedness of the group members.

Emphasize Homogeneity

The worker must actively stress the homogeneity of the members' problem. This process involves identifying a common theme in the group, reflecting it to the members, and using it as the glue that bonds the members. Once verbalized, this theme must be referred to repeatedly, in some sense grounding the group to their purpose and their shared plight.

Be Attentive to Group Process

Support group work necessitates that the leader attend carefully to the process of the group, not merely the content. Although observations of process should not be stated aloud frequently in the support group setting, the worker's knowledge of process serves as a crucial tool in the building of cohesion. Only by attention to process can the leader assess which strengths of a particular group are fostering a sense of connection and therefore are deserving of reinforcement. Conversely, only then can the worker be aware of the weaknesses in the process that are undermining cohesion, which generally require immediate, skillful intervention.

Minimize Social Distance

To strengthen cohesion, the leader will most likely need to take a position in the group that reduces the social distance characteristic of many therapy groups. Primarily this is done by a willingness to step out of the expert role at times and to join the members through self-disclosure. This is similar to what Rosenberg (1984) describes as worker transparency. With this action, the leader is modeling the risk taking inherent in reaching for a human bond.

Use Consensus in Decision Making

A final practice that enhances cohesion is what Guerney and Jordon (1979) term "consensus-reaching techniques." When at all possible the worker should attempt to achieve group consensus on decisions, through discussions, give and take, and open communication. Consensus goes beyond the rule of the majority and aims for agreements that all members are content to follow. As a very democratic philosophy, this concept promotes support group survival.

Safety

One cannot stress enough the importance of a support group's need for a safe, almost protective environment. The isolated, the stigmatized, and the despairing do not seek further positions of vulnerability but rather the comfort of a secure atmosphere. If the support group is to flourish, it is essential that the worker provide such a setting, using the following suggestions.

Avoid Demands for Self-Disclosure

Euster, Ward, Varner, and Euster (1984) identify the importance of avoiding demands on the member for self-disclosure. They stress the advantage of allowing the member to determine his own level of participation. The minute pressure to disclose is felt, the safeness of the group decreases. To insure a secure, trusting group, the worker must respect the need for self-determination and respect the individual's ability to regulate his level of exposure.

Accept Differences

As the worker attempts to point out similarities as a way of building cohesion, she must also model tolerance and acceptance of differences, to guarantee a sense of safety. This is crucial.

Avoid Focusing on Personal Change

Earlier it was pointed out that the focus of the support group is not one of personal change. Workers must not focus on attempts to alter behavior; rather, they must remember that the purpose of the group is support and mutuality. While at times this may be difficult, particularly for the worker accustomed to conducting therapy groups, the worker must view personal change as a secondary gain and not the primary goal of a support group. This, again, requires the ability to accept and tolerate differences in members.

Avoid the Use of Interpretation

There should be minimal use of deep, intrapsychic interpretation in a support group setting. With such an intervention the goal is usually personal change and can be quite anxiety provoking where not desired or expected. Interpretations should be limited to process notations, which benefit the group as a whole. Of course there are probably exceptions to this rule, but it is offered as a general guideline.

Use Cotherapy to Avoid Transference

In psychotherapy groups, the need for interpretation is often felt by the worker in respect to transference issues. The worker in the support group setting should note transference processes but not actively share them with the group. It is suggested that a cotherapy relationship be used in such cases, which will usually reduce intense transference reactions (Lakin, 1985).

Maintain Sufficient Control

In order to communicate a feeling of safety, the worker must maintain a delicate balance of control over the group at the same time she is eliminating some of the social distance. This element of control or authority is necessary to provide a sense of protection. As Lakin (1985) notes, any group has a powerful potential for both positive and negative outcomes. For this reason, the worker should never relinquish all control, for undoubtedly the time will arise for limit setting. In fact, (Galinsky & Schopler, 1977) view the process of limit setting as an integral part of the worker role.

Use Humor

A final technique that promotes a safe environment is the ability of the worker to maintain at times a certain lightness and humor in the group. Often the emotionality of the group needs to be lightened, instilling a sense of hope in the members. Several clinicians (Lonergan, 1982; Grotjahn, 1978) credit humor as an enhancer of group vitality and security.

Support

When a sense of cohesion and safety is beginning to develop, the element of support can evolve in the group. Clearly this is the pivotal quality of this form of group work and may be encouraged using the following ideas.

Introduce the Concept of Mutual Aid

The worker must actively voice the potential for mutual aid, thus introducing this concept, which present-day society has somehow devalued. By doing so, the worker steers the group toward "cooperative interdependence," as described by Rook (1984). Permission is given to reach out and act to benefit one another. It is the worker who must plant this seed and support efforts or approximations of mutual aid.

Highlight Empowerment

As mutual aid is introduced, the worker can simultaneously offer another form of support to the member by calling attention to the inherent sense of empowerment that accompanies the self-healing process. Jacobs (1980) suggests, in fact, that empowerment should be considered one of the primary emphases of the group. This form of support is a tool the member can take away with her, even after group termination.

Show Empathy

One of the most supportive techniques available to the worker is the appropriate use of empathy. By demonstrating empathic responses, the worker not only enters the isolated world of the member but models the concept of mutuality for the rest of the group. Empathy must continually be utilized in the support group format; it is the primary tool for facilitating bonding and evoking affective expressions.

Model Support

Related to the demonstration of empathy is the co-workers' need to model support among themselves. The supportive expression between co-leaders offers a powerful experiential learning opportunity for the members. The importance of this indirect teaching of the support process cannot be overemphasized.

Reinforcement

It is the intention of the support group to provide a strengthening, healing experience; it therefore follows that positive attention would play a critical rôle in the group process. The worker may use reinforcement in the following ways.

Focus on Positive Aspects

Work in the support group format should focus on the positive, healthy aspects of individuals and the group, not on the negative and pathological. By attending to the positive, these qualities are naturally reinforced.

Focus on Productive Aspects

Similarly, giving attention to the productive and adaptive aspects should be used with respect to individual behaviors in the group. As discussed earlier, every group develops a culture or set of norms. By attending to the appropriate behaviors or approximations of such, workers will reinforce, encourage, and shape such actions. The counterpart of this technique is the ability to ignore inappropriate behaviors when possible, unless the act is in some way physically hazardous or destructive of property. Withholding attention, in conjunction with skillful use of positive reinforcement, will promote the adaptive behaviors.

Promote Self-Esteem

As a result of using reinforcement, the worker is also inherently building the members' self-esteem or what Rosenberg (1984) describes as "strengthening the central core of individuals" (p. 181). If the worker keeps in mind the intent of promoting positive feelings in members, the use of reinforcement comes easily. Frequently, improvements in self-esteem appear quickly with the use of positive attention.

Stress Reduction

Lakin (1985) describes members' expectations of a group, with regard to reduction of stress, as follows: "The group represents a hope of relief from stress, a promise of personal betterment. One comes to the group with the expectation that the group experience will provide answers to one's problems" (p. 68). Clearly, to provide relief from stress is a primary goal of the support group. To attain this there are particular guidelines for workers, some of which are quite different from the focus in the traditional psychotherapy group.

Attempt to Reduce Discomfort

In psychotherapy groups, the intention is often to raise anxiety to a certain level, to elicit the motivation needed for change. In the support group setting, however, the focus is the opposite. The worker does not make interventions designed to evoke anxious feelings, but generally attempts to reduce stress and anxiety. If the worker observes anxiety stemming from within the individual, supportive action is taken to soothe and reduce the discomfort. If the cause of anxiety appears to be interpersonal, stemming from group interactions, the worker uses himself and supportive group members as buffers to absorb, redirect, and soften the anxious feelings.

Provide Appropriate Structure

Related to this concept is the level of structure needed. This assessment must be geared to each particular group and the level of member functioning. A group in high need of structure will become anxiety ridden if the necessary boundaries are not provided. Likewise, the membership in need of low structure will feel anxious and most likely constricted in a highly rigid setting. Thus, the worker must be attuned to the requirements of the group when establishing a format that promotes the reduction of stress and anxiety.

Plan for Enjoyment

A final possibility for reducing the stress level of group members is to plan activities that are relaxing, fun, and action oriented. This step will also promote the cohesion needed by the support group.

Information Giving

Support groups often have an additional function of imparting information to members. This process may be from leader to member or from member to member. The support group, as well as having this sort of educative purpose, may also have a problem-solving element. The following two points are important for the worker to follow.

Be Well Informed

It is essential for the worker to be familiar with the subject at hand. Specific knowledge of the disability or problem area is the *sine qua non* of conducting a support group. The better the worker is informed, the better the members can be educated and the greater their sense of empowerment and self-esteem.

Explore Ideas as a Group

One of the most helpful tools in dealing with the information needs of the group is for the worker to be open to the use of an exploratory discussion format. In this way, by leading an interchange, members share ideas, learn from one another, and often participate more actively than would have been expected. This approach also proves helpful in problem solving. Group participation in problem solving not only models the process itself but lends a sense of unity which stems from the members' mutually aiding one another.

As the worker moves to promote cohesion, safety, support, reinforcement, stress reduction, and the sharing of information, the individual leadership style, the group purpose, and the climate or culture of the microsociety will clearly affect intervention decisions. The guidelines discussed here are offered with a spirit of flexibility. The worker should approach the leadership role creatively and without the rigidity that often becomes associated with other treatment modalities. Above all, the worker's role is to foster a supportive environment in which members can develop their own mutual-aid system. The worker serves to model and facilitate a sense of connectedness. Presenting herself as a caring and respectable professional who is a living representation of the values of support group work, she implicitly teaches the helping process (Tropp, 1976). Just as the support group leader respects the members' individually while building a collective mutuality, she must work with her unique resources and skills as a clinician to find her own intervention style, by which she can successfully lead the group to bonding and cohesion.

CONCLUSION

While knowledge of the theory and practice of support groups is limited, there is sufficient positive evidence about their efficacy to encourage social workers and other mental health professionals to engage in their study and application. Building mutual aid in the support group process implies that mental health professionals themselves begin to adhere to the philosophy of mutual aid, that its principles be embodied within their own work organizations. Only then can the concept become an organic part of professional and client existence.

REFERENCES

Anderson, J. (1984). *Counseling through group process*. New York: Springer.
Avery, N., & Wayne, J. (1978). Group development and group therapy for

nonnurturing mothers. *Social Work with Groups, 1*(3), 287-298.

Beaulieu, E. M., & Karpinski, J. (1981). Group treatment of elderly with ill spouses. *Social Casework, 62*(9), 551-556.

Bernstein, L., Purcell, K., Rosenblum, S., Wasserman, H., Stewart, A., & Metz, J. R. (1963). Organization and functions of the psychological services at the Jewish national home for asthmatic children. In E. Harms (Ed.), *Somatic and psychiatric aspects of childhood allergies* (pp. 203-250). New York: Macmillan.

Breton, M. (1979). Nurturing abused and abusive mothers. *Social Work with Groups, 2*(2), 161-174.

Budman, S. H. (1975). A strategy for preventive mental health intervention. *Professional Psychology, 6*(4), 394-398.

Carbino, R. (1982). Group work with natural parents in permanency planning. *Social Work with Groups, 5*(4), 7-30.

Denney, L. (1983). I'm not the only one: Report on a diabetic support group. *Journal of Visual Impairment and Blindness, 77*(5), 215.

Euster, S. D., Ward, V. P., Varner, J. G., & Euster, G. L. (1984). Life skills groups for adolescent foster children. *Child Welfare, 68*(1), 27-36.

Galinsky, M. J. & Schopler, J. H. (1977). Warning: groups may be dangerous. *Social Work, 22*(2), pp. 89-94.

Garland, J. A., Jones, H.E., & Kolodny, R. C. (1965). A model for stages of development in social work with groups. In S. Bernstein (Ed.), *Explorations in group work* (pp. 1-28). Boston: Boston University School of Social Work.

Garvin, C. D. (1984). The changing contexts of social group work practice: Challenge and opportunity. *Social Work with Groups, 7*(1), 3-19.

Getzel, G. S., & Masters, R. (1983). Group work with parents of homicide victims. *Social Work with Groups, 6*(2), 81-92.

Grotjahn, M. (1987). *Group communication, group therapy with the aged.* New York, NY: Gardner.

Guerney, L., & Jordon, L. (1979). Children of divorce: A community support group. *Journal of Divorce, 2*(3), 283-294.

Harris, P. B. (1979). Being old: A confrontation group with nursing home residents. *Health and Social Work, 4*(1) 152-166.

Holman, S. L. (1979). An early intervention program for developmentally at-risk toddlers and their mothers. *Clinical Social Work Journal, 7*(3) 167-181.

Jacobs, M. (1980). Foster parent training: An opportunity for skills, enrichment and empowerment. *Child Welfare, 59*(10), 615-624.

Kaplan, M., & Glenn, A. (1978). Women and the stress of moving: A self-help approach. *Social Casework, 59*(7), 434-436.

Klein, A. F. (1972). *Effective groupwork: An introduction to principle and method.* New York: Association Press.

Lakin, M. (1985). *The helping group: Therapeutic principles and issues.* Reading, MA: Addison Wesley.

Lee, J. A. & Park, D. N. (1978). A group approach to the depressed adolescent girl in foster care. *American Journal of Orthopsychiatry, 48*(3), 516-527.

Lee, J. A., & Swenson, C. R. (1986). The concept of mutual aid. In A. Gitterman & L. Shulman (Eds.), *Mutual aid groups and the life cycle* (pp. 361–377). Itasca, IL: F. E. Peacock.

Levine, B., & Schild, J. (1969). Group treatment of depression. *Social Work, 14*(4), 46–52.

Lieberman, M. A., Yalom, I. D., & Miles, M. B. (1973). *Encounter groups: First facts*. New York: Basic Books.

Ludlow, B., & Epstein, N. (1972). Groups for foster children. *Social Work, 17*(5), 96–99.

Mackey, R. A. (1980). Developmental process in growth-oriented groups. *Social Work, 25*(1), 26–29.

Mayfield J., & Neil, J. B. (1983). Group treatment for children in substitute care. *Social Casework, 64*(1), 579–584.

McFerran, J. (1958). Parents' groups in protective services. *Children, 5*(6), 223–228.

Papell, C., & Rothman, B. (1980). Relating the mainstream model of social work with groups to group psychotherapy and the structural group approach. *Social Work with Groups, 3*(2), 5–23.

Phillips, N. K., Gorman, K. H., & Bodenheimer, M. (1981). High-risk infants and mothers in group. *Social Work, 26*(2), 157–161.

Rook, K. S. (1984). Promoting social bonding. *American Psychologist, 39*(12), 1389–1406.

Rosenberg, P. P. (1984). Support groups: A special therapeutic entity. *Small Group Behavior, 15*(2), 173–186.

Rosenberg, S. A., & McTate, G. A. (1982). Intellectually handicapped mothers. *Children Today, 11*(1), 24–26, 37.

Schulman-Miller, J., & Rubin, D. (1982). *Parents in transition groups*. Unpublished manuscript.

Schwartz, W. (1961). The social worker in the group. In *New perspectives on services to groups* (pp. 7–34). New York: National Association of Social Workers.

Schwartz, W. (1976). Between client and system: The mediating function. In R. W. Roberts & H. Northen (Eds.), *Theories of social work with groups* (pp. 171–197). New York: Columbia University Press.

Shulman, L. (1979). *The skills of helping: Individuals and groups*. Itasca, IL: F.E. Peacock.

Tropp, E. (1976). A developmental theory. In R. W. Roberts & H. Northen (Eds.), *Theories of social work with groups* (pp. 198–237). New York: Columbia University Press.

Turner, V. (1974). *Dramas, fields and metaphors*. Ithaca, NY: Cornell University Press.

Wayne, J. L. (1979). A group work model to reach isolated mothers: Preventing child abuse. *Social Work with Groups, 2*(1), 7–18.

Yalom, I. D. (1975). *The theory and practice of group psychotherapy*. New York: Basic Books.

III Examples of Professionally Led Support Groups

Introduction

The next four chapters will provide the reader with a bird's-eye view of the range and types of professionally led support groups in four fields of practice: health, aging, family and children's services, and mental health.

Why are social workers increasingly employing support groups as a mode of intervention in each of these respective fields? What is the rationale and justification for forming such groups? Which targeted populations are joining support groups? What are the benefits that members derive from the support group experience? Finally, what are some of the primary issues and problems in regard to professionally led support groups which emerge from the analysis? These are some of the queries that are addressed in these chapters. Some elicit straightforward answers; others remain perplexities at this stage of social support group theory and practice.

7 Support Groups in the Health Field

Illness and disabilities can be divided into acute and chronic types. The former can usually be treated effectively with the high-technology armamentarium of modern medicine. While psychosocial correlates to acute illness are often disruptive of an individual's or family's normal life processes, psychological and social sequelae are usually not of long duration. In contrast, chronic illnesses and disabilities necessitate quite a different treatment approach, one in which the patient's long-term psychosocial functioning demands as much attention and concern as physical impairment.

Roback (1984) makes a critical point when he declares that "many health care professionals now recognize the importance of providing psychological interventions for 'normal' as well as psychologically impaired persons who have suffered the devastating blow of learning that they have a debilitating, painful, or terminal illness, or that a close family member has such an illness" (pp. 2–3). The onset and ongoing course of a chronic organic illness threaten the psychic integrity of persons who usually enjoy good mental health as well as the "normal" functioning of a solid, cohesive, loving family.

The major emphasis of this chapter will be on chronic illness and disability, and the place of support groups in patients' quest for enhanced well-being. While the lives of these persons are to some considerable extent shaped by the biology of their conditions, chronic illness and disability are also social phenomena affecting every aspect of living in society. For such people, everyday existence revolves around regular contacts with physicians and a variety of health professionals; chronic stress punctuated by acute and often unpredictable bouts and flare-ups; treatment by palliative methods; the possible deterioration and breakdown of organ systems other than the one of central concern; a host of limitations such as dietary regimes, special physical regimes and exercise, radiation, and chemotherapy; prosthetic devices that include a multitude of therapeutic and maintenance interventions which require major adjustments in perspective and lifestyle; financial problems in meeting the high costs of treatment; restrictions on employment possibilities; the troubles and anguish attendant to physical immobility; and, most painfully, the social isolation and stigma that plague people as they try to cope with the physical and psychic pain of their conditions.

In addition to the aforementioned burdens of chronic illness and disability, Cohen and Lazarus (1979) point to six kinds of threats that accompany illness: (1) threats to life itself; (2) threats to bodily integrity and comfort; (3) threats to self-concept and future plans; (4) threats to emotional equilibrium; (5) threats to the accomplishment of customary roles and activities; and (6) threats associated with the demands of adjusting to a new physical or social environment.

Given, then, the potential massive bodily, social, and psychological consequences of chronic illness and disability, the hypothetical role of social workers as the front-line professionals in helping patients regain, maintain, and strengthen their psychosocial functioning is of major importance.[1] The relatively recent advent of professionally led support groups covering a variety of patients with different illnesses and disabilities represents a possibility of creative intervention for the social work profession. That possibility revolves around helping patients cope with their difficulties—strengthening psychosocial functioning—through the support group experience. Meeting with other people in the same or similar circumstances is perhaps the most effective way of combating social isolation and the stigma of impairment. The raising of self-esteem ensues with the diminishment of negative social and self-valuations. A prescient Dr. Joseph H. Pratt as far back as 1907 in his group work with tuberculosis patients observed that his patients rallied as a consequence of a "common bond in a common disease" (Roback, 1984, p. 533).

TARGET POPULATIONS

A reading of the social work literature in the health field indicates that professional social workers are increasingly utilizing the support group as a mode of helping patients cope with illness and disability. Social

[1]A reading of the medical social work literature indicates that social workers in the health field have experienced an uneven acceptance from the major health professionals—physicians and nurses.

support groups are formed on both inpatient and outpatient services. The group approach in hospitals and clinics recognizes the inherently social nature of illness and disability, and it increasingly affirms people's right and obligation to participate in there own care.

Both patients and their families are recruited to join support groups, most usually around the homogeneous factor of a specific illness or disability. Patients of all ages and from all racial and ethnic populations join support groups where, singly and together, they can seek their highest level of well-being.

The following is a brief list of a few kinds of support groups for people suffering from chronic illness and disabilities, or their families. These examples give the reader some preliminary notions of a few patient and family populations with whom professionally led support groups have been formed, as well as the literature describing work with each type of group.

1. *Adult cancer patients:* Adams, 1979; Baker, 1977; Gustafson & Whitzman, 1978; Herzoff, 1979; Jerse, Whitzman & Gustafson, 1984; Spiegel, Bloom, & Yalom, 1981; Spiegel & Yalom, 1978; Whitzman, Gustafson, & Coleman, 1979; Wood, Milligan, Christ, & Liff, 1978; Wood & Tombrink, 1983.
2. *Parents of children with cancer:* Adams, 1978; Chesler & Yoak, 1984; Hymovich, 1976; Knopp & Hansen, 1973; Martinson & Jorgens, 1976; Ross, 1979; Stolberg & Cunningham, 1980.
3. *Terminally ill patients:* Brachfield & Myers, 1980; Ferlic, Goldman, & Kennedy, 1979; Franzino, Geren, & Meiman, 1976; Spiegel & Yalom, 1977.

According to Kerson and Kerson (1985) people with chronic disorders can be classified into nine categories of illness and disability:

1. Physical disability
2. Arthritis
3. Cancer
4. The dementias
5. Diabetes
6. The epilepsies
7. Heart disease
8. Respiratory disease
9. Stroke

Professionally led support groups are proliferating in all of these chronic illness and disability categories. To this list we would add AIDS, with the expectation that we will see increasing numbers of support groups for AIDS victims and their loved ones. Informational and institutional resources for the chronically ill in these categories are listed in Kerson and Kerson (1985). Professionals in the health field are encouraged to familiarize themselves with these resources, since they include references on support and self-help groups.

PLANNING FOR SUPPORT GROUPS IN A HOSPITAL ENVIRONMENT

While there is general accord among the professions of the health field that the psychosocial factors of illness and disability have a powerful influence on bodily processes, and vice versa, this accord seems to be essentially rhetorical in nature and is often not evident in the organization and operation of medical facilities. Physicians, nurses, and other health workers in their everyday ministrations and dealings with patients do not always concern themselves with the psychosocial dimensions of patients' medical problems. Thus social workers historically have had to "make a case" for their presence in the health field, particularly in hospitals. It has not been self-evident that social work is absolutely necessary in helping patients get well, at least, not in the same way that people clearly see the imperative presence of physicians and nurses. Thus social work as a profession has yet to persuade the other professions and the consumers of health services that it is an important component in patients' recovery from illness and in ameliorating the effects of disability. Since patients' recovery of health and maintenance of optimal well-being are the main goals of the health professions, social work has to make its case in terms of these goals. In this time of emphasis on cost-effectiveness, however, institutions generally require objective proof of the value of a treatment. Social work cannot clearly show, through research, that support groups or any other of its services contribute to patients' recovery.

Planning a support group for a particular set of patients in a hospital or an outpatient clinic, particularly in the beginning days of introducing social work groups to a facility, is an exercise that demands from the putative group leader knowledge of the power structure in a clinic or on a ward. This means that the social worker should know who makes the important decisions, who has solid connections with the more powerful persons in the organization, and who is potentially a willing collaborator in the creation of support groups. It is critical, too, that the social worker who initiates the groups demonstrate at the outset a willingness to share group leadership with members of the other professions (Lonergan, 1982a).

In Chapter 5, Kurland's (1978) six components of careful planning were identified and discussed. We will use them again here, in regard to social work operations in the health field. The sixth component, pre-group contact, is included in the discussion of the other five.

Need

Social workers have to be concerned about assessing the needs of both patients and a multidisciplinary staff. What do patients perceive as their "educational" needs in regard to their medical condition? What kinds of information do they think they need? Do they have any problems or difficulties in the hospital that they would like to discuss with others? Do they have any questions about their illness? Patients can be approached on a one-to-one basis, which is probably the most effective way in reaching (and persuading) them to join a group. A personal memo announcing a "patients' discussion group" might also be sent to all eligible patients, followed up with individual interviews.

In the health field, the open-ended nature of the majority of support groups frequently makes it impossible to screen patients carefully before they enter a support group. The usual method is to welcome all of the patients, except the grossly psychotic and those who are seen to be exceedingly agitated and disruptive. Lonergan (1982a) does not veer away from including social isolates in groups where they often are excluded. She has observed some of them to be surprisingly productive in groups.

Physicians' and nurses' opinions about the usefulness of groups and their possible interest in co-leading them are critical components of the planning process. Without their agreement, and particularly that of the most powerful doctors or nurses in the service, there will be no successful support group program. Eliciting these professionals' opinions and interest about support groups is more than an exercise of professional diplomacy and courtesy, but an integral part of a process that embraces nurses and physicians as potential co-leaders of groups. These professions represent the requisite authority for leading the discussions on the more purely medical aspects of patients' conditions. They are the information givers, the educators about the physical aspects of the illness. Social workers, on the other hand, take a large responsibility in the co-leader team in guiding the group process and leading discussions on the more psychosocial aspects of illness. Social workers in health settings have the professional obligation to learn as much as they can about the illness and disabilities with which they are in daily contact, but they are not nurses and physicians and do not carry the implicit authority to provide medical information in any sustained, systematic way. Thus the issue of co-leadership of support groups is crucial in their functioning and future development. Social work standing alone in the promotion of support groups in the health field will probably not be sufficient to assure their continued or expanded use.[2]

Purpose

The general purpose of support groups in the health field is to assist in the treatment of patients and to enlist the supportive efforts of the intimate caregivers—usually family members—of those suffering from organic illnesses and disabilities. All efforts in the medical enterprise are directed toward patient recovery and enhanced well-being. Frequently, one of the most difficult issues faced by the chronically ill is the drudgery of routine and the need to comply with a tiresome regimen. This problem of compliance often becomes a central purpose of support groups, a purpose that doctors and nurses readily support.

Beginning with the social work principle of "starting where the client is," and translating that dictum into the medical idiom, support groups focus initially on the physical facts of the illness. This is the major point of patients' concern and worry, and the same is true of their family members. Thus co-leaders' activities are guided by the purpose of imparting correct information to patients and family members, attending to their psychological states through giving emotional support and understanding, and maintaining a sense of hopefulness even in the face of the stark reality some patients face.

Let us consider, for example, the monumental psychological effort the parents of children with cancer have to engage in, in order to grapple with the combined intellectual, instrumental, interpersonal, emotional, and existential stresses of their children's grave illness. These are shown in Table 7-1, taken from Chesler and Yoak's (1984) group work with this population. Central to these parents' preoccupations and diverse tasks and undertakings is the possibility that their children may die. It has only been within the past 10 to 15 years that parents might reasonably hope for a successful outcome. Both parents and children observe during the

[2]Nurses have become increasingly active in support group work. Often they are the initiators of groups in hospitals and clinics.

TABLE 7–1 Stress and Social Support for Parents of Children with Cancer

Category of stress	Relevant coping tasks and strategies	Forms of social support	Agents of social support	Self-help group activities
Intellectual	Getting information about cancer and treatment procedures Interpreting medical jargon Protecting against information overload Getting information about the hospital	Information Ideas Books, newsletters	Medical staff Social service staff Scientists	Lectures by staff Writing handbooks Establishing library of articles Printing newsletters Information sharing by parents
Instrumental	Getting help at home (child care, housekeeping) Getting help at work Negotiating with hospital Making financial plans Solving other problems Caring for the sick child	Problem-solving activities Practical assistance at home or work Financial aid Transportation Negotiations with hospital	Social service staff Family members Neighbors and co-workers Institutional representatives	Collecting and distributing funds for wigs, prostheses, parking Arranging parent lodging Efforts to improve local medical care Fundraising for research or added services

Interpersonal	Maintaining relationships with family members and friends Creating new social roles Talking and sharing with others Relating to the medical staff Informing others (and avoiding stigma)	Affection Listening Caring Being there	Family members Close friends Medical social service staff	Reference group processes Meeting new people Having someone to talk with
Emotional	Getting counseling Finding love and affirmation Dealing with hope, anger fear, and despair Stabilizing self Monitoring somatic reactions Feeling efficacious in providing care	Affirmation Counseling Clarifying feelings	Close friends Spouse Social service staff	Professional counseling Peer counseling Sharing intimate feelings
Existential	Seeking meaning and explanations for the illness Creating new social identity Relating to God and fate Reordering life plans and dreams	Reflection on God and fate Creating a community	Clergy Philosophers	Talking about religious beliefs Sharing the struggle

Source: *Helping Patients and their families cope with medical problems* (p. 496) by M.A. Chesler and M. Yoak, 1984, San Francisco, CA: Jossey-Bass. Reprinted by permission.

course of the illness that some children live and others die. And thus in their own individual and support group experiences, both children and parents are helped to talk about their anticipations, fears, doubts, and hopes.

Further inspection of the activities listed in Table 7–1 under the heading "Self-help group activities" expands usual notions and conceptions about support group possibilities. Under the "intellectual" and "instrumental" categories, there is a host of activities and tasks which delineate the necessity of undertaking and executing concrete, specific plans and programs. In sum, all support group activities are directed to the central purpose of helping patients and families cope with chronic illness, with the hope of achieving optimal physical and mental health functioning.

Some children on oncology wards die. Grieving parents and the remaining siblings can be helped to cope with their loss through support groups composed of those who have suffered a similar loss (Chesler & Yoak, 1984). Parental grief over time is partially transformed into communal grieving, and all of the existential questions that surround the mysteries of life and death become the focus of intense interchange among group members. During this phase the support group functions as a small, nondenominational religious community.

Composition

Rosenberg and Neill (1982) found that most medical support groups were organized around the type of illness rather than the demographic variables of age, marital status, sex, or ethnicity. These variables, with the exception of age,[3] do not form the basis of social support groups. Patients are usually grouped together in services and wards according to type of illness, and the organization of support groups is facilitated by that physical arrangement.

Following the practice of forming medical support groups on the basis of a mixture of homogeneous and heterogeneous factors, it might be well to employ this principle in social support group formation as well, unless there appear to be some common-sense or practical reasons for not doing so. It is quite clear that in crisis groups people can tolerate great socio-demographic differences, given the overpowering fact of a common illness (Block, 1985). Yet the social worker is professionally obligated to make an assessment of the effects any given mix of patients might have on an individual patient.

[3]Children, for instance, usually have separate hospital facilities.

The question also arises as to whether or not patients and family members should be seen together in support groups or should maintain separate groups. While there is a great deal of evidence that family support is of central influence on patients' motivation and compliance behavior (DiMatteo & DiNicola, 1982), there are no clear-cut data that dictate whether separate or together is preferable in achieving the desired effect. Family members, like patients, often have little understanding of the nature of the illness or disability. They may foster excessive dependency in the patient or, on the other hand, may resist and resent the dependency inherent in the patient's physical situation. The patient's feelings of depression, anxiety, and helplessness may be mirrored by their spouses and children or, again, may be the object of rejection and attack. It appears that this issue must be answered, where possible, on a case-by-case basis.

The recommendations in the literature are also mixed. For cancer patients in crisis, Block (1982) encourages patients and family members to attend sessions together. On the other hand, Brown, Glazer, and Higgins (1983) began with mixed patient-family groups for open-heart-surgery patients but found they were not effective. The group leaders felt that neither patients nor families were able to express freely their thoughts and feelings. Thus they opted for separate groups. The issue of mixing patients and families in support groups has not been resolved, and perhaps there is no grand principle or rule to be established.

Structure

In large medical facilities such as hospitals in urban areas, there is a growing trend toward both inpatient and outpatient support groups. The former are generally open groups, a structure that reflects the increasingly rapid turnover of hospitalized patients. Many hospital groups are of the single-session type (Lonergan, 1982a). Whether or not single-session groups can be reasonably defined as support groups is doubtful. Yet the promoters of this type of hospital group testify to the development of cohesion and bonds among people as an outgrowth of the powerful factor of universality (Johnson & Stark, 1980). Short-term inpatient groups are comprised of patients afflicted with either acute or chronic illness.

Outpatient groups also tend to be of the open kind, although the closed format is more common than among inpatient groups. Their memberships are composed primarily of chronically ill and disabled patients. Turnover is not on the same scale as that of inpatient support groups. Long-term groups in the community usually take the form of self-help groups, in contrast to those in hospitals, which are under professional auspices.

Another unresolved structural issue in the health field revolves around the inclusion of patients who are in different phases of their illnesses, such as occurs with multiple sclerosis and cancer patients. Both Johnson and Stark (1980) and Block (1985) report that patients who are suffering from cancer and are in a crisis phase (the beginning stage, a recurrence of the illness, or showing signs of the beginning of the terminal stage) can come together in group sessions and develop feelings of intimacy and strong bonds within a single session. The different phases of the illness do not prove to be a barrier to the communication of empathic supportive feelings within the group. In self-help groups such as the Wellness Community in Los Angeles, people finding themselves in all phases of the illness, including those who have apparently recovered, attend meetings and join together in small groups for mutual support and aid. And yet it should be recognized that the crisis group and the community self-help groups of the Wellness Community type represent special contexts which can absorb the wide range of illness stages. It is quite possible that in noncrisis hospital support groups some patients in the beginning stages of a serious illness may become extremely upset in the presence of patients dying from that illness. This issue of mixing patients from different stages of illness deserves much study and deliberation, case by case. The needs and sensibilities of every potential group participant must be assessed before the composition of a support group is finally decided upon.

Content

The principal topics of discussion in medical social support groups are (1) the nature of the illness and/or disability and (2) how people cope with their situations. There is a great deal of difference in the emotional intensity of a short-term support group composed primarily of adult male cardiac patients, versus a long-term group of women who have undergone mastectomies; of a one- or two-session group of presurgery male patients, versus a long-term group of the parents of children hospitalized for leukemia. In the former situations, the patients may easily enter into discussions about their illnesses but typically will be reluctant to reveal their feelings. In the latter, the patients' wounded self-esteem, sense of isolation and helplessness, and death anxieties are openly expressed.

As an example of how these content issues may be played out, let us consider an actual long-term group for parents of asthmatic children. This was a six-month group conducted by a social worker and a pediatrician in a facility for severely ill asthmatic children (Bernstein et al., 1963). The beginning sessions were taken up with the physician's explanations of the nature of this mysterious illness. Interspersed with this didactic/educational approach were the parents' detailed stories of how they had "shopped" the asthma treatment market, going from one physician to another, and how little help their children had received. They had all suffered in varying degrees from the frustrating experience.

The next several weeks of discussion revolved around parents' problems in dealing with the sick child. Frequently they disagreed on how to handle asthmatic attacks. In some cases, one of the child's two parents could not bear being with the child during an attack. Parents suffered universally from disruptions of sleep, since attacks seemed mostly to occur at night. Conflict between the parents seemed to be endemic to the presence of a seriously ill asthmatic child. The reaction of siblings to the sick child, combined with those of extended family members and friends, ranged from compassionate and supportive to uncaring and distant. Siblings often felt neglected by virtue of the great amount of attention and concern directed toward the sick child.

The content of this long-term parents' group can be best understood as a delineation of the ecology of severe childhood asthma. At some point in the support group, the following "systems" and their content were discussed:

1. The child
   a. Anxiety about dying.
   b. Cannot often play with other children.
   c. Often absent from school because of illness.
   d. Panic during asthmatic attacks.
   e. Sleeps poorly because attacks often come at night.
   f. Suffers from low self-esteem.
   g. Feels isolated.
   h. Feels stigmatized, different from "normal," healthy children.
2. The family (parents, child and siblings)
   a. Anxiety about the child dying and what the future holds.
   b. Parents sleep poorly; anticipate asthmatic attack.
   c. Parents sometimes disagree on how to respond during asthmatic attacks.
   d. Constant trips to hospital emergency room doctors.
   e. Financial worries stemming from child's illness.

f. Parents feel worn down physically and emotionally; often blame each other for child's illness.
g. Parents are sometimes blamed by professionals (physicians, mental health professionals) who believe that asthma is a "psychogenic" illness; doctors often disagree as to the etiology of the illness.
h. Parents feel stigmatized.
i. Parents feel they have been "punished" by God or some unknown source.
j. Siblings often feel neglected by parents.
k. Relationship difficulties between sick child and siblings.
l. Social life outside the walls of the home.
m. Need for respite from everyday involvement with child.
n. Need to talk to "someone" who *understands* their plight.
o. Need to know that they are not bad parents; need to lessen guilt and shame.
p. Need to deal with whatever abrasions have arisen between them as an outgrowth of the child's illness.
q. Need to relate to sick child and siblings in different ways.
r. Need to become further educated about their child's illness and the need to educate others (teachers, children) about the child's difficulties.

3. The schools
   a. Parents, teachers, and principals have to deal with attendance problem and child keeping up with school work.
   b. Provisions for alerting parents if child has severe attack in school.
   c. Instructions to school personnel about the type of play the child can safely undertake.
   d. Medical and social work consultations with teachers and principals.
   e. Group meetings for teachers of several ill asthmatic children. Groups will be co-led by pediatricians and social workers.

The support group provided these parents with new knowledge about their children's illness and an experience in correcting distorted perceptions and relationships. Through the process of social comparison, parents were able to compare, for instance, their ways of relating to their sick children and their siblings with those of the other parents. The group also provided an experience of genuine acceptance, which is the caring, human feeling that is the necessary solvent for feelings of guilt, shame, isolation, and stigma.

The processes of acceptance and comparison are intrinsic to the health of a support group. These positive forces can be deflected and finally blocked, by internal group conditions, a disruptive patient, or an incompetent group leader or by external influences such as a last-minute change of meeting place. The forces of mutual acceptance and social comparison provide the group and the group leaders with the possibilities of cohesion.

Successful "copers" in support groups provide models for those who, at the beginning stages of illness and disability, need encouragement and hope for the future. Those who have coped successfully can offer assurance and guidance (affective and cognitive aids) to others (Lonergan, 1982a).

A PRACTICAL VIEW ON CHRONIC STRESS AND DISABILITY

In regard to chronic illness and disability, medical inpatient and outpatient support groups represent only one significant element in the rehabilitative process. People leave hospitals, move back into their homes and communities, and sometimes enter nursing homes for temporary and permanent stays. They continue to need the sustainment and care of families and support and self-help groups. Every hospital and clinic and all of the professional personnel who lead support groups, especially social workers, should be conversant with the recognized self-help groups in the community and should maintain working relationships with them.

While collaboration is the optimal relationship, Froland (1980) depicts a total of four possible modes of interaction; conflict, competition, cooperative co-existence, and collaboration. The informal self-help and self-care[4] movements have now become an integral part of the American health care system, and the collaboration between self-help groups and the formal, professional system depends upon their mutual acceptance and respect. First, professional workers (doctors, nurses, social workers) in the health field have to recognize that self-help groups serve an important therapeutic function which is not supplied by the professional community. Second, while some self-help movements have taken an antiprofessional stance (this is particularly true in the field of mental health), this has generally not been true in the health field. The most effective

[4]*Self-care* emphasizes the individual's effort in engaging in healthful practices without necessarily involving the influence of mutual aid.

and stable self-help medical groups encourage their members to adhere to their doctors' guidance and prescriptions. Third, there are some important roles that social workers can play in working with self-help groups. Toseland and Hacker (1982) write that these roles include "(1) providing material support to maintain a self-help group, (2) serve as a linkage by connecting traditional services, clients, and self-help groups to one another, (3) serving as a consultant to a self-help group, and (4) initiating and developing a self-help group" (p. 341). Fourth, when self-help groups need consultation around matters that affect their functions, social workers are increasingly being asked to supply that consultation. Baker (1977) asserts that a collaborative relationship between the formal and informal systems exists when they actively exchange information and material and human resources. Tuzman (1982) expresses the opinion that until quite recently social workers and other professionals have resisted working with self-help groups, since they were seen as threats to professional control over the provision of services.

Black, Dorman, and Allegrante (1986) have worked on an ecological model for the chronically ill in which the voluntary agency is the focal organization in health promotion. Self-care education, health education, and social work collaborate to establish the information and social support requirements that the chronically ill need in order to live a decent existence in terms of their health needs.

ISSUES AND PROBLEMS

There are some issues and problems that commonly arise in the leading of support groups in the health setting. Some are internal to social work, while others inhere within many of the environments in which medical social workers find themselves.

Internal Social Work Issues

Some observers have noted that clinical social workers in general are reluctant to become group leaders, that the possibility of treating people in a group is a frightening idea (Gitterman, 1982; Lonergan, 1982a). Although there are very few hard data on this issue, there are nevertheless some indications that, in the field of health, social workers are running groups, either alone or as team co-leaders. The larger practice issue revolves around medical social workers' convictions as to the therapeutic efficacy of support groups. Having reluctant or skeptical social workers attend support groups as observers might be one way of exposing them to this modality of treatment in a relatively nonthreatening way.

Another issue connected to the aforementioned is the problem of training social workers and other professionals in the group method, which emphasizes mutual-aid factors. Spiegel, Bloom, and Yalom express the opinion that: "The skills to conduct such groups may be obtained by persons from many health disciplines over a few months' time through group observations and supervision" (p. 531). Assuming that this opinion is valid, the question of supervision is central to the training process. Where will knowledgeable and skilled group-work supervisors come from who can make a difference in the numbers of patients who might benefit from support groups?

The most important internal problem is the deep ideological orientation that health professionals, including many social workers, ascribe to, namely, that illness and disability are strictly within the private realm of the individual and his family. The social and interpersonal aspects of coping with illness and disability are not as readily perceived and understood.

Social Work Issues Within Health Environments

Health environments have, in the main, tolerated the presence of social workers, but they have not often become natural contexts in which social workers view themselves or are viewed as truly belonging. While health professionals give lip service to the importance of psychosocial factors in illness and disability, there is a profound ideological conviction within the medical community that advances in the physical and biological sciences and their consequent technologies will be the principal sources of helping patients overcome their illnesses and disabilities, including ultimately those of a chronic nature. Thus, psychosocial factors and the interventions of the social work type are considered as "frosting on the cake," an effort and an expense which hardly bear the investment in professional time (and money) that they take. This may be a too-gloomy picture of the present state of social work in the health field. There are, of course, outstanding medical environments where social work flourishes, but there are many places where social work is barely tolerated.

It is difficult to show, by the accepted criteria of scientific research, that social support groups help patients deal with anxiety, depression, damaged self-concept, social isolation, and so on. Very few researches have been mounted. Spiegel, Bloom, and Yalom (1981) made an evaluation of the process and outcome of support groups created for the potential benefit of 86 women with metastatic breast cancer. This was a controlled study in which the women were divided into three separate support groups. A fourth control group received only regular medical care and the "equivalent chemotherapy" that the women in the support groups received. On the outcome measures, the women in the three support groups showed greater improvement in psychosocial functioning than their counterparts in the control group. On some measures there were no differences between the treatment and control groups. The point to be made here is that one way that social work can make a better fit in health environments is to push for this type of comparative research, which tests the effectiveness of any treatment, including social support groups. Schools of social work, many of which now have doctoral divisions, might be good sources of research consultation for social work departments in the health field.

Perhaps the overriding issue within the health field is the recent emergence of large numbers of people suffering from chronic illness and disability. The health care systems historically were organized to treat acute illness. Chronic illness necessitates not only doctors and nurses, but a host of medical personnel with specialized skills, such as those who make prosthetic devices; physical, art, and occupational therapists; health educators; home helpers; and so on. All of these people's efforts have to be integrated into a workable system. Chronically ill patients need not only health education (knowledge about the illness and disability), but self-care education and social work, which includes individual and family counseling and participation in professionally led support and community self-help groups.

This is a new world of illness and disability, of treatment and care. Social support and self-help groups have significant contributions to make toward patient recovery and enhanced well-being.

CONCLUSION

A chronic illness is an invasive and disruptive force in the life of an afflicted individual and his or her family and community. These three entities represent the primary triad of human existence. When one of them is weakened, so are the others. The strengthening of one automatically invigorates the others. Thus chronic illness is as much a group and collective phenomenon as it is individual. Support and self-help groups represent mediating social structures that not only help patients and families cope with illness and reinforce ties with the larger community and its resources, but re-imagine and invent new ones. They have now become indispensable tools in the protection and restoration of people's physical and mental health.

REFERENCES

Adams, J. (1979). Mutual-help groups: Enhancing the coping ability of oncology clients. *Cancer Nursing 2,* 95–98.

Adams, M. (1978). Helping the parents of children with malignancy. *Journal of Pediatrics, 93*(5), 734-738.

Baker, F. (1977). The interface between professional and natural support systems. *Clinical Social Work Journal, 5*(2), 139–148.

Baker, K. (1977). Oncology support groups for outpatients. *Hospital Topics, 55*(1), 40–42.

Bernstein, L., Purcell, K., Rosenblum, S., Wasserman, H., Stewart, A., & Metz, J.R. (1963). Organizations and functions of the psychological services at the Jewish National Home for Asthmatic Children. In E. Harms (Ed.), *Somatic and psychiatric aspects of childhood allergies* (pp. 203–250). New York: Macmillan.

Black, R.B., Dornan, D.H., & Allegrante, J.P. (1986). Challenges in developing health promotion services for the chronically ill. *Social Work, 31*(4), 287-293.

Block, L.R. (1985). On the potentiality and limits of time: The single-session group and the cancer patient. *Social Work with Groups, 8*(2), 81–99.

Brachfield, C.D., & Myers, R.A. (1980). Make today count: A mutual support group for the dying. *Mid-American Review of Sociology, 5*(2), 91–100.

Brown, D.G., Glazer, H., & Higgins, M. (1983). Group intervention: A psychosocial and educational approach to open heart surgery patients and their families.*Social Work in Health Care, 9*(2), 47–59.

Chesler, M.A., & Yoak, M. (1984). Self-help groups for parents of children with cancer. In H. Roback (Ed.), *Helping patients and their families cope with medical problems* (pp. 481–526). San Francisco: Jossey-Bass.

DiMatteo, M.R., & DiNicola, D.D. (1982). *Achieving patient compliance.* New York: Pergamon Press.

Ferlic, M., Goldman, A., & Kennedy, B.J. (1979). Group counseling in adult patients with advanced cancer. *Cancer, 43*(2), 760–766.

Franzino, M.A., Geren, J.T., & Meiman, E.L. (1976). Group discussion among the terminally ill. *International Journal of Group Psychotherapy, 26*(1) 43–48.

Froland, C. (1980). Formal and informal care: Discontinuities in a continuum. *Social Service Review, 54*(4) 572–587.

Gitterman, A. (1982). The use of groups in health settings. In A. Lurie, G. Rosenberg, & S. Pinsky (Eds.), *Social work with groups in health settings* (pp. 6–24). New York: Prodist.

Gottlieb, B.H. (1983). *Social support strategies: Guidelines for mental health practice.* Beverly Hills, CA: Sage.

Guŝtafson, J.P., & Whitman, H.H. (1978). Towards a balanced social environment on the oncology service: The cancer patients' group. *Social Psychiatry, 13*(2), 147-152.

Herzoff, N. (1979). A therapeutic group for cancer patients and their families. *Cancer Nursing, 2*(6), 469-474.

Hymovich, D. (1976). Parents of sick children: Their needs and tasks. *Pediatric Clinics of North America, 23*(3), 225-232.

Jerse, M.A., Whitman, H.H., & Gustafson, J.P. (1984). Cancer in adults. In H. Roback (Ed.), *Helping patients and their families cope with medical problems* (pp. 251-284). San Francisco: Jossey-Bass.

Johnson, E.M., & Stark, D.E. (1980). A group program for cancer patients and their family members in an acute care teaching hospital. *Social Work in Health Care, 5,* 335-349.

Kerson, T.S., & Kerson, L.A. (1985). *Understanding Chronic Illness.* Glencoe, IL: Free Press.

Knopp, V., & Hansen, H. (1973). Helping the parents of children with leukemia. *Social Work, 18*(4), 70-75.

Kurland, R. (1978). Planning: The neglected component of group development. *Social Work with Groups, 1*(2), 173-178.

Lonergan, E.C. (1982a). *Group intervention.* New York: Jason Aronson.

Lonergan, E.C. (1982b). The use of groups in health settings. In A. Curie, G. Rosenberg, & S. Pinsky (Eds.), *Social work with groups in health settings* (pp. 30-38). New York: Prodist.

Martinson, I., & Jorgens, C. (1976). Report of a parent support group. *Home Care for the Dying Child.* New York: Appleton-Century-Crofts.

Rosenberg, G., & Neill, G. (1982). Group services and medical illness: A review of the literature—1964-1978. In A. Lurie, G. Rosenberg, & S. Pinsky (Eds.), *Social work with groups in health settings* (pp. 39-53). New York: Prodist.

Ross, J. (1979). Coping with childhood cancer: Group intervention as an aid to parents in crisis. *Social Work in Health Care, 4*(4), 381-391.

Spiegel, D., Bloom, J.R., & Yalom, I.D. (1981). Group support for patients with metastatic cancer: A randomized prospective outcome study. *Archives of General Psychiatry, 38,* 527-533.

Spiegel, D., & Yalom, I.D. (1978). A support group for dying patients. *International Journal of Group Psychotherapy, 28*(1), 233-245.

Stolberg, A., & Cunningham, J. (1980). Support groups for parents of leukemic children. In J. Schulman & M. Kupst (Eds.), *The child with cancer* (pp. 26-36). Springfield, IL: Charles C. Thomas.

Toseland, R.W., & Hacker, L. (1982). Self-help groups and professional involvement. *Social Work, 27*(4), 341-347.

Tuzman, L. (1982). Professional role in self-help groups. In A. Lurie, G. Rosenberg, & S. Pinsky (Eds.), *Social work with groups in health settings* (pp. 44-56). New York: Prodist.

Whitman, H.G., Gustafson, J.P., & Coleman, F.W. (1979). Group approaches for cancer patients: Leaders and members. *American Journal of Nursing, 79*(5), 910–913.

Wood, J.D., & Tombrink, J. (1983). Impact of cancer on sexuality and self-image: A group program for patients and parents. *Social Work in Health Care, 8*(4), 45–54.

Wood, P.E., Milligan, M., Christ, D., & Liff, D. (1978). Group counseling for cancer patients in a community hospital. *Psychosomatics, 19*(9), 555–561.

Yalom, I.D., & Greaves, C. (1977). Group therapy with the terminally ill. *American Journal of Psychiatry, 134,* 396–400.

8 Support Groups with the Frail Elderly

The elderly are generally classified as those persons who are 65 or older. They represent many different kinds of persons who can be categorized according to age, health status, social class, ethnicity, place of residence, and so on. To think about the elderly, then, is to be aware that they are not a monolithic group; on the contrary, they exhibit the diversity of the entire human spectrum.

Professional workers in the field of gerontology can be heartened by the fact that the elderly in general are very willing to meet in groups. They naturally seek out groups as places to make acquaintances and friends as well as to exchange information and ideas.

According to Schneider, Decker, Freeman, and Syran (1984), group meetings of the aged are held in a variety of settings, including:

Acute-care hospitals
Board-and-care facilities
Churches
County mental health centers
Domiciliary care by Veterans Administration
Foster homes
Hotel-apartment residence
Hotels in geriatric ghettos of cities
Low-cost housing units
Mobile home units
Nonproprietary intermediate-care facilities
Nonproprietary skilled-nursing facilities
Nutrition sites
Outpatient departments

Prisons
Private offices
Private residences
Proprietary intermediate-care facilities
Proprietary skilled-nursing facilities
Recreation and park centers
Rehabilitation hospitals
Religious homes for retired persons
Retirement homes
School settings
Service centers
State mental hospitals
Veterans Administration hospitals
Volunteer centers

This seeming ubiquity of groups for the elderly is an indication of their high sociability and the desire for human connection.

The great majority of the elderly are not sick. They are people who carry out the functions of everyday life, even though many do suffer from one or more serious ailments (Hartford, 1985). The vulnerable and frail elderly represent a special group within the aged population who do not conform to this general rule of social activity. They represent a numerically minor but significant segment of the aged and stand as a special challenge to health and social work professionals. Whether in nursing homes, board-and-care homes, or their own homes, living with or without permanent caretakers, they are essentially invisible and inaudible.

Large numbers of the ill aged have dropped out of the mainstream, by virtue of their isolation and, for some, a correlative tendency to withdraw into themselves. Their isolation and insularity are reinforced by the exclusionary strategies that healthy people, including the well elderly, tend to employ (Sheehan, 1986). In brief, the elderly ill suffer from isolation and stigma in a massive way. Thus the question arises; How can these elderly citizens maintain their self-esteem? What are the kinds of informal and formal supportive measures that would sustain and perhaps even enhance their sense of living fuller lives?

TARGET POPULATIONS

In the main, support groups for the frail elderly are not always organized around a specific illness, although there are self-help and support groups, for example, for stroke and Alzheimer's disease victims, as well as others. The aged ill are often organized into groups primarily on the basis of their being more or less disabled by virtue of their being both old and sick. Some live in their own homes, either alone or with a family member (often a spouse) or a family surrogate, and they are sustained by a combination of formal supports (Social Security, visiting nurses, part-time home health aides, and so forth) and informal supports (family, friends, and neighbors). Others live in boarding and nursing (or convalescent) homes, that is to say, in congregate settings. Those who live in their own homes might be living in a single-family house, a large apartment house complex, or a variety of living arrangements. Those frail ill living in nursing homes might, if they are well-to-do, enjoy a certain physical luxury; however, the great bulk live in nursing homes where the level of care ranges from quite excellent to grossly inferior and inadequate. Thus their living conditions vary tremendously. The physical circumstances are of enormous importance, for they represent the material conditions underlying psychosocial possibilities. In this sense, some inferior nursing home environments negate the whole concept of support and care. It is difficult, if not impossible, to mount and maintain helpful support groups in environments that do not promote health and sanity.

While there is not an extensive literature on work with the frail elderly in groups, the works cited in this chapter can serve as an inspiriting orientation for the reader.

PLANNING FOR SUPPORT GROUPS

While the social work literature does not give much detail on the planning phase in forming groups with the frail elderly, Feil (1983), in an article on "Group Work with the Frail Elderly," discusses the rudiments of the process within an institutional setting. Prior to the organization of the group, she developed rapport with "each prospective group member" (p. 58). The professional staff selected the prospective members. "Criteria for group membership were: withdrawal from group participation or from interpersonal relationships and some capacity of verbalization" (p. 58). The participation of the staff in the selection process is critical for two reasons: (1) it provides the staff with a sense of participation in the formation of the group and in monitoring the impact of the group on the individual member's morale and behavior, and (2) it negates the subjectivity of a single person who might do the selecting.

Friedlander (1983) describes the planning process in the development of a group of handicapped elderly who "had been locked into their homes for as many as seven or eight years'' (pp. 34–35). The agency began by selecting a small group of people who had been with the agency many years and who were receiving both home care and social services. Using the individual relationships with the social workers, a small planning committee was formed. As Friedlander describes it, ''Five potential members met for a series of planning sessions to work out with the staff the possible program. In terms of the agency's planning, it was felt important to focus on the services most needed by this client group'' (p. 35). What is critical to understand about programs for the frail elderly living in their own homes is that there are workers in all the professions who believe that people can be brought together in small groups to regain and recover their self-esteem through mutual aid.

It is no exaggeration to stress that bringing together several frail elderly people, living in their own homes, to meet regularly at a designated setting is a formidable, difficult enterprise. The people are old, weak, and often physically handicapped. They need to be helped to go from their homes to specially constructed cars or vans and then to the meeting place. Food has to be prepared and served. Proper toilet accommodations have to be arranged. In brief, the members of the agency staff who attempt to form and maintain a support group for the homebound aged must possess a solid general knowledge about the capacities and disabilities of the frail elderly, and they must know in specific, concrete terms the particularities of the individual elderly person.

Need and Purpose

The frail elderly very often find themselves in situations where they have been ''shut away and forgotten for so long that the thought of reentering a social situation was overwhelming'' (Friedlander, 1983, p. 36). The fundamental need is to become resocialized, to be with others who are beset by similar life circumstances, to break out of the chains of a physical limitation, and to reassert one's participation in the life process. One of the creative activities that the elderly, including the chronically ill, engage in is reminiscing. And surely one of the underlying motivations for the tendency toward reminiscing is the search for significance in one's existence. As Ernest Becker wrote, ''What man really fears is not so much extinction, but extinction with *insignificance*. Man wants to know his life has somehow counted if not for himself, then at least in a larger scheme of things, that is, he left a trace, a trace that has meaning'' (quoted in Getzel, 1985, p. 9).

Until recently reminiscing was thought of as a regressive activity on the part of the aged person. Family members and others either actively discouraged this activity or passively dissuaded the reminiscer through inattention. In 1963, Butler reframed the concept. He viewed recalling the past as an activity unconsciously aimed at achieving better self-understanding. Reminiscing can be a part of support group activity. In a professional framework it is optimally undertaken when a list of topics has been thought through, topics that are at once important and sufficiently general to elicit the interest of all of the members. For example, Matteson (1984) structured eight sessions for a group of depressed elderly around the following subjects: (1) birth and childhood, (2) courtship and marriage, (3) child bearing and child rearing, (4) the Great Depression, (5) World War II, (6) jobs, (7) the advent of television, and (8) holidays. Matteson's observations of this short-term group led her to believe that the structured reminiscing activity was particularly helpful to moderately depressed individuals, among whom there are many frail elderly.

Reminiscing in a group is another vehicle in the process of resocialization. In speaking about oneself and listening to the life experience of others, similarities and differences become striking and one begins to see oneself as a member of a larger humanity. This is a significant gain, given the tendency of many of the frail elderly to turn inward and become self-absorbed.

On a more prosaic but highly important level, the process of resocialization signifies the relearning of old social roles and the learning of new ones. This surely is one of the primary purposes of attempting to "mainstream" the elderly ill—"the restoration of self-esteem by establishing new roles" (Friedlander, 1983, p. 35).

All elderly people, regardless of health status, are confronted with the constancy of loss through death of spouses, sometimes adult children, extended family, friends, and acquaintances. Widow and widower self-help and professionally led support groups are now quite common. Their purpose is to help people work through a grief reaction in which the concern and care of others is one of the principal components of support. These groups are usually of a short-term kind.

Where the bereft person needs an ongoing support group, an appropriate referral can be made to a longer-term group. While all elderly live in environments where the death of "significant others" is an existential fact for all elderly, the frail elderly, particularly those who live in congregate care (nursing homes, board-and-care homes, and hospices) are constantly faced with death and dying and thus with the contemplation of their own demise. Support groups of the frail elderly cannot avoid these central issues, for to do so would be an act of reinforcing the pathological trend of treating death as a taboo subject. While some members of a support group of frail elderly will resist dealing with the topic, others will be ready to do so. The catharsis of talking about the taboo, the confrontation with the dreaded topic, frequently leads to the partial lifting of depression and to a higher integration of the self, even though this may be a temporary phenomenon (Orr, 1986).

Composition

As previously stated, groups of the frail elderly are normally composed of chronically ill people who suffer from a variety of illnesses, although there are support groups made up of those who represent a single major illness such as Alzheimer's disease. Nevertheless, not all of the frail elderly can benefit from a support group experience, and some should be excluded because they are so mentally impaired that they cannot contain their impulses or they are incontinent. Burnside (1984) cites Judith Altholz in regard to her recommendations for excluding some aged persons from a group: "disturbed, active, wandering persons; incontinent persons; patients with a psychotic depression; patients recommended solely by the staff; individuals having bipolar disorders; deaf persons; [and] hypochondriacal persons" (p. 113) should be excluded from support groups.

The issue of who should be excluded from a group cannot simply be done by reliance on diagnostic categories. Lee (1983), for example, directed a successful group-work program for "the more confused and disoriented patients who did not fit in other hospital or community programs" (p. 44). Many were "severely disoriented," some "seriously depressed," each with medical and social problems compounding their sense of loss.

Realistically, sound work with the frail elderly, like all social work, has its successes and failures. Failure in this context simply means that some frail elderly will gain little or nothing from the support group experience. In some instances, the motivational, intellectual, and affective capacities of some individuals may be too shattered for them to benefit from the group experience.

Feil (1983) writes, "After five years, I found that mixing mildly disoriented residents with severely confused residents was not helpful" (p. 58). Readers might wonder why it took five years for Feil to come to this conclusion. One can only surmise that doing group work with the frail elderly, a clientele that is essentially new for social work, necessitates taking a long time to arrive at a decision that *excludes* some people from a process that one believes is potentially helpful. Social workers who undertake what is a daunting task, namely, the resocialization of the frail elderly, begin philosophically with a sense of hope that all people can be helped to lead fuller, more satisfactory lives. Reality teaches, however, that some people—due to the combined impacts of advanced age and serious illness and disabilities and their sequelae—cannot use a group experience beneficially. It is a difficult lesson to absorb when one begins from a position of social idealism.

Excluding severely confused people from groups is understandable in that they tend to disrupt the group process. Yet this exclusion is one of many social "rejections" they experience. These people should be seen in individual treatment by a staff member, presumably a social worker, to help them regain a firmer sense of reality. Sometimes, regrettably, this is not possible, but too often it is a foregone conclusion, even before an attempt to help has been made.

The question arises as to whether the severely confused elderly can benefit from their own support groups. There is so little recorded experience in working with groups composed of the severely mentally impaired, that no definitive statement can be made in regard to their viability.

On the other hand, the handicapped aged and the nonhandicapped aged were brought together to hold membership in the same group (Friedlander, 1983). Here is an instance of widening the circle of empathy by breaking out of the segregation model. This conforms to the ideal that the frail elderly can move from a position of isolation and insularity to their own support group, and then to a mixed group with the relatively healthy elderly, and then progress to a support group composed of different generations. While studies show a goodly amount of intergenerational familial interaction in the form of two-way mutual aid (Cantor, 1975; Shanas, 1979), there is nevertheless a genuine need for professional reaching out to the frail elderly who can benefit from a peer support group experience.

Structure

The frail elderly would probably benefit most from closed support groups of five people. Closed groups would assure constancy of environment—the same people meeting together over a period of time with the aim of building mutual support. While a group of five people is on the small side, it is optimal for people who become easily confused and bewildered by an excess of conversations and random activities. To be practical and realistic, the usual support group structure is open and has a variable attendance. Many elderly sick and/or disabled people cannot regularly attend meetings, due to illness or some conflicting appointment, such as a physician's visit or an unexpected treatment. In reality there are some days in which the group will be composed of 3 people and on others 10.

In creating groups for the frail elderly, the group leader must expect potential members initially to resist joining, but most join when the social worker demonstrates an attitude of kindly persistence (Silverston & Burack-Weiss, 1984). The group leader must expect to have more than a single pre-group contact with individual elderly persons before some will agree to join a group. The group leader's attention and patience will pay off in getting people to "risk" group membership. Once a group has begun to meet it is important to encourage participants by praising their efforts. The more reticent members' presence should be acknowledged with the recognition and appreciation that they were present.

One of the critical aspects of the social workers' pre-group work is her contacts with other staff as to their observations of a putative member's behavior in social situations. Nurses, physicians, caretakers, and physical, recreational and occupational therapists have many contacts with patients, and their observations provide information from different points of view about the possibilities of a person's group membership. In order to elicit the cooperation of the facility, the pre-group contact must be carried out on the highest administrative levels. In brief, the owners and managers of nursing homes, and the directors of social agencies and hospitals have to be approached and won over to the idea of support group formation for the frail elderly.

While professionally led support groups often meet once a week for $1^1/_2$ hours, in the case of the frail elderly it is advisable to meet for approximately 45 minutes, once a week. Limited attention spans, restlessness, physical discomfort are all limitations that dictate shorter meetings.

Content

The content of support group sessions with the frail elderly is significantly influenced by the group leader's role and the group process. In general, group leaders are more directive than they are in other kinds of support group work (Burnside, 1984). Scharlach (1985), who conducted a "task-centered," eight-session welcoming committee training group for institutionalized frail elderly, notes that this type of group, which has significant mutual-support elements,

> is considerably more structured than is commonly found in social group work. By exerting control over the content and intensity of group discussions, the worker attempts to make sure that demands on the group will occur at the optimal point in the group's development, and in a manner consonant with the particular needs and goals of the group members and the institutional milieu within which they live. Moreover, the structure format facilitates the transfer of personal gains to the larger context, and maximizes the likelihood that interpersonal skills and mutual support will be maintained long after the group has ended. [p. 45]

Lee indicated that mentally impaired older persons are capable of undertaking a variety of activities. In general, these activities are designed to restore and maintain social skills; to help people move out of isolation toward the making of new relationships; and to provide the kinds of human interaction that promote enjoyment.

Lee's finely drawn analysis of the use of activities in the group and the social worker's professional obligation to understand the members as individuals accentuates the complexity of the work and the broad knowledge and skill needed to do that work sensitively and effectively. Lee (1983) comes to the following conclusion about her work with mentally impaired older people:

> A sense of self is restored through community, through providing opportunities for recall through doing together with some assurance of success, and the opportunity to talk, share feelings and help each other . . . It must be overwhelmingly concluded that this population has strengths in making relationships and mutual aid which are usually underestimated. And this group/ milieu approach is a most effective way to serve the mentally impaired elderly. [pp. 53–54]

Saul (1983a) describes the work of an admissions group of frail elderly in a nursing home.* The group consisted of six frail elderly people from the ages of 74 to 88, one of whom was a new admission. In this article Saul has transcribed a tape of the third session of this group; the content of which centered around (1) the recent death of the spouse of the newly

*Welcoming committees and admission groups are the same thing: small groups of elderly patients whose main purpose is to welcome a newcomer to an institutional setting. They are formed with the awareness that the transition from living-at-home (or the temporary stay in a hospital) to a strange permanent place such as a nursing home is a severe social-psychological jolt.

admitted person and (2) the beginning friendship of two of the group's members. While these two topics do not seem to relate directly to the adjustment problems of admission to a congregate living facility, in actuality they do. In the first, for instance, three of the group members engaged in either grieving or reminiscing activities, which provide relief from depression and anxiety; moreover, in sharing their past histories, they experienced a sense of integration and resiliency (Burnside, 1984). From this one might conclude that, while leaders of frail elderly groups are advised to be directive in structuring group tasks, room and time must be allowed for people to speak spontaneously about deeply held feelings that do not fit precisely with the agenda of a given session.

The content and process of groups for the frail elderly include such topics as adjusting to advanced age and illness, adapting to an institutional setting, relearning old social roles and learning new ones, taking on new responsibilities, and developing new relationships.

Friedlander (1983), in her work with groups of the handicapped elderly, comments as follows on content and process:

> Analysis of work with chronically ill patients shows how the shared experience and the accepting atmosphere of the group can encourage mutual support and discussion of the full impact of members' conditions. So members began to trust, understand, and tolerate each other. They began to admit their vulnerabilities and share their anger, frustration, helplessness and fears and their grief over loss of animate and inanimate objects and the deaths of loved ones. They began to recognize their shared struggles, to help and accept one another and to share jointly in problem solving, both for the program and each other. [p. 37]

The content, then, of support groups of the frail elderly is at once particular and universal. It is particular in its reference to their specific circumstances and universal in the quest for making life more tolerable, more decent, and if possible, sweeter.

Burnside (1984) has some critical advice to give leaders of groups for the elderly. Based on her wide experience, she advocates the following attitudes and behaviors:

> Group leaders need to provide much support, encouragement, and empathy because the elderly often have special problems that must be recognized and dealt with. On the emotional level, elderly people may be preoccupied with loss and death and may refer to these topics again and again. A major objective in group work is to alleviate this general anxiety by helping group members solve immediate problems. . . .

> Group leaders must also contend with the physical problems of the elderly. Sensory defects, for example, require special techniques. Speaking slowly and clearly, sitting close to the members, and keeping the groups and circles small are all helpful. Assessing the energy level for each member is another important aspect of group work with the elderly. [pp. 24–25]

Professional social workers and those of other professions interested in working with the frail elderly and their families can only do so effectively if they view old age, frailty, and death as a part of life. One cannot enter into this kind of professional work with a completed philosophy; one has to achieve it through a lived experience with those who are old and frail. As Gadow (1983) writes,

> The very frailty which made possible the encounter with intensity is itself suffused with new life and rendered intense; *it becomes the new form for the life,* it is itself experienced with the passion that once was directed into other forms. And to the extent that it is the focus of energy, frailty becomes in turn the source of still more life. [p. 146]

Perhaps not many of the frail elderly reach this fusion of energy, passion, and frailty, this "new form for the life"; but for workers in the field it is crucial to believe that some can reach this high state of being.

WORKING WITH THE FAMILIES OF THE FRAIL ELDERLY

As noted earlier, Bronfenbrenner (1979) wisely counsels professional workers that parent education should not focus on "who cares for the children, but on who cares for those who care" (p. 777). This ecological principle is being increasingly fulfilled in the recent proliferation of groups of family and friends—caretakers—of the frail elderly. It appears that one of the most significant recent developments in the formation of these groups is the organizing activity of caretakers of Alzheimer's disease victims. These groups are usually led by professionally trained group workers, primarily social workers and nurses.

Family caretakers are mostly the spouses and adult children of frail elderly persons. Sometimes an adult child is the principal caretaker of both disabled parents. The development of support groups for caretakers "is an attempt to assist them in discovering the universality of their condition and to find the meaning of the caregiving role, which is often misunderstood, denied, and unappreciated in society (Getzel, 1983, p. 91).

Support groups for caretakers are usually short-term, closed groups that meet for 8 to 10 sessions for 1½ to 2 hours per session. The age range is wide. Very often the caretakers are in their middle years. Some still have children for whom they are responsible. Others who already can be classified as the "young-old" (65 to 70 years old) may be struggling physically and/or psychologically with their own advancing age and, possibly, frailty.

The format is most frequently of the didactic/interactional type. The educational part focuses on the aging process, including normal and pathological developments, psychosocial developments, and death and dying (Cohen, 1983; Hartford & Parsons, 1983). The participants may be caretakers of relatives suffering from the same disease or from a variety of illnesses. Little is known about which composition is more effective. Hartford and Parsons (1983) believes that the mixed group may be more beneficial because members can "share with each other some of their different experiences" (p. 81).

Cohen (1983) has outlined the specific goals of caretaking groups:

1. To provide support for the families of elderly persons and a place where feelings could be shared and similarities as well as unique problems could be recognized
2. To provide information about adult development, the aging process, and available community resources and services
3. To help those who need to make specific decisions
4. To teach skills in self-care
   a. Assertiveness skills
   b. Stress management
   c. Communication skills
5. To provide a setting within which group therapy could occur as it relates to issues such as guilt, role reversal, unresolved childhood conflicts, and sibling rivalry. [pp. 248–249]

The burden of the full-time caretaker of an elderly, ill person is enormous, particularly in those situations where the afflicted one tends to be uncooperative, self-centered, and more or less incapable of engaging in rational conversation. The caretaker has to be at once nurse, cleaning person, bath giver, cook, feeder—in sum, the all-giving, good parent who frequently receives little or no sustaining feedback from the cared-for person.

Wasow (1986) points out several cultural dilemmas that emerge out of work with the families of Alzheimer's disease victims. The first relates to the composition of groups: Should family members of the ill persons be mixed or kept separate? Should family members of ill persons in various stages of the illness be mixed? Should the group be open or closed? The second relates to the fact that some caretakers' health is at risk as they attempt to give total care. Professional workers have to be sensitive to the physical and mental health of both parties, and choices have to be made. Wasow suggests that some caretakers should be helped in letting go when they are overburdened with their responsibilities. The rub is that there is a shortage of first-rate facilities for Alzheimer's patients or, for that matter, the frail elderly as a group. The third dilemma is that, while the main content of family groups is centered around coping strategies for dealing with the ill person, there can be an overload of discussion in this domain. Family caretakers spend 24 hours a day with Alzheimer's disease, so going to a group where nothing else is discussed week after week can be burdensome for some people. Wasow suggests that in a longer-term group here might be "a gradual shift to a recreational focus" (p. 95).

As noted previously, family support groups are of short duration. While the professionals who have led them firmly believe in their helpfulness, the issue of sustained peer group support arises. It would seem that the support group might well become a self-help group in which professional consultation is at hand when desired and needed. Caretakers' morale and physical stamina are at risk. A self-help group could be a source of sustainment and encouragement of a more permanent kind.

Working with the families of the frail elderly represents a genuine advance in social work and mental health practice. In this connection, the Community Service Society of New York began a research-and-demonstration project in 1976, entitled The Natural Support Program. It was aimed at directing social group activities toward the network of family and friends. Since then this program has become institutionalized and operates support groups in many parts of New York City. Clinical social work services continue to be extended to both the frail elderly and their families, when this treatment approach is the right one for the situation.

A NOTE ON ECOLOGY AND RESPECT

From the point of view of how the external environment can sustain and make life more satisfactory for the chronically ill in general and the frail elderly in particular, the proper mix of formal and informal supports is at issue (Lawton, 1983; Tietjen, 1981). A nurturing environment is a human creation whose inspiration is undergirded by a set of values respectful of those weakened and debilitated by the ravages of illness. The care of close family, extended kin, neighbors, and friends, mixed with first-rate medical, rehabilitative, and social services and the contributions of a host of social institutions and organizations can do much to fortify people's spirits. Everything depends on what society wishes to invest in. County, state, and federal budgets, particularly the latter, are testimonies to a society's values and priorities. Perhaps the antecedent issue to a proper mix of formal and informal supports is what society wants and is willing to pay for. Values are expressed in the priorities of budgets.

CONCLUSION

The frail elderly are people who to some considerable extent have been turned into an abstraction, a collective mental image connoting weakness, debility, and impending death. Certainly physical and frequently mental limitations are a part of their reality. Yet what is missing from this image is the capacity—the possibility—for human connection, for mutual aid, for giving and receiving from others such feelings as pleasure and joy, and for learning.

Professional workers often share in this restricted collective view of the frail elderly. To some considerable extent the frail elderly represent the opposite of another abstraction, the YAVIS (young, attractive, verbal, intelligent, successful), a cohort of people purported to be the most desirable psychotherapeutic clients. Thus, for the professional helping community, including social workers, the frail elderly represent a moral responsibility and challenge. A question emerges: Unwittingly, unconsciously, is "the survival of the fittest" still the guiding principle of social policy and professional mental health practice? Or is there truly a commitment to the most vulnerable, to the "least fit," whose principal need is to live decent lives as long as they live?

REFERENCES

Berman-Rossi, T. (1986). The fight against helplessness and despair: Institutionalized aged. In A. Gitterman & L. Shulman (Eds.), *Mutual aid groups and the life cycle* (pp. 333–360). Itasca, IL: Peacock.

Bronfenbrenner, U. (1979). *The ecology of human development.* Cambridge, MA: Harvard University Press.

Burnside, I.M. (1984). *Working with the elderly: Group processes and techniques* (2nd ed.). Monterey, CA: Wadsworth.

Butler, R.N. (1963). The life review: An interpretation of reminiscence in the aged. *Psychiatry, 26*(1), 65–76.

Cantor, M. (1975). Lifespace and the social support system of inner city elderly of New York. *The Gerontologist, 15*(1) 23–24.

Cohen, F., & Lazarus, R.S. (1979). Coping with the stresses of illness. In G.C. Stone, C. Cohen & N.E. Adler (Eds.), *Health psychology—A handbook* (pp. 217-254). San Francisco: Jossey-Bass.

Cohen, P.M. (1983). A group approach for working with families of the elderly. *The Gerontologist, 23*(3), 248–250.

Feil, N. (1983). Group work with disoriented nursing home residents. *Social Work with Groups, 5*(2), 57–65.

Friedlander, H. (1983). Differential use of groups in mainstreaming the handicapped elderly. *Social Work with Groups, 5*(2), 33–42.

Gadow, S. (1983). Frailty and strength: The dialectic in aging. *The Gerontologist, 23*(2), 144–147.

Getzel, G.S. (1983). Group work with kin and friends caring for the elderly. *Social Work with Groups, 5*(2), 91–102.

Getzel, G.S. (1985). Critical themes for gerontological social work practice. *Journal of Gerontological Social Work, 8*(3/4), 3–12.

Hartford, M.E. (1985). Understanding normative growth and development in aging: Working with strengths. *Journal of Gerontological Social Work, 8*(3/4), 37–54.

Hartford, M.E., & Parsons, R. (1983). Uses of groups with relatives of dependent older adults. *Social Work with Groups, 5*(2), 77–89.

Lawton, M.P. (1983). Environment and other determinants of well-being in older people. *The Gerontologist, 23*(4), 349–357.

Lee, J.A. (1983). The group: A chance at human connections for the mentally impaired older person. *Social Work with Groups, 5*(2), 43–56.

Matteson, M.A. (1984). Group reminiscing for the depressed institutionalized elderly. In I. Burnside (Ed.), *Working with the elderly: Group process and techniques* (pp. 287–297). Monterey, CA: Wadsworth.

Orr, A. (1986). Dealing with the death of a group member: Visually impaired elderly in the community. In A. Gitterman & L. Shulman (Eds.), *Mutual aid groups and the life cycle* (pp. 315–332). Itasca, IL: Peacock.

Roback, H.B. (Ed.). (1984). *Helping patients and their families cope with medical problems.* San Francisco, CA: Jossey-Bass.

Roback, H.B. (1984). Conclusion: Critical issues in group approaches to disease management. In H.B. Roback (Ed.), *Helping patients and their families with medical problems* (pp. 527–543). San Francisco, CA: Jossey-Bass.

Saul, S.R. (1983a). An admissions group in a skilled nursing facility. *Social Work with Groups, 5*(2), 67–76.

Saul, S. (1983). *Groupwork with the frail elderly.* New York: Haworth Press.

Scharlach, A.E. (1985). Social group work with institutionalized elders: A task-centered approach. *Social Work with Groups, 8*(3), 33–47.

Schneider, R.C., Decker, T., Freeman, J. & Syran, C. (1984). *The integration of gerontology into social work educational curricula* (CSWE series in gerontology). Washington, DC: Council on Social Work Education.

Shanas, E. (1979). The family as a social support system in old age. *The Gerontologist, 19*(2), 144–169.

Sheehan, N.W. (1986). Informal support among the elderly in public senior housing. *The Gerontologist 26*(2), 171–175.

Silverstone, B., & Burack-Weiss, A. (1983). Social work practice with the frail elderly and their families. Springfield, IL: Charles C Thomas.

Tietjen, A. M. (1981). Integrating formal support systems: The Swedish experience. In J. Gabarino, S.H. Stocking et al. (Eds.), *Protecting children from abuse and neglect* (pp. 15–36). San Francisco: Jossey-Bass.

Wasow, M. (1986). Support groups for family caregivers of patients with Alzheimer's disease. *Social Work, 31*(2), 93–98.

9 Support Groups in Child and Family Practice

In recent years, child and family work has caught media attention and, at times, has been under fire. Publicity has landed most heavily on child physical and sexual abuse as well as the plight of protective service agencies faced with understaffed, undertrained workers who struggle with overwhelming caseloads and limited resources. Time and again, alarming statistics appear, highlighting the prevalence of domestic violence, such as spouse battering, child sexual assault and physical abuse, rape, elder abuse, parent battering, and sibling violence. An extremely sobering statistical example comes from a rather rigorous piece of research in which Wyatt (1985) concluded, "Considering the prevalence of sexual abuse before 18 years of age for this sample of women (a multistage stratified probability sample of 17-36 year old Los Angeles County residents), 1 in 2.5 Afro-American women experienced some form of abuse involving body contact as did 1 in 2 white American women" (p. 518).

While such information may shock some clinicians, others may receive it as mere confirmation of previously suspected levels of family and social dysfunction. Either way, as Star (1983) points out, "So prevalent is violence in the family that it prompted members of the National Commission on the Cause and Prevention of Violence to comment that the general public had more to fear from family and friends than from violence in the streets committed by strangers" (pp. 3–4).

Statements of this magnitude inherently imply that an enormous population exists that is in need of family and child services. This is clear even without mentioning other families faced with nonviolent crises, such as teenage and unwanted pregnancies, poverty, disabled parents, abandoned children, unemployment, divorce, or parental death. Most social workers have experienced at one time or another a deeply gripping moment when the enormity of the problems faced by families and children has seemed overwhelming. This may not always occur with graphic encounters, but some image breaks through the professional distance or detachment, causing a poignant visceral stirring and a pulling of the heart.

Prompted by such personal glimpses of reality, much thought has been focused on the cause of this state of pervasive social disorganization. While some theorists point to the dramatically increasing divorce rate, claiming the demise of the American family, other thinkers assume a more hopeful stance. For example, Finkelhor (1984) points out that "the availability of divorce has certainly rescued many children from what might have once been chronic and inescapable torment and abuse" (p. 7). Others suggest that the family unit is here to stay, but that the time has come to rethink the family concept, particularly from a feminist perspective, in light of the increasing numbers of single female heads of households (Thorne & Yalom, 1982).

Unquestionably, parents have begun to rethink their ways of coping in this period of rapid change and stress. As parents enlist in and commit their energy to such self-help organizations as Parents Anonymous, Parents without Partners, or Parents United, they are not only acknowledging a need for support but a recognition that this can be achieved through mutual aid. The growth of such organizations speaks to the need for some sense of society, of connection, and of decreased isolation. In discussing strategies for preventing child abuse and neglect, Garbarino and Stocking et al. (1981) make a relevant point:

> The family is, after all, one of the few remaining private affairs in a world in which the government and a host of lawyers exercise increasing power over people's lives. But social isolation is one of the costs of this cherished privacy. One way to deal with this situation is to extend the value we place on sharing and reciprocity to include people's emotional lives. . . . But people who don't naturally take part in this kind of emotional sharing need to be brought into new social settings where they can have contact with new reference groups that will offer acceptance and a sense of belonging. [p. 58]

The social work profession can bring isolated individuals and families into these new "social settings," which offer emotional sharing through the use of support groups. It is particularly important to have professional involvement in child and family support work, in light of the delicate balance between the sanctity of the family and society's responsibility to nurture and protect children. Workers have begun to take this role in support group work in the field of child and family practice.

In this discussion, *child and family* refers not only to the formal child welfare system concerned with supportive, supplementary, and substitute care for children, but also to the numerous programs run by Child Guidance Centers, Family Service Agencies, and private social service organizations. All of these systems of service delivery offer some examples of support group work in this field.

TARGET POPULATIONS

Children in Foster Care

With the increasing emphasis on permanency planning, the child welfare system has directed more effort toward working with natural parents of neglected or abused children who are in placement. Support groups have become a more common part of the services offered to such parents. Carbino (1982) offers detailed descriptions of her group work with natural parents. Using an open-ended, open-membership format, group meetings were held in a local church, with provisions for child care and transportation. Focus was placed on "providing an opportunity for mutual support and sharing of common problems, becoming better informed about foster care, and improving the ways natural parents are treated in the foster care system" (p. 20). Reflecting on the group experience, Carbino writes,

> Parents reported feeling uninformed, isolated and negatively labeled and treated in foster care. They were active in meetings from the beginning and used the first several meetings to air their anger, hurt, guilt and concerns. . . . It is very promising that, given the ongoing demands on the energies of natural parents, group work can still have quite positive results. Parents became better informed about foster care, no longer felt isolated, contributed and received support and encouragement and generally were able to interact with the foster care system more effectively. [p. 26]

For further information on support groups with this population, see Hess & Williams (1982).

Approaching the issue of substitute care from the other side, that is, from the children's point of view, we find that support groups have also been helpful (Lee & Park, 1978; Ludlow & Epstein, 1972; Mayfield & Neil, 1983). Mayfield and Neil give an excellent, step-by-step description of their support group for children in substitute care, a program called Sunday's Child. (For a discussion of this program, please see the Chapter 6 section entitled "Group Process in Short-Term Support Groups.")

Physically and Sexually Abused Children

One of the most creative uses of the support group format can be seen in Breton's (1979) "hairdressing group" for neglectful and abusive mothers (see Chapter 6). While she does not label the program as a support group, much of the focus is on nurturing and supporting the mothers. Seven mothers met for weekly 4-hour sessions with two social workers, during which the mothers had their hair done and shared lunch. Breton believed that, through empowering the mothers by using mutual aid, steps could be taken to prevent and decrease child abuse. While she found the group process to be slow, the mothers who received nurturing themselves seemed to have more to give to their children and a better sense of appropriate parenting. Other clinicians have also demonstrated this ability of support and mutual aid to reduce hostility and abusive behavior (Kruger, Moore, Schmidt, & Wiens, 1979; McFerran, 1958; McNeil & McBride, 1979).

In the area of sexual abuse, perhaps the most famous treatment program is Giarretto's (1982) program, Integrated Treatment of Child Sexual Abuse. While this program does not strictly fit the definition of a support group used in this text, support and mutual aid are primary elements. Few experiences evoke such intense feelings of isolation and shame as do incest and child molestation. The ability to share these feelings with other victims, with other perpetrators, and with other parents and families is paramount. The following is quoted from a member of one of Giarretto's groups: "When my stepfather started molesting me in third grade, I thought I was the only one this had happened to in the whole world. I felt isolated and was sure none of the other kids would have been able to understand it. . . . So I learned not to trust people with my confidences" (p. 240).

The chance to share her experiences with other girls who suffered similar abuse can be invaluable to an incest victim. It is likewise valuable for mothers and fathers of the victims as well. As a social worker in a group of mothers of molested girls, time and again one of us (Danforth) has observed with great respect the mutual aid process as the members, with their shared trauma, helped one another in a way no amount of clinical training could duplicate.

Children of Divorced Parents

In a more preventive vein, many agencies have begun to attend to the needs of divorcing parents and their children. Several support groups for single parents are noted in the literature (Armstrong-Dillard, 1980; Bonkowski & Wanner-Westly, 1979). Of special quality, however, is a group formed by Bonkowski, Bequette, and Boomhower (1984) for children experiencing parental divorce. The group of eight children and three leaders met for eight 1 1/2-hour sessions of structured activities and discussion, focusing on the divorce experience. The workers concluded that one of the most therapeutic elements for the group members was the children's experience of meeting with other peers who were in the midst of a similar loss.

Summary of Populations Reported in the Literature

Support groups have emerged for various populations in child and family practice. A partial listing with references is offered here for the interested reader:

1. *Natural parents with children in foster care:* Carbino, 1982; Hess & Williams, 1982; McFerran, 1958
2. *Children in foster care:* Euster, Ward, Varner, & Euster, 1984; Lee & Park, 1978; Ludlow & Epstein, 1972; Mayfield & Neil, 1983
3. *Foster parents:* Jacobs, 1980; Lee, 1979; Park, 1979
4. *Neglectful and abusive parents:* Breton, 1979; Kruger et al., 1979; McFerran, 1958; McNeil & McBride, 1979; Wayne & Avery, 1980
5. *Sexual abuse of children:* Giarretto, 1982
6. *Single parents:* Armstrong-Dillard, 1980; Schulman-Miller & Rubin, 1982
7. *Children of divorce:* Bonkowski et al. 1984; Bonkowski & Wanner-Westly, 1979; Guerney & Jordon, 1979
8. *Wife batterers:* Bern & Bern, 1984; Pardy & Nickle, 1981; Saunders, 1984; Star, 1983
9. *New parents:* Wandersman, Wandersman, & Kalm, 1980
10. *Adolescent pregnancy:* Blythe, Gilchrist, & Schinke, 1981; Erf, 1981
11. *Parents of adolescents:* Cohen & Irwin, 1983

PLANNING A SUPPORT GROUP IN FAMILY AND CHILD PRACTICE

Need

The earlier discussion of statistical prevalence of abuse, neglect, and family violence speaks to the need for intervention. In addition, the change in recent years to emphasis on permanency planning demands that dysfunctional family systems receive supportive services. When the risk factors discussed in Chapter 4 are applied to people in family and child social service systems, an alarming need for support usually is evident. This is particularly true with child sexual abuse, due to the high level of stigma and powerlessness (Finkelhor, 1984) and the pressure of secrecy (Summit, 1983).

Purpose

Support groups in this field often not only focus on decreasing stigma, isolation, guilt, and shame, but also have a strong educational component which is used to break a cycle of abuse or dysfunction. Thus purpose statements often include goals for improving parenting skills.

In beginning a support group for abused or abusing populations, a fine line develops between support and treatment. Because there is an absolute need for a behavior change—that is, the abusive action must stop—it is recommended that support group work be conducted in conjunction with (but not necessarily simultaneously with) treatment programs such as individual, family, or group therapy. This does not lessen the importance of the mutual-aid experience or the impact a peer support system may have on deterring impulses to repeat abuse.

Composition

Again, it is usually recommended to separate parents and children into different group meetings. This becomes particularly important when dealing with physical and sexual abuse, due to the victim/perpetrator relationship. Without separation in this case, neither party can experience the safety necessary to engage in the mutual-aid process. This does not always mean there should be absolutely no contact between victims and perpetrators, but it is an issue that requires careful therapeutic consideration. For instance, in the treatment of sexual abuse, some Parents United programs meet initially with all the families together, for business aspects of the evening, and then break down into their respective mothers', daughters', or fathers' groups.

Another factor that needs to be considered in composing groups of children, particularly sexual abuse victims, is their developmental stage and social age. The sensitivity of intimate feelings and discussions that may arise should be shared only with children of similar age and sophistication.

Structure

In most cases, it is recommended that physically and sexually abusing families be in therapy in addition to the support group. For several reasons, it is imperative that the group leader arrange for a structure that allows contact with the primary clinician. Often the focus of treatment between children and their parents is to achieve eventual reunification. Movement toward this goal is sometimes slow and requires constant evaluation. The delicacy of this situation, and the assessment of the family's psychological readiness, will impact the amount of contact tolerable between victim and perpetrator. The support group leader cannot responsibly intervene with the family or adequately protect a child if she does not have a handle on the family's treatment progress.

Contact with the primary therapist as well as the legal system is also important, so the group leader understands legal conditions for contact between children and their parents. Group leaders must be aware of stipulations for no contact or for monitored visitations and the assigned responsible persons authorized to monitor parent/child visits. Leaders are cautioned not to rely on parent or child reports with regard to visitation and contact arrangements. It is advisable to verify information with the therapist, the Children's Service worker, the attorney, or the court.

This leads to the next point with respect to structure. In working in the field of family and child practice, several systems are usually interfacing. A structure for contact between the group leaders, treating therapists, Children's Services, the police, the courts, the schools, and other health providers is essential. This implies a cooperative, working relationship among these systems, securing the appropriate releases of information needed to allow communication. Agencies must also establish a system of documentation suitable to meeting the needs of these departments. Of most importance, in the midst of all of this interdepartmental communication, workers should keep the family advised of the information being shared. These systems should also have a prearranged mechanism for intervention if reabuse should occur or complications arise.

In structuring the group time itself, several issues should be addressed. It is often helpful to hold the group in a neutral setting, instead of a stigmatized, threatening environment. Consideration must be given to child care and transportation, if at all possible. Meeting times and lengths will be affected by children's eating and sleeping schedules. Offering food as a form of nurturance to this population is often recommended. Finally, thought should be given to mechanisms for outside contact between group members, as this will invariably come up. At times this outside support is quite valuable, while at others it may become a problem as a result of extreme neediness and difficulty with boundaries. As McNeil and McBride (1979) observe:

> Sometimes relationships with other couples were so intense that a couple or member became too intimately involved in the family conflict of another. In general, these were families who often had difficulty handling their own problems. . . . The group, though, served as a safety valve because caution could be expressed if potentially volatile situations seemed to be developing. [pp. 39–50]

If possible, due to the intimate material shared in many child and family groups, memberships should be closed. Duration of the group life depends highly on the purpose of the meeting and chronicity of the problem. Self-help organizations are often beneficial sources of support after termination of the group.

Content

As noted earlier, groups in family and child work often have an educational component, particularly in the realm of parenting skills. Focus also can be placed on helping parents negotiate the many social service and legal systems. Themes of isolation, stigma, shame, and guilt consistently arise. In addressing those themes, a recurrent point in the literature is the need to nurture the parents. As Carbino (1982) writes, "Abusive parent group members were in seriously disadvantaged circumstances economically, socially and personally. They were isolated, lacking familial and community supports. . . . They are in obvious need of nurture and attention for themselves as well as on behalf of their children" (p. 15).

Leaders must be well versed on the issue facing the group. Issues are frequently specific to the particular problem area, as in the case of sexual abuse, where content will be quite different for parents and children. A father who perpetrated incest will often experience the following:

Intense guilt and shame, humiliation, and loss of self-esteem
Fear of losing his family

Fear of incarceration
Anger with the child who disclosed
Anger with the involvement of outside systems
Severe isolation and depression
Rigid denial of the abuse
Increased financial stress, as he generally is required to move out of the home if the child remains there
Anxiety, confusion, and despair, often heightened if disclosure elicits memories of his own abuse as a child
A sense of inadequacy due to role loss
Increased impulsivity or self-destructive behaviors
Desires to flee
Often frustrated desires to have ''apologetic contact'' with the child before the child is ready

The mother of the victim faces the following:

Shame and guilt for not knowing or acting sooner
Pain of actual or feared separation from children
Mistrust of social/legal systems
Rage at spouse
Anger with the child who disclosed
Sexual inadequacy
Depression, confusion, panic
Disbelief, particularly if memories emerge of own victimization
Denial of incident(s)
Loss of supports
Material/survival issues, especially when the spouse leaves the home (child care, transportation, financial support, etc.)
Less emotional energy and availability to children

The victimized child, meanwhile, grapples with the following:

Feelings of responsibility for family chaos after disclosing the secret
Separation from parents
Exquisite guilt and shame for both the abuse and disclosure
A desire to retract statements
Anger with parental denial
Isolation and loneliness, particularly if separated from mother
Unsettling experiences with social and legal professionals, often a form of revictimization
Rejection from family, most intense when the perpetrator remains at home and the child is extracted

Confusion about her own reality, wondering if she imagined it or dreamed it all
Belief that she's the only child who has had this experience
Physical trauma
Depression, anxiety

It is beyond the scope of this work to discuss the dynamics of abuse, neglect, foster care, or the array of problems dealt with in support groups. The reader is referred to articles referenced earlier, to review specific content areas.

Pregroup Contact

Several issues should be addressed in pregroup contact with members. Arrangements for confidentiality, interfacing with other involved systems and agencies, and reporting of abuse or neglect should be reviewed. Needed releases of information should be obtained. If treatment is court mandated, this should be discussed, along with mechanisms for reporting progress and attendance.

The most important reason for pregroup contact with this population, however, is to establish a safe, trusting rapport. Children have often been exposed to system-induced trauma (Conte, 1984), due to insensitive handling of situations or the mere ordeal of separation from their families. By the time parents arrive at the group leader's door, they, too, are often distrustful, particularly of social workers as a result of unfortunate sterotypic ideas about the professional role. One widowed mother poignantly taught one of us (Danforth) that lesson. At the point of termination, after five months of intensive work, she turned to give me an embrace, saying, "You've restored my faith in social workers." Seeing my look of bewilderment, she tearfully whispered, "You didn't take my child away." This fear, often unspoken, needs to be addressed if a trusting alliance is to ensue.

A NOTE ON VALUES AND COUNTERTRANSFERENCE

Work with families and children often elicits intense feelings in the social worker, particularly when dealing with abusive or violent families. The support group leader must maintain an awareness of her own reactions and feelings about the group members, knowing that the work ahead can be emotionally draining and unsettling. Workers may find themselves experiencing judgmental or critical thoughts or feeling anger or pain, or they may find themselves caught in fantasies of rescuing particular children. Whatever the case, the worker's feelings must be monitored through self-awareness and supervision. This is often particularly true for the social worker who experienced abuse or neglect as a child. For these reasons, it helps to have a co-worker and not to do groups alone. There will be times when the workers must treat their own feelings with the same gentleness they afford their clients, if a support group is to remain vital and nurturing.

SUMMARY OF IMPORTANT POINTS

The following are general guidelines for conducting support groups with children and their families:

1. Often a fine line exists between the process of support and psychotherapeutic treatment. As a result, careful liaison and smooth cooperation between support group leaders and other treating clinicians are essential to differentiating these components.
2. As a general rule, separate groups for victims and perpetrators.
3. Clarify legal stipulations, both civil and criminal, on any given case, particularly with regard to parent/child contact.
4. Be sure material is appropriate to the emotional and social age of children. Usually it is most helpful to separate children by developmental stages, such as the latency and adolescent periods.
5. Be sensitive to the need for educational information, especially in the areas of parenting skills and in the negotiation of the social/legal system.
6. Be certain to address issues of confidentiality, abuse reporting, and the procedures for interagency contact.
7. Be alert to countertransference issues, for the sake of group members as well as group leaders. This population is frequently so draining and difficult that groups are best done with co-workers, along with periodic supervision.

Child and family practice workers approach their tasks with hopes of helping families function in an optimal manner, thereby enabling children to enjoy the nurturance, protection, and caring needed for healthy physical and emotional development. Along that developmental path, there is enormous need for support, even at relatively low-stress times in family life. One can easily conceptualize the preventive possibilities of early supportive intervention prior to problem development, as well as the invaluable benefits support could provide in moments of acute family stress and pain. The support group offers a mutual-aid network which can shore up the family system and augment a child's connection with other nurturing adults and peers. Faced with the overwhelming number of families and children in need of support, it only makes sense to tap the inherent healing aspects of human relatedness and assist families in helping one another.

REFERENCES

Armstrong-Dillard, P. (1980). Developing services for single parents and their children in the school. *Social Work in Education, 3*(1), 44–57.

Bern, E. H., & Bern, L. L. (1984). A group program for men who commit violence toward their wives. *Social Work with Groups, 7*(1), 63–77.

Blythe, B. J., Gilchrist, L. D., & Schinke, S. P. (1981). Pregnancy-prevention group for adolescents. *Social Work, 26*(6), 503–504.

Bonkowski, S. E., Bequette, S. Q., & Boomhower, S. (1984). A group design to help children adjust to parental divorce. *Social Casework, 65*(3), 131–137.

Bonkowski, S. E., & Wanner-Westly, B. (1979). The divorce groups: A new treatment modality. *Social Casework, 60*(9), 552–557.

Breton, M. (1979). Nurturing abused and abusive mothers: The hairdressing group. *Social Work with Groups, 2*(2). 161–174.

Carbino, R. (1982). Group work with natural parents in permanency planning. *Social Work with Groups, 5*(4), 7–30.

Cohen, M., & Irwin, C. E. (1983). Parent-time: Psychoeducational groups for parents of adolescents. *Health and Social Work, 8*(3), 196–202.

Conte, J. R. (1984). Progress in treating sexual abuse in children. *Social Work, 29*(3), 258–263.

Erf, L. A. (1981). A moratorium for growth: Group work with adolescent mothers. *Clinical Social Work Journal, 9*(1), 44–56.

Euster, S. D., Ward, V. P., Varner, J. G., & Euster, G. L. (1984). Life skills groups for adolescent foster children. *Child Welfare, 43*(1), 27–36.

Finkelhor, D. (1984). *Child sexual abuse: New theory and research.* New York: The Free Press.

Garbarino, J., Stocking, S. H. et al. (1981). *Protecting children from abuse and neglect.* San Francisco: Jossey-Bass.

Giarretto, H. (1982). *Integrated treatment of child sexual abuse: A treatment and training manual.* Palo Alto: Science & Behavior Books.

Guerney, L., & Jordon, L. (1979). Children of divorce: A community support group. *Journal of Divorce, 2*(3), 283–294.

Hess, P., & Williams, L. B. (1982). Group orientation for parents of children in foster family care. *Child Welfare, LXI* (7), 456–466.

Jacobs, M. (1980). Foster parents training: An opportunity for skills enrichment and improvement. *Child Welfare, 59*(10), 615–624.

Kruger, L., Moore, D., Schmidt, P., & Wiens, R. (1979). Group work with abusive parents. *Social Work, 24*(4), 337-338.

Lee, J. A. (1979). The foster parents workshop: A social work approach to learning for new foster parents. *Social Work with Groups, 2*(2), 129-143.

Lee, J. A., & Park, D. N. (1978). A group approach to the depressed adolescent girl in foster care. *American Journal of Orthopsychiatry, 48*(3), 516-527.

Ludlow, B., & Epstein, N. (1972). Groups for foster children. *Social Work, 17*(5), 96-99.

Mayfield, J., & Neil, J. B. (1983). Group treatment for children in substitute care. *Social Casework, 64*(10), 579-584.

McFerran, J. (1958). Parents groups in protective services. *Children, 5*(6), 223-228.

McNeil, J. S., & McBride, M. L. (1979). Group therapy with abusive parents. *Social Casework, 60*(1), 36-42.

Pardy, F., & Nickle, N. (1981). Practice principles for working with groups of men who batter. *Social Work with Groups, 4*(3/4), 111-122.

Park, D. N. (1979). A workshop for foster mothers of special children. *Social Casework, 60*(3), 171-175.

Saunders, D. G. (1984). Helping husbands who batter. *Social Casework, 65*(6), 347-353.

Schulman-Miller, J., & Rubin, D. (1982). Parents in transition groups. Unpublished manuscript.

Star, B. (1983). *Helping the abuser: Intervening effectively in family violence.* New York: Family Service Association of America.

Summit, R. (1983). The child sexual abuse accommodation syndrome. *Child Abuse and Neglect, 7*, 177-193.

Thorne, B., & Yalom, M. (1982). *Rethinking the family: Some feminist questions*. New York: Longman.

Wandersman, L., Wandersman, A., & Kalm, S. (1980). Social support in the transition to parenthood. *Journal of Community Psychology, 8,* 332-342.

Wayne, J. L., & Avery, N. C. (1980). *Child abuse: Prevention and treatment through social group work*. Boston: Charles River Books.

Wyatt, G. (1985). The sexual abuse of Afro-American and White-American women in childhood. *Child Abuse & Neglect. 9*, 507-519.

10 Support Groups in Mental Health

In a broad sense, the earlier discussions about the fields of health, aging, and family and child practice address uses of support groups to promote mental health, in that the support process enhances psychosocial functioning and abilities to cope with stress. This chapter, however, speaks specifically to the use of support groups in formalized mental health delivery systems.

Over the past several decades, portions of the mental health field have unquestionably recognized the benefits of support. In fact, the most significant movement in the field, the Community Mental Health Centers (CMHC) Program, theoretically incorporated the importance of support. As deinstitutionalization became the thrust of the mental health field in the 1960s, CMHCs intended to provide humane, therapeutic treatment at lower costs to the mentally ill, through community-based care designed to support the client in dealing with outpatient living (Bachrach, 1983). Bachrach points out that, as deinstitutionalization failed to fulfill many of the roles institutions once had, "the quest for *support networks* that would help implement these functions emerged as a major planning emphasis" (p. 8). However, despite this call for support, the upsurgence of support groups in mental health has been a relatively recent phenomenon.

TARGET POPULATIONS

Perhaps the most publicized mental health population utilizing the support group modality is the chronically mentally ill. Society's problems in meeting the needs of these people have been so pervasive that professionals, families, and clients frequently search for imaginative use of supportive resources (Pepper & Ryglewicz, 1984). Many existing mutual-aid groups for the chronically mentally ill or their families are not professionally led and have arisen as a result of extensive and justifiable disillusionment with professionals (Lamb & Oliphant, 1978). Organizations such as the Alliance for the Mentally Ill, Parents of Adult Schizophrenics, Project Return, and England's National Schizophrenic Fellowship exemplify these mutual-aid and advocacy groups.

Historically, a rift has formed between the mental health professions and such mutual-aid groups. The similarity in goals and, at the same time, the contrasting means of achieving those goals provide a fertile place for conflict. Speaking for the National Institute of Mental Health and sounding a conciliatory note in reference to mutual-aid groups, Silverman (1978) warns, "Mental health workers are bound to fail when they do not recognize their own limitations and when they try to maintain a superordinate position as the 'helping experts'" (p. 5). It appears that mental health professionals are beginning to heed this advice, after referring clients to mutual-aid groups and recognizing their healing potential. The next step has been the incorporation of the mutual-aid aspect into the professional sphere, through the formation of professionally led support groups.

Atwood and Williams (1978) offer a description of a support group formed for relatives of chronically mentally ill day-treatment clients. The group was closed and time limited, running 1½ hours for 8 consecutive weeks. Support remained the primary focus of the group; the hope was "to bring about interpersonal communication among a group of people sharing a common problem: how to understand and cope with the mental illness of their family member and its effect on the family unit" (p. 418).

Support groups in mental health have focused primarily on the chronically mentally ill, but there have been some creative uses of groups with other populations as well. A listing of some examples follows, with references provided if more information is desired. This sample does not include the field of developmental disability (mental retardation, autism, and so forth), an area that has also begun to utilize the support group format quite effectively.

1. *Chronically mentally ill*: Atwood, 1983; Atwood & Williams, 1978; Dincin, Selleck, & Streicker, 1978; Zolik, 1962
2. *Depressed clients*: Coates & Winston, 1983; Gordon, 1982; Leon, Mazur, Montalvo & Rodriguez, 1984
3. *Adults molested as children*: Gordy, 1983

4. *Spouses and families of inpatients*: Hill, Raley, & Snyder, 1982
5. *Significant others of rape victims*: Rodkin, Hunt, Cowan, & Dunstan, 1982

For one of the most descriptive accounts of a program that epitomizes not only the essence of a support group, but also the values of the social worker in the mental health field, one is referred to Leon, Mazur, Montalvo, and Rodriguez's (1984) article, "Self-Help Support Groups for Hispanic Mothers." They effectively designed a group to serve poor, minimally educated Hispanic mothers of children in outpatient psychiatric treatment. Initially these groups of 6 to 10 mothers, held in the South Bronx, ran for 12 sessions, but to date they have been extended to 30 sessions due to the severity of the families' difficulties and the quest for more successful outcomes. The goals were (1) to help the mothers understand the mental health system; (2) to help them find alternative solutions to environmental and emotional problems; (3) to return a sense of responsibility and control to the mothers, lessening traditional Hispanic fatalism; (4) to allow ventilation of feelings; (5) to increase self-esteem; (6) to provide a peer network, thereby discussing isolation; (7) to highlight cultural and language differences in a positive light; and (8) to provide better parenting models.

The mothers viewed the primary purpose as *desahogo*, or "an emotional release achieved through ventilation of problems" (Leon et al., 1984, p. 265). Sensitive to the importance and fragility of bonding in this group, the leaders followed a format of spending the first half of each session discussing problems, while the women crocheted and had coffee and cake during the second half. They also utilized guest speakers to provide a psychoeducational component to the program. As a result of compassionate and astute planning, the leaders saw "a mutual aid system among the group members emerge as participants began to break through their walls of isolation and respond to one another's needs" (p. 266). As the group progressed and the mutual-aid phenomenon took hold, leaders took a less directive, less active role in supporting the group life.

PLANNING SUPPORT GROUPS IN MENTAL HEALTH

Need

Again, the first step in developing a mental health support group is to identify the population in need of supportive services. Groups can be formed around common problems, losses, diagnoses, life events, or life transitions. Chapter 2 discusses the relationship of stress to an individual's experience of stigma, shame, guilt, isolation, loneliness, and diminished self-esteem. Frequently, mental health clients suffer the impact of these feelings more than any other population. As a result, the need for support groups in mental health is pervasive and often self-evident. However, when questions arise as to how needed a group is, making reference to the flow charts in Chapter 4 can be helpful. Whether the prospective group is facing acute or chronic stressors, mental health populations tend to be so underserved that the additional service of a support group is usually welcomed.

Purpose

Due to mental health professionals' training in psychotherapy, the mental health system's bias toward psychotherapy, and mental health clients' familiarity with psychotherapy, a clearly defined support group purpose is critical. With the mental health population, perhaps the greatest risk exists for overlap between support group work and psychotherapeutic interventions. Many families and clients seek a support group experience as a result of unsatisfactory or incomplete help from traditional therapeutic modalities. If members join a group with this motivation, it is all the more important to differentiate the support and mutual-aid purposes from the psychotherapeutic approach.

At times this separation can be quite difficult, since many support group members concurrently receive individual or family treatment, particularly during inpatient hospitalizations. Anyone familiar with the psychotherapeutic process knows that a time arises when sessions can be painful and when the client experiences vulnerability and struggle. Often families associate this discomfort with any mental health contact. It is not an uncommon experience, when inviting people to attend a support group meeting affiliated with a mental health setting, for the first question to be something like, "Now, this is just a support kind of thing, a place to talk, right? It's not going to be like therapy, is it?" People need reassurance and clarification of the supportive focus.

In mental health settings, as a result of individual or family treatment, problem behaviors and dynamics have often been pointed out to the group members. This is particularly true with families of the chronically mentally ill, where the parents may be aware of their emotional overinvolvement and the child's need for increased independence. In such situations one purpose of the support group can be to augment the therapeutic process, if the member so chooses.

Purpose statements in mental health support groups invariably address the need to increase self-esteem, deal with stigma and isolation, and often help cope with denial of problems and illness. Frequently purposes also include education, for example, understanding bipolar illness or teaching management techniques for chronic schizophrenic patients. Parents' groups often aim to assuage the guilt associated with having a mentally ill child and allow ventilating of the chronic sorrow that seems so common.

Composition

Although exceptions arise, the rule for mental health support groups is to separate clients and significant others. Part of the group function is to provide a safe, accepting environment in which members can feel free to ventilate their frustrations, anger, and guilt. Atwood and Williams (1978) maintain that separation enhances ventilation. Without separate groups, the client often feels restricted in his expression, for fear of eliciting guilt in significant others; while the family members censor their statements in the hope of protecting the "fragile" client.

Another issue relating to composition arises with respect to clients' problem areas or diagnoses. Often in psychotherapy groups, clinicians are trained to compose a group of people artfully, mixing clients with varying personality styles or diagnoses. When composing a support group, however, this is not always the best method. As Yalom (1975) writes,

> There appears to be a general clinical sentiment that heterogeneous groups have advantages over homogeneous groups for intensive interactional group therapy. Homogeneous groups are believed to "jell" more quickly, to become more cohesive, to offer more immediate support to the group members, to have better attendance, less conflict, and to provide more rapid symptomatic relief. [p. 261]

It is clear that, while the characteristics of a homogeneous group may not serve the purposes of psychotherapy, they are very much in harmony with the goals of support groups. Thus, in an intense psychotherapy group, a membership of only depressed women may not be desirable, but for a support group such a composition may be quite workable.

In working with children, another issue of composition may arise if parents are divorced or separated. Case-by-case evaluation is necessary when divorced parents are considering joint attendance. The worker must assess the level of cooperation and the parents' ability to tolerate one another's presence, before both join the group.

Structure

Several issues arise concerning the preplanning of structure in a mental health support group. One issue, discussed earlier in the text, is often the advantage of holding group meetings in a neutral, nonmental-health setting. Clearly this is not always possible, but the worker should be cognizant of the stigma members face and fear as they enter mental health facilities.

Another important factor is sensitivity to the timing of the meetings. For example, in running an outpatient support group for the chronically mentally ill, it may be quite useful to schedule the group just after members have come in for a medication clinic with their psychiatrist. This provides an immediate opportunity for members to discuss their successes, frustrations, or concerns about their progress. However, with parents of psychiatrically hospitalized children, conducting a support group just after some members have completed an intense family session sometimes backfires. Parents may be too emotionally stirred up or drained to be able to connect with the group, and they may want some decompression time.

Length of the group meeting also becomes an issue where the specific needs of the group must be addressed. A group of depressed teenagers may tolerate a longer meeting than a group of attention-deficient children. These variables of age and diagnosis also affect the amount of external structure the leaders must provide. For an example of extremes, conduct-disordered adolescents would require a very different kind and amount of limit setting than overly compliant anorexics.

In addition, leaders must preplan the structure for assuring confidentiality and the liaison process with other professional involved with a group member. Inherently these issues relate to concerns about clinic liability and documentation. The literature on mental health support groups does not appear to address these issues. Nonetheless, it is suggested that these problems be clarified prior to the group's beginning, with an understanding between leader and agency. When the group is formed or a new person joins, the agreement must be clearly communicated to the member.

In many cases the support group leader would not be the primary therapist or case manager for an identified client. If a member is in treatment, it may be advisable to have a routine release signed, permitting the group leader and primary clinician to consult with one another. If the first sign of schizophrenic decompensation is observed in a support group setting, the professional leader may need to enlist the help of the primary clinician. Many mental health settings, more than other fields of practice, can be expected to require documentation of support group progress, as a result of clinical liability and justification of the service. One needs to clarify this position with institutional or agency policies.

With regard to open versus closed formats or short-term versus long-term groups, mental health groups are similar to other support groups. Short-term groups often do best with closed membership, while longer-term groups can frequently tolerate more membership variability. Stress level and problem area often dictate duration of the group. For example, developmental, transition-focused groups are often shorter term, while the chronically mentally ill faced with chronic stress would benefit from a long-term group (Atwood, 1983).

Content

As with all support groups, content needs to be geared to the common problem binding the group together. In mental health, this often requires that at least one leader be knowledgeable about such topics as medication and side effects, symptomatology, parenting techniques, mental health regulations, community resources, and course and prognosis of a disorder. Many mental health support groups not only encompass components of mutual aid and education, but also involve political advocacy for the underrepresented mental health population. Again, group consensus about important matters of content should be achieved.

While content issues are often specific to diagnoses, the makeup of group membership, and the like, some common issues in mental health support groups are

- Feelings of stigma, isolation, and loneliness
- Questions about diagnosis
- Questions and complaints about medications and side effects
- Concerns about or anger with the mental health profession and treatment
- Fears of hospitalization or rehospitalization
- Feelings of defectiveness; fears of prognosis and the future
- Loss of family/social support

Repeated failures in relationships and employment
Fear of having no control over one's illness
Financial/survival difficulties
Issues of dependency
The unfairness of one's plight; struggling to make sense of one's world
Guilt on the part of parents, with concerns of overinvolvement
A chronic sense of loss

One difficult content issue often arises in mental health support groups that are ancillary to individual therapy. Group leaders may find themselves in the position of hearing vehement complaints or idealized statements about primary or family therapists. Frequently those therapists may be colleagues or peers of the group leader. Inevitably this brings up feelings in the group leader, and sometimes awkward situations arise. The trick here is (1) to be aware of the internal feelings this evokes, (2) to avoid defensive or personal discussion about the colleague, while at the same time normalizing the client's feelings about the therapist, (3) to find a common experience in the group, and (4) to refer the member back to deal with the professional under discussion.

A similar boundary issue arises when members introduce highly intimate material or a problem more appropriately dealt with in individual treatment. Again, the leader should, with sensitivity, refer the member back to the primary therapist, while educating the membership about purpose and appropriate content.

Pregroup Contact

Pregroup contact is highly recommended in mental health groups, to develop early rapport with the individual and to screen for appropriateness of membership. The structural issues regarding confidentiality, fees, and liaison with other professionals should be clarified. Any needed releases of information should be signed. Assessment should be made for psychotic and/or aggressive behavior. For patients with intractable delusions or hallucinations, clinical judgment must be used in determining the advisability of group membership.

If members are in treatment, it is helpful to know the reason for treatment, particularly for patients with major psychiatric disorders, personality disorders, substance-abuse histories, aggressive histories, and/or victimization experiences. If the patient is agreeable to the social worker contacting the primary therapist, it is a good idea to do so before the group begins, rather than wait to learn about a patient's inner experience the hard way. Finally, since many mental health clients have had previous treatment, it is helpful to find out if the experience was considered positive or negative. In short, with this population, any information obtained prior to group initiation may be helpful.

Summary of Important Points

To emphasize specific issues and problem areas in planning mental health support groups, the following points are highlighted:

1. The mental health population deals with a high level of stigma, guilt, denial, and isolation. Expect these themes to pervade group discussions.
2. Because many support group members will simultaneously be in or will have previously been in therapy, the boundaries between therapy and support become fluid and diffuse. The group leader must make a special effort to maintain the support focus.
3. In most cases, set up separate groups for identified clients and significant others.
4. If possible, hold groups in nonstigmatized, neutral settings.
5. Special ethical and legal issues may arise with this population. Be sure to formulate plans with regard to (a) sharing information with other treating professionals, (b) documentation of group meetings, and (c) clarification of clinical liability.
6. Carefully screen group members if at all possible, to evaluate advisability of group membership.
7. At least one group leader should be skilled at performing a mental-status examination with clients. In working with certain populations, one of the leaders should be experienced in handling a potentially aggressive or psychotic client.
8. In any mental health support group, there should be a preexisting plan for crisis intervention. If a member should become suicidal, homicidal, or psychotic, a preplanned course of action will facilitate resolution of the crisis.

Clients coping with mental health difficulties, whether of a chronic or situational nature, find that their struggle pervasively impacts their lives. Pressures are felt in the social, emotional, familial, and work spheres. Amidst these stresses, the individual can find himself deluged with feelings of defectiveness, loneliness, and helplessness. Many mental health workers expend great effort to reduce the demoralizing effect of psychological turmoil. For the client, however, a week can stretch out as an enormously expansive time between individual therapy sessions or appointments for medication follow-up. A support group can provide a crucial piece of contact and treatment for many mental health clients. In addition, the healing effects of experiencing commonality and universality in a support group are invaluable and difficult to duplicate with any other modality.

CONCLUSION

The last four chapters have offered a brief overview of some uses of support groups in practice. Other fields using support groups have not even been touched upon, such as education, corrections, substance abuse, the workplace, and developmental disabilities. The modality of support is so flexible and the need for mutual aid is so universal that social workers face a myriad of possibilities through the support group format. It is particularly exciting to see innovative workers stake out a theoretical base, engage in some creative thinking, and form programs that thrive on people's needs for connectedness and support in the face of stress.

REFERENCES

Atwood, N. (1983). Supportive group counseling for the relatives of schizophrenic patients. In W. R. McFarlane (Ed.), *Family therapy in schizophrenia* (pp. 189–205). New York: Guilford Press.

Atwood, N., & Williams, M. E. (1978). Group support for the families of the mentally ill. *Schizophrenia Bulletin, 4*(3), 415–425.

Bachrach, L. L. (1983). An overview of deinstitutionalization. *New Directions for Mental Health Services,* (17), 93–106.

Coates, D., & Winston, T. (1983). Counteracting the deviance of depression: Peer support group for victims. *Journal of Social Issues, 33*(2), 169–194.

Dincin, J., Selleck, V., & Streicker, S. (1978). Restructuring parental attitudes: Working with parents of the adult mentally ill. *Schizophrenia Bulletin, 4*(4), 597–608.

Gordon, V. C. (1982). Themes and cohesiveness observed in a depressed women's support group. *Issues in Mental Health Nursing, 4*(2), 115–125.

Gordy, P.L. (1983). Group work that supports adult victims of childhood incest. *Social Casework, 64*(5), 300–307.

Hill, B., Raley, J., & Snyder, D. (1982). Group intervention with parents of psychiatrically hospitalized children. *Family Relations, 31*(3), 317–322.

Lamb, H. R., & Oliphant, E. (1978). Schizophrenia through the eyes of families. *Hospital & Community Psychiatry, 29*(12), 803–806.

Leon, A. M., Mazur, R., Montalvo, R., & Rodriguez, M. (1984). Self-help support groups for Hispanic mothers. *Child Welfare, 63*(3), 262–268.

Pepper, B., & Ryglewicz, H. (1984). Treating the young adult chronic patient: An update. *New Directions for Mental Health Services: Advances in Treating the Young Adult Chronic Patient*, (21), 5–119.

Rodkin, Z., Hunt, E. J., Cowan, S., & Dunstan, S. (1982). A men's support group for significant others of rape victims. *Journal of Marital and Family Therapy, 8*(1), 91–97.

Silverman, P. R. (1978). *Mutual help groups: A guide for mental health workers.* U.S. DHEW Publication No. (ADM)78-646. Rockville, MD: National Institute of Mental Health.

Yalom, I. (1975). *The theory and practice of group psychotherapy* (2nd ed.). New York: Basic Books.

Zolik, E. S., Des Lauriers, A., Grayfill, J. G., & Thomas, H. (1962). Fulfilling the needs of "forgotten" families. *American Journal of Orthopsychiatry, 32*(1), 167–185.

IV Looking Forward

11 Possibilities for the Future

RECONSTRUCTED SOCIAL WORK

Currently the primary social work direct-practice model is one in which a clinical social worker treats a client (usually an individual, less often a family) who needs help in dealing with some life problem(s). This model, which is coeval with the profession itself, will undoubtedly continue to be the predominant form of practice in the years to come. Its primacy is due to two reasons. First, when individuals or families have difficulties that touch upon the intimate details of their lives and which they see as theirs alone, they cannot easily conceive of revealing these "secrets" to a group of people who are strangers. The desire for and the claim to privacy is a high-level value in the American scheme of things. Social work has from its beginnings honored that value. A correlate to the factor of privacy is the general feeling among Americans that "I, as an individual, deserve to be treated in a way that is in accord with that which I am—an individual person, not one of the masses, not an anonymous member of a collectivity, including a small group." A culture in which the individual and her or his rights are historically at the pinnacle of the hierarchy of values would naturally choose the one-to-one, direct-practice approach.

The second reason for the continuing supremacy of individual (and now, increasingly, family) treatment is the inherent belief within the clinical social work community that these are superior forms of treatment, although each has its ardent adherents who disparage the other. The one-to-one and the one-to-family treatment ideologies carry the authority of tradition behind them, and, since the introduction of insurance schemes that cover psychotherapeutic services, the lubricatory power of money that maintains therapists' livelihoods. Given these formidable forces at work, the advent of professionally led mutual-aid and support groups may well strike a discordant note in some places.

Social work with groups (but not group psychotherapy) fell into disfavor in the 1950s, and it is only within the past few years that schools of social work as well as practitioners in the field have rediscovered the power of group work, especially in the form of professionally led support or mutual-aid groups. It can be expected that most social work practice of the future will continue to be primarily with individuals and families. Yet, more frequently, one sees professional journal articles on professionally led support groups (and other kinds of helping groups), which are referred to as discussion, therapy, friendship, and mutual-aid groups, and so on. Work with groups will be seen increasingly as a powerful helping modality in its own right, and not simply as an adjunct to individual treatment or a cheaper, "wholesale" way of covering more clients.

What is of critical importance is the philosophical mind-set of social workers and other professionals who are going to lead support groups. This is the amalgam of beliefs, values, and attitudes a professional helper holds toward those who are the recipients of a helping service. In the case of support groups, the professional helper who regards the members of the group as people bound together in search of relief from the anxiety and pain of stress holds a philosophical mind-set that eschews psychiatric terminology and labeling. Even support group members who are psychiatric patients are not regarded as objects to be changed, but rather simply as people who have to contend with troublesome feelings, thoughts, and behaviors as manifestations of stress and who can learn to cope with these in healthier ways. The universality of their experience; their growing willingness to listen, care, and learn from each other; and their increasing cohesiveness as a group—all of these forces together provide relief from stress and sometimes bring about significant changes in attitudes and behaviors.

To carry this line of thinking somewhat further, the expansion of the support/mutual-aid group idea can be envisioned as the performing of social work functions in new and old social contexts, which are physically close to where other people live and work. Examples include reimagined and reappropriated social service contexts such as settlement houses, neighborhood personal and family services (Brown, Finch, Northen, Taylor, & Weil, 1982), community-based agencies that offer both treatment and developmental/socialization services (Kahn & Kamerman, 1982). These kinds of new/old agencies could be centers of support group activity, depending upon the demographic nature of the neighborhood and the kinds of problems people were facing in common. People's needs would be the factor determining the services they received. Such agencies could become *the* major social work institution, whose presence in a multitude of neighborhoods could provide familiarity and easy access. In brief, the neighborhood-based social service agency might well be conceived of as a front-line social work institution coming into touch with people at any time in their lives. It could provide family crisis services, be an information center for children's day-care services, and offer support groups for people going through divorce or for older people who are isolated and feel their aloneness as a painful burden.

The potential support groups that such a neighborhood-based agency could offer in the name of front-line treatment, information and referral, and developmental/socialization services, carry the potential of being the most powerful psychosocial preventive service that social work could contribute to this broken world. In brief, a recreated social work, in which social support/mutual-aid groups formed an important component, could be part of a larger movement of social reconstruction in this society. Working for the common good is a basic assumption in traditional social work philosophy.

SOCIAL AGENCIES AND SUPPORT GROUPS

Social agencies that are interested in initiating support groups must first identify the commonalities of their current clients' problems, experiences, and stressful situations. For example, a child-placing agency in which significant numbers of children are placed in foster homes may perceive an immediate need for support groups comprised of foster children, foster parents, and biological parents. Each could learn about themselves and their roles, about the other two, as well as the agency system, the law, the courts, and how these affect them.

Just as important, the support group idea compels an agency to look beyond its own traditional boundaries. A family agency dealing with the elderly is cognizant of the fact that some elderly take large numbers of medications, often to their disadvantage. Is it possible that the agency might assist a health maintenance organization in initiating a support group around the proper use of medications, compliance problems, and so on? Or, since some of the elderly have complained to their social workers during treatment hours about conflicts with their adult children, how might the agency enlist the involvement of those children into an exploration of difficulties with their parents? The possibilities and examples are unlimited. An organization adopting the support group idea assumes a proactive stance and engages in community-based work involving a large measure of community responsibility.

A support group emphasis in an agency further implies a potentially greater degree of interagency communication and cooperation. This necessarily arises in a situation where a group can only be formed from clients of different agencies, such as a support group for parents of kidnapped children or a support group for adult women who were sexually molested as children. Since agencies, like other organizations, possess strong "turf" feelings, there may be a tendency to think immediately that a raid is being made on one's natural constituents (clients), where no raid is intended. Thus the need to meet, talk, explain, and finally understand on the highest administrative levels is imperative. Cooperation is only possible under these conditions. In addition, agencies undertaking a support group thrust have to sustain that effort, as they do for all programs, by providing funds and time for staff learning, training, and professional involvement with groups.

With assistance from experts within the mental health and legal professions, an agency has to explore issues of confidentiality that arise out of group processes, and possible issues of agency liability vis-à-vis client involvement. These may not be different from issues of possible agency liability in work with individual clients, but they are worth exploration and discussion.

As previously noted, support groups, as potentially effective instruments for the prevention of serious mental health problems, should add to and fortify an agency's view of itself as a place where the preventive function rivals in importance those of amelioration and restoration. Support groups are only one means of prevention, but necessarily an important one.

THE ACADEMIC CURRICULUM

The social work curriculum in schools of social work is beginning to reflect increased time allotted to the study of the theory and practice of helping groups. This is not a finding from a research study, but simply an impression one gains by reading through current curriculum offerings. This is a hopeful sign.

Persons holding the Bachelor and/or Master's of Social Work degree should be encouraged to study support group theory and practice, with the purpose of eventually undertaking group leadership roles. Like all professionals who do this kind of work, learning and training in all aspects of group work is imperative. Supervision by experienced persons should be mandatory, particularly in supervision of beginning workers.

The expansion of support/mutual-aid groups within social work practice ought to be undertaken with the consultation and guidance of the Committee for the Advancement of Social Work with Groups. Their contribution to the learning, training, and supervision aspects of support group leadership is critical.

UNTAPPED POSSIBILITIES FOR SUPPORT GROUPS

Social workers have only begun to provide support groups to populations in need. The possibilities are limitless. In schools, children of minority groups who are a numerical minority might well benefit from group discussions and support. A school might reach out to parents who are going through divorce and their children whose schoolwork is being negatively affected. Both groups might well be sustained socially and psychologically through mutual-aid groups.

In the school structure, there is a fine line to be drawn between the creation of a support group, such as for children with learning disabilities, and an unintended increase in stigmatizing simply by selecting certain children for a group. This is a caveat that merits a great amount of exploration and discussion.

In the field of corrections, support group formation could take place with juveniles awaiting ajudication and/or sentencing, the spouses of prisoners, and the children of prisoners.

In industrial or occupational social work, beyond the popular alcoholism groups, the stresses and strains arising from the work situation may well be a commonality worth exploring. Clearly a social work type of employee assistance program (EAP) should be as concerned about the workplace as an environment as it is about the psychology of the individuals who work there. A potential "stress and strains" support group would have to be worked out with the responsible management people, who might see a threat in such a development. The EAP professionals would have to be ready to show how such a group would be helpful, not only to the personnel involved but to the firm itself.

Within the social work profession itself, support would be offered among workers. Groups of oncology social workers, child sexual abuse specialists, or prenatal social workers could share their common stresses, discussing the threat of burnout and professional isolation. Support groups could be mounted in public welfare units, particularly in neutral sites such as churches and schools. AFDC parents; hard-to-reach elderly, blind, and disabled people; and even General Relief recipients could use support groups for both informational and more broadly psychosocial services. The same would be true for county public health clinics, which see many single parents, unemployed parents, patients suffering from a particular illness, and so on. The public health clinic contains a plethora of support group possibilities.

RESEARCH

The research possibilities are rich and varied. The kinds of research mentioned here do not pretend to be exhaustive; they are simply suggestive of some avenues critical to the understanding of support group work.

Short-Term versus Long-Term Groups

Much more has to be known about the effects of both short- and long-term support group experiences. What are the benefits and costs to people suffering, for instance, from serious chronic physical disabilities (e.g., multiple sclerosis, rheumatoid arthritis) or chronic psychological upset and pain (women molested as children; parents whose children have been murdered), when they are exposed to short-term support group programs? What are the outcomes? Are some people helped? Others harmed?

Longitudinal studies of clients in both types of groups are called for. Do short-term beneficial effects tend to stretch out into the long term, say, three to five years after termination? Are some people harmed by either the long- or short-term experiences? In brief, evaluation studies are needed to get a deeper understanding of differential responses to the support group experience as well as a more profound understanding of the forces and dynamics of help and those of harm.

Closed versus Open Support Groups

Given two groups formed around a common problem such as unemployment, which type of group, open or closed, seems to be more helpful to its members? What are the advantages and disadvantages of both types? What are the conditions under which open groups are optimal? What about closed groups?

Clients and Their Families in Support Groups

Support group theory and practice needs a keener understanding of when it is and is not good to mix clients and patients with their family members (parents, spouses, children). Should cardiac patients be mixed in a support group with their spouses? What are the factors and/or conditions within an environment that need to be evaluated or understood before deciding on a mixed or unmixed group? Should the purposes and goals of a support group, to some degree, determine the choice in terms of mixed or unmixed? There are many related questions.

The Newly Discovered Ill and the Long-Term Afflicted

Should newly diagnosed cancer patients be placed in support groups with those who have been battling the illness for longer periods of time? Are there differential effects? What are the factors that determine different outcomes? Do they tend to be of an individual psychological nature, or do they tend to be environmental, such as group composition or group leadership?

Support Composition with Respect to Ethnicity, Race, and Social Class

The factors of homogeneity and heterogeneity are at issue. The democratic social ideal might hold for a mix of people from different races, backgrounds, cultures, and social classes. Among the unemployed, would it be advisable to mix blue- and white-collar workers, professional and nonprofessional, or would it not be advisable? If it might not be advisable to mix the unemployed from different life experiences, would the same hold true for renal dialysis patients? Again, the importance of understanding more clearly the conditions under which support groups' formation and composition take place seems to be critical.

Who Can and Who Cannot Use a Support Group Beneficially?

If it is posited that there are people who either do not want to be members of a support group or who should not be, then how might they be identified? There are undoubtedly many people in our society who, when seeking help for some personal problem or difficulty, cannot abide the thought of joining a group in the quest for relief, improvement, or problem resolution. Do they represent fairly large numbers? What are their principal objections?

Who should be excluded from support groups? There are people who display gross kinds of disturbed behavior, easily detectable to the senses, which identify them for exclusion. There are the less clear, "borderline" kinds of behavior, which make for group-leader uneasiness and anxiety. If, through leader observations and/or formal screening, a person tends to be withdrawn and very quiet, or, the opposite, extremely talkative and a potential "monopolist" within the group, should these types be included or excluded? What are the factors, beyond a leader's countertransference distortions, that might determine inclusion or exclusion?

Comparative Research on Clients Receiving Different Kinds of Treatment Intervention

Given a common problem, such as mild, reactive depression, a researcher might assign clients to three different modalities—individual treatment alone, individual and support group combined, and support group alone. A comparison of the outcomes could possibly determine the most effective mode of intervention.

CONCLUSION

A reconstructed social work envisions a theory and practice in which the individual, family, small group, and community constitute an interdependent quartet. This requires, on the theoretical level, an internally consistent set of concepts and, in everyday life, a web of human connections. The health and strength of each component depends on the health and strength of the others.

The professionally led support group is one type of small group that can become an important subcomponent in an array of community services. Its power in helping people is grounded on the commonality of situation, the commonality of stress and suffering revealed in group interaction, and the care and mutual aid that the group members render to and receive from each other. There is yet much to be learned about the organization, composition, leadership, and dynamics of the support group process. In some modest way, support group practice research may be helpful in illuminating some of the perplexing issues and questions that abound in this new endeavor.

REFERENCES

Brown, J.H., Finch, W.A., Northen, H., Taylor, S.H., & Weil, M. (1982). *Child Family Neighborhood.* New York: Child Welfare League of America.

Kahn, A.H., Kamerman, S.B., & Sheila, B. (1982). *Helping America's families.* Philadelphia: Temple University Press.

Epilogue

People contend with stress in myriad ways. In this book we have shown that people can cope with stress with some measure of hopefulness when they join others facing the same difficult, frequently painful situation. The good support group is a firsthand experience in mutual aid, in trusting and being trusted, caring and being cared for, and helping and being helped. Sustaining and being sustained by other humans who are neither relatives nor friends is an unusual experience for many, many people in our society.

We believe that, among all the human service professions, social work adheres to a philosophy and bears a tradition in which caring for people is a cardinal value. It is our hope that the concept of mutual aid, which is linked to the fundamental idea of human cooperation, will be incorporated into the theory and practice of all social work; that, wherever social workers are engaged in practice, they will search out the possibilities of embodying mutual aid programmatically.

At this juncture of social work history, the dark side of humanity has been accorded a great deal of study and attention and has been absorbed into our theory and practice. Because they have been witnesses, social workers know much about the ubiquity and power of the irrational in human affairs. It is not our aim to deny what we know. Yet the dark side of our individual and collective lives cannot illuminate the possibilities of hope with which our work must be suffused. One aspect of hope is people joining each other in a mutual quest to accomplish some purpose, whether that be the relief of stress or something as commonplace as having a stoplight installed at a dangerous intersection.

From a philosophical point of view, we are not posing a theory of human goodness to counterpoise a history of human badness. We speak only of the possibilities of human cooperation and mutual aid. If we are to "choose life" in these days of incessant turmoil and death through violence, then we are obligated to seek charted and uncharted ways of doing so in our personal and professional lives. One such way, we believe, is to pursue mutual aid through social support and reinforcement of the human bond.

Appendix
Support Group Planning Guide

A step-by-step procedure for planning a support group is offered below. Remember these are general guidelines, and the worker must use clinical judgment and a certain creativity in forming the most beneficial group for the unique members involved.

Step 1: *Identify Need*

a. Identify a group with a common problem, experience, or situation in need of support.
b. Be aware of the risk factors applicable to that population.
c. When identifying a population in need, take advantage of
   - Formal social service needs assessment research
   - Client/community requests for service
   - Clinical judgment.
d. If several groups are identified and resources are limited, you may use Table 4–2 to prioritize those most urgently in need of intervention.

Step 2: *State Purpose*

a. Identify whether stress facing potential members is generally acute, ameliorable, or permanent.
b. Identify the probable psychosocial correlates (Table 4–1) of the stress.
c. Formulate a purpose statement, usually aimed at reducing or relieving the psychosocial correlates; keep it within the realistic possibilities of the group.
d. Be sure to emphasize the support focus of the group.

Step 3: *Propose Composition*

a. Plan your group composition, remembering that homogeneity is important in support group, with regard to the problem at hand.
b. Usually it is most beneficial to offer separate groups for victims or identified patients and their significant others.
c. Keep in mind that support groups can generally tolerate heterogeneity in terms of socioeconomic status, ethnicity, religion, and so on.

Step 4: *Design Structure*

a. Determine the duration of the group, whether time limited or open ended. Usually longer-term stressors need longer-term groups.
b. Decide upon open or closed membership. Closed is usually best for short-term groups.
c. Plan frequency and length of meetings; a typical format is one time per week for 1 to 2 hours.
d. Carefully decide upon meeting place.
e. If indicated, address needs such as
   - Transportation
   - Child care
   - Handicapped access.
f. Arrange for interagency communication and release of information, if needed.
g. Consider using food and drinks to facilitate interaction and bonding.

Step 5: *Plan Content*

a. Be well versed on the problem at hand.
b. Identify personal values that relate to the problem area.
c. Adapt the content to be appropriate for the age, emotional and educational level of members.
d. Remain open to members' contribution to content; eventually, group members may increasingly determine content.

Step 6: *Clarify Agency Commitment*

a. Present proposed group to sponsoring agency, to assure commitment to the plan.
b. Educate staff and referral resources on the benefits of support and on your plan for the group.

Step 7: *Initiate Pregroup Contact*

a. Recruit potential members through staff referrals, community contacts, and flyers; be creative.
b. If possible, meet with potential members individually.
c. Screen for appropriateness of group membership.
d. Inform potential members of purpose, structure, and other specifics of the group format.

Index